R.d V. Bleeck Pinxit. 1716. F. Morellon la Cave *Sculpsit*. 1754.

M.r Kellom Tomlinson

AUTHOR of the Original *ART* of DANCING, Compofer, Writer of *DANCES*, and their *Music*, for the Ufe & Entertainment of the *Public*.

THE
ART
OF
DANCING

Explain'd

by

KELLOM TOMLINSON, *Dancing-Master.*

First design'd in the year 1724 and publish'd by the author in 1735.

Revised and restored
in the year 2021 by
KATHERINE OKTOBER MATTHEWS.

HOUSE OF OKTOBER

HOUSE of OKTOBER

House of Oktober is an arts publisher based
in Amsterdam, The Netherlands.

houseofoktober.com

THE ART OF DANCING EXPLAIN'D
Tomlinson, Kellom

Subjects: Dance; Dance Instruction and Manuals; Minuet.

First printed for the author in London, 1735.

Digitized and archived for the public domain by the Library of Congress.
https://www.loc.gov/item/20010870

ISBN 9789493075054

— Tulit alter honores.

THE
CONTENTS.

BOOK I.

BOOK II.

NOTES
FROM THE EDITOR.

My interest in *The Art of Dancing Explain'd* was born naive: I liked the pictures. The writing, on the other hand, I found so entrenched with old-fashioned notions of class, gender, and formality, to say nothing of the verbose dealings of Baroque dance steps, that I nearly abandoned it. Nearly.

Dotted throughout the text are gems of intrigue, salacious accusations, obsequious flattery, and stroppy complaints dressed up in genteel language. While the vernacular and format make it difficult for modern eyes, the longer I stayed with it, the more I was rewarded for doing so.

Kellom Tomlinson's book is not what we would nowadays call, "a labour of love," but seems rather a burden of which the author could not rid himself sooner. His writing is impatient, constantly hedged by commentary that he has gone on for long enough and trusts he need not say anything more. While it might be argued that these asides count as conventions of formality or evidence of an oral capture of writing, his frustration seethes off the page. His *Preface* starts with an excuse for the great delay of his book due to difficulties and obstructions, recriminations for the sabotage of his intellectual property, as well as explanations for his mistaken identity. By Book II, he has reached sufficient need to tell us about the "great pains, trouble, and expense" he has taken in completing this book—all of which was motivated only for the public good! His bitter words spark with the injustice of being put upon, and the publication of his book affords him the opportunity to have the last word.

He name-drops one of his successful students, only to state that she stopped working with him, without further explanation. The gossip is given and withheld. His *Dedication* of the book to Viscountess Fauconberg is so rich with servile sycophantry that, to modern ears, it reads as obvious irony, or evidence of some entanglement with her. His overt declaration that he hopes the dedication to her will save him from "such unjust censures as malice or envy ordinarily produce," is pure snark, a backhanded compliment spicing up a melodramatic linguistic performance of admiration.

The added signed statements, provided by witnesses, which attest to the book's authoring by such-and-such date seemed to me at first unnecessary proclamations of pomp, adding not much more than administrative bloat. Yet, after reading a recent article by Gabriella Karl-Johnson on Tomlinson's book and its role in Baroque dance notation, even more things clicked into place about the book as an object and its difficult path to being published. For this reason, I am so grateful that she has agreed to extend and update her article for this publication, which you can read here as the *Foreword*.

This brings you some context on my decisions as an editor. While there are many facsimile editions of Kellom Tomlinson's book now available online, I wanted to remove some of the barriers to its accessibility and easy reading. For this edition, I've entirely re-typeset the text, so it's clearer than the original's scanned pages, which bear much distortion and noise. The transcribed text itself also provides some hurdles in the form of archaic spelling and the use of the long-s character (ſ). I've modernized these because, though a sharp reader can parse the writing in its original form, it does require parsing, which makes reading slower and more tiresome.

I decided to preserve intact the authorial content, and to edit only typesetting choices, and spelling or grammar idiosyncrasies that are now obsolete, such as the convention of capitalizing nouns. This effort presented many delightful puzzles, such as trying to decide what to do with a seemingly haphazard system of footnote identifiers, as well as the INCONSISTENCIES in *words* put into SMALL CAPS or *italics* with apparent *abandon* but probably occupying an INTERNAL LOGIC, of which I have tried to make sense. When uncertain, I deferred to the original. This process, performed digitally, gave me an immense appreciation for the physical and mental effort to typeset the book in 1735.

This edition also includes the original *List of Subscribers' Names*, which is fascinating as proof of an early model of subscription-based funding for an artist. Moreover, at 169 contributors, the list demonstrates that despite Tomlinson's frustration with the book's slow path to publication, he had an incredible amount of support. He was a crowdfunder, and a successful one at that.

It has been my goal that this edition preserves the spirit and intentions of the original, while gaining readability. It's unclear why that became meaningful to me. I imagine, half in earnest, the ghost of Kellom Tomlinson striving in a Sisyphean bind to save his book, across the ages, once more.

— Katherine Oktober Matthews
May 2021

THE
FOREWORD.

by GABRIELLA KARL-JOHNSON

ABSTRACT

The late seventeenth century gave rise to a powerful innovation in Western European social and theatrical dance: the art of dance notation. The new representational technology of dance notation provided a means to broadcast fashionable dances emerging from the French court as well as new compositions from dancing masters operating in London and elsewhere. In the first three decades of the eighteenth century, dance notation quickly reached faddish heights, with published dance manuals in high demand among upper levels of English society. One publication from the era, Kellom Tomlinson's *The Art of Dancing Explained by Reading and Figures,* provides a window onto the descriptive tool of dance notation, its function in society, and its eventual decline. While providing a previously unimagined communicational technology, the completeness and specificity of the dominant form of dance notation ultimately spelled its demise. An addendum describing the physical aspects of the printed book follows the essay delineating the book's content and context.

From the PAGE *to the* FLOOR

Baroque dance notation and Kellom Tomlinson's
The Art of Dancing Explained.

ANCER and historian Irmgard Bartenieff remarked in 1963, "Dance notation is not an invention of modern times. Like music notation, it has a history extending over several centuries" (1963, 2). Both now and at midcentury when Bartenieff was active, most people with any knowledge of dance notation, either within or outside the field of dance, would point to the early twentieth-century choreographer and scholar Rudolf von Laban as the primary figure in the development of dance notation. His highly systematized and abstract notation method, known as Laban Kinetography, or Labanotation, provides a comprehensive means to record both dance and ordinary movement, but it is hardly the genesis of dance notation. The first substantive, fully developed systems of dance notation emerged in the late seventeenth century in France and Germany. In the first incarnations of dance notation, debates arose among dance teachers and choreographers (known as "dancing masters," in the era's parlance) about the formal and creative implications of dance notation, conflicts that ultimately contributed to the waning of dance notation's popularity.

Dance notation originally arose out of the French court, where dance played a highly important role for nobility as well as courtiers. King Louis XIV himself performed dances at court, and elegance and grace in performance were highly revered qualities for both a ruler and his subjects. The dance notation system that ultimately attained precedence, Beauchamp-Feuillet notation, was commissioned by Louis XIV, apparently intended as another element of cultural achievement to augment the glory of the Sun King's reign. In the Baroque era, social dance and stage dance were strongly interlinked in France, with dances performed on stage being the same as or highly similar to those dances performed socially.[1] Prior to the Baroque invention of dance notation, dance was an art taught and transmitted almost exclusively through bodily communication, that is, conveyed both orally and through physical movement. While notes about scenography or costuming could be readily conveyed and easily comprehended on paper, written notes about choreography would require human interpreters to actualize. Once the notation system commissioned by Louis XIV was in place, dancing masters were able to communicate to new, physically distanced audiences the steps and movements of popular dances of the day, as well as their own creations. With the first publications of French dances, the conveyance of choreography was no longer exclusively achieved through the human body and voice but could be transported by the printed page as well.

In the first decades of the eighteenth century, translations of the French dancing masters' texts were published in London, and English dancing masters added their unique compositions and notational variations to the printed corpus of Baroque dance notation. This article surveys the emergence and significance of the primary system of dance notation in the Baroque era and examines the appearance of French notation and dance composition in English-language translations, and specifically investigates one unique published example of dance notation, Kellom Tomlinson's 1735 work *The Art of Dancing Explained*

---

1. At this time social dance would have been practiced in the royal court and in private homes of nobility or the very wealthy. In France, stage dance was performed largely in such venues as the Royal Opera, and in England, in London theaters such as Lincoln's Inn Fields.

by Reading and Figures. Written in an augmented form of Beauchamp-Feuillet notation with detailed figural illustrations, Tomlinson's *The Art of Dancing* was both the apotheosis and swan song of dance notation of the Baroque era.

HISTORY OF DANCE NOTATION

As with any system of notation or representation, dance notation engages in varying levels of abstraction. Unlike standard musical notation, which is an entirely disembodied, abstract form of notation that maintains no direct reference to physical objects or space, early dance notation utilizes iconographic representational elements that can be recognized as components of the physical world. Chiefly the most recognizable of such elements is the correlation of page space to the space of the dance floor. As will be discussed in further detail below, additional recognizable elements can be viewed in notation of the Baroque era.

As the Baroque choreographic repertoire and Baroque dance notation began to emerge through the work of Pierre Beauchamp and Raoul-Auger Feuillet, both masters of performance and of notation, the emphasis on the floor plane and movement path tracings established during the Renaissance remained constant and highly important. The earliest known forms of dance notation that arose during the Renaissance were defined by the tracing of dancers' paths across the floor onto a surrogate of the floor in the form of a leaf of paper. In some cases those recorded paths might define the contours of a plan-view image, one example of which is the almost mystical-seeming image of the rose pattern from Fabritio Caroso's *Nobiltà di Dame* of 1600 (see fig. 1).

An exemplary case such as this shows the primacy of the danced or notated path as seen in plan, a choreographic feature

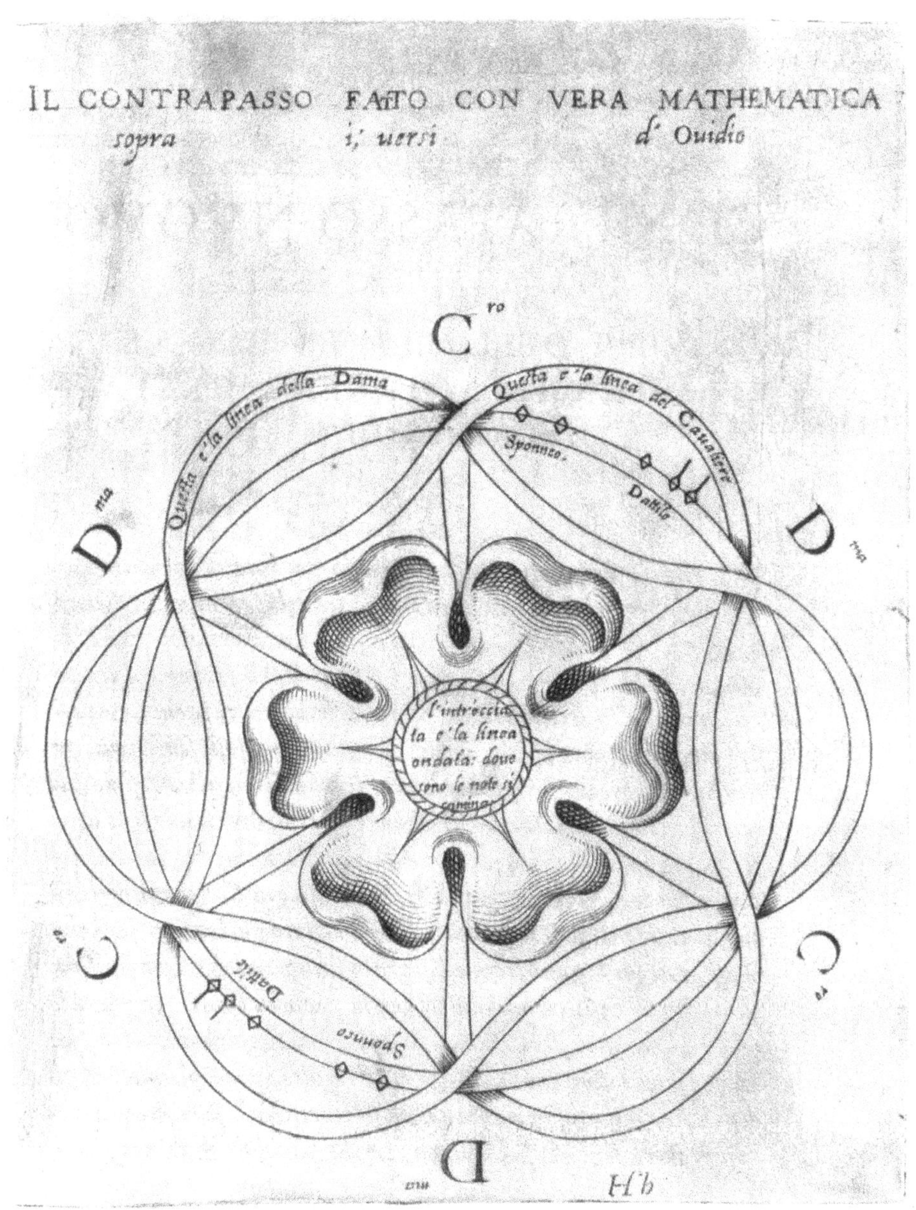

Figure 1. The rose-shaped floor pattern traversed by the dancers in Fabritio Caroso's
Nobiltà di Dame (1600).

that is not readily visible from the perspective of a spectator or audience member viewing the dance in performance. Other early examples of dance notation are characterized by either their indication of points on the floor occupied by performers at a particular moment or by the lines traced by the movement paths of dancers throughout the duration of a work. In addition to this, written description often would have accompanied such tracings or point maps; and generally speaking, no dance documentation or notation, when viewed alone, would have provided sufficient information to restage a dance, until the introduction of Beauchamp-Feuillet notation, which began to approach completeness of representation for the first time.

The development of a systematic movement representation scheme either requires a complex, abstract, highly detailed system of representational elements to accommodate every possible movement variation, or the system itself must have a narrower scope of representational aims, a more limited intent for communication, and a smaller movement lexicon. The dominant notation scheme of the Baroque era fell into the latter category and represented only those movements already established in the dance vocabulary of the day.

In his history of French dance notation of the late seventeenth century, Ken Pierce (1998, 287) describes several rival dance notation systems that emerged nearly concurrently in France, with no shortage of disputes between their respective authors. These disputes were not merely moral or interpersonal, but extended to lawsuits brought up for judgment in French courts. Only one name became inextricably associated with Baroque dance notation, that of Raoul-Auger Feuillet, whose seminal *Choréographie* was published in 1700. Feuillet, however, is commonly held not to be the inventor of the notation scheme that now bears his name, but rather he is recognized as the first person who documented and published (and perhaps also adapted and modified) the notation system developed by Pierre Beauchamp, a French ballet master affiliated with both the Paris Opera and the court of Louis XIV. Beauchamp had been commissioned by the king to develop a method for notating and recording dances; or, in Pierce's words, "Sometime around 1674 Louis XIV ordered Pierre Beauchamp, dance director at the Académie Royale de Musique (the Opéra) and Louis's dancing master, to find a way to put dance on paper. … We do not know whether Louis gave a reason for this order, beyond the formulaic *'Car tel est notre plaisir'*" (287).

Beauchamp was responsible for devising and developing the system later known as Feuillet notation, and indeed he was recognized in one of the lawsuits mentioned above as the creator of said notation system, but it was Feuillet who popularized Beauchamp's notation method through an energetic agenda of notating, publishing, and circulating printed dances. *Choréographie* is Feuillet's best known and most translated work. With this work and those that followed shortly after, Feuillet facilitated the transmission of French ballet choreography and of Beauchamp's notation system to a geographically dispersed audience across Europe and England. In 1706 two English translations of *Choréographie* were published in England by two different dancing masters active at the time. A version entitled *The Art of Dancing* was published by P. Siris, about whom little is known (Thorp 1992); the other was titled *Orchesography, or the Art of Dancing*, by John Weaver, who was well known in English stage dance and private dancing instruction. Of the two versions, Weaver's translation appears to have become more popular for reasons possibly related to personal influence. Weaver's version of Feuillet's text was accompanied by an additional original text by Weaver titled

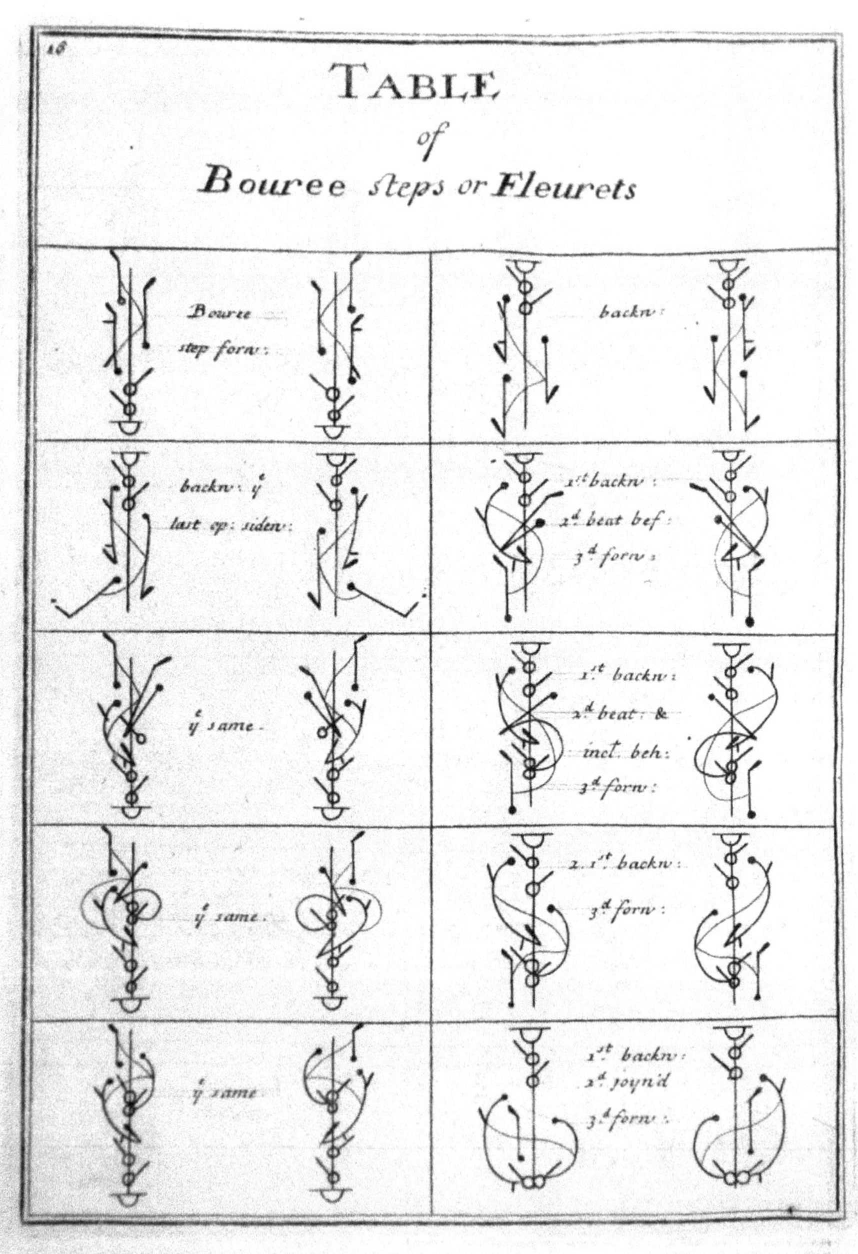

Figure 2. Feuillet's table of bourrée steps, as printed in *Orchesography* (1706),
John Weaver's translation of Feuillet's *Choréographie* (1700).

"A Small Treatise of Time and Cadence in Dancing, Reduced to an Easy and Exact Method Shewing How Steps, and their Movements agree with the Notes, and the Division of Notes, in each Measure." As Weaver explains, this exposition was missing from Feuillet's original text, and the simple insertion of numbers correlated between the musical notation and the dance notation enables the clarification of steps. This notational evolution was not the invention of Weaver, but rather was presented by Feuillet himself in his 1704 work "Recueil de Dances," a collection of ballets composed by Louis-Guillaume Pécour and notated by Feuillet, which Weaver notes that he found enlightening in the preparation of his treatise.

Feuillet's influential first publication presents, in a somewhat dry, matter-of-fact manner through tables, diagrams, and textual description, the full range of movements commonly utilized in Baroque dance. The space of the dance floor, as mentioned above, is represented either by a rectangle set within the page or by the page space itself, always oriented with the top of the page, or top of the rectangle, as the front of the room, where the figure of nobility or rank would be seated. To quote from Weaver's translation, "You must understand, that each Page, on which the Dance is described, represents the Dancing-Room; and the four Sides of the Page, the four Sides of the Room, viz. The upper part of the Page, represents the upper end of the Room; the lower part, the lower end; the right side of the Page, the right side of the Room; and the left side, the left" (Weaver 1706, 34). Feuillet's representation of the foot presents another element that is relatively recognizable from its real-life counterpart (fig. 2). The feet are represented as heel and angle of foot, with a circle for the heel and an extended line for the direction of the toes. The basic foot positions, divided into "true positions" (toes pointing outward) and "false positions" (toes pointing inward), are the basis of the foot positions still used in ballet of the current day, although the so-called false positions are no longer part of common ballet vocabulary.

Feuillet's system of notation, as laid out in *Choréographie* and in Weaver's translation, includes over forty tables of precisely defined steps and foot movements. Weaver's translated tables reproduced those of Feuillet nearly identically, replacing French with English, although many movement terms were simply imported (bourrée, pirouette, etc.) rather than translated. As Wendy Hilton notes, "At first glance, it seems that the vocabulary of steps was enormous, but Feuillet is showing every possible variation of each step as well as the different ways of notating each variation. There are ninety-four examples of pas de bourrée, each drawn to account separately for execution with the left or the right foot" (1997, 47). The textual portion of the book, roughly forty pages long, is written with plodding detail but some lack of clarity for a reader unfamiliar with the era's customary dances.

Feuillet's notation system reached predominance quickly, and the first two decades of the eighteenth century saw numerous publications in dance notation. John Weaver, the translator of Feuillet mentioned above, was among those dancing masters who published regularly during these years. In the early 18th century, the ability to read dance notation was considered to be a necessary complementary skill when learning to perform the social dances of the day. In eighteenth century society, dancing held a place of prominence for which there is little equivalent today. As Eric McKee (2011, 2) states in his study of the minuet and waltz in this era, "The ubiquity and far-reaching influence of social dancing in the eighteenth and nineteenth centuries cannot be overestimated. The activity of dancing was a vital part of social life and was without question the most common form of social entertainment. ... For the lower classes, dancing provided a diversion from the toils of the day; the upper classes used it as a way of defining themselves individually within their class and collectively apart from the lower classes; and for all levels, the activity of dancing was a vehicle for courtship, ceremonies, and celebrations." Among the upper classes, learning to read dances seemed to be nearly as important as learning to perform the dances themselves. As Ann Hutchinson Guest states, "Dance literacy was an expected skill of an educated man. Indeed, one reads of complaints from the clergy of ladies having books of dances instead of Bibles on their bedside table" (1990, 64).

In this era of dance literacy mania, another influential French publication hit the London scene by way of Pierre Rameau's new work titled *Le Maître à Danser*, published in Paris in 1725. Rameau's book committed numerous pages to elucidating the positions and movements of the dancer's arms, a topic relatively unaddressed by Feuillet in his influential text of two decades earlier. Also in contrast to Feuillet's seminal work, Rameau's text included illustrated plates of human figures performing the positions and movements; human figures were not included in Feuillet's work. Rameau also provides readers with a glimpse of the performance and viewing experience of the era's dances through inclusion of an oversized illustrated plate included in *Le Maître à Danser* (fig. 3). Rameau's detailed depiction of the dancing room supplies the visual context into which readers can imagine the isolated figures and diagrams that punctuate Rameau's text.

The illustrated plates of etchings included in *Le Maître à Danser* were delineated by Rameau himself; while his depictions of the human figure might be kindly characterized as naïve, the illustrations were also entirely sufficient for the purpose. The unembellished lines and smiling countenance of Rameau's figures

Figure 3. Oversized illustrated plate of the dancing room, from Pierre Rameau's
Le Maître à Danser (1725).

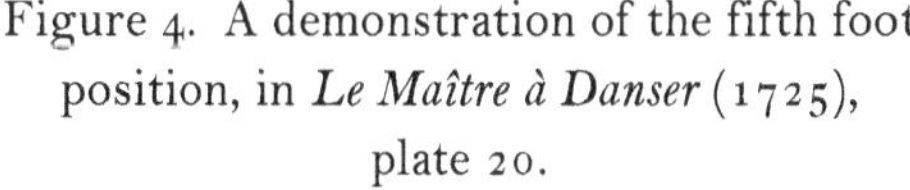

Figure 4. A demonstration of the fifth foot
position, in *Le Maître à Danser* (1725),
plate 20.

Figure 5. A demonstration of the fifth foot position,
in *The Dancing Master* (1728), John Essex's translation
of *Le Maître à Danser*, plate 12.

provide a pleasant counterpoint to the rather dry text (fig. 4).

An English translation of *Le Maître à Danser* was published in London by John Essex in 1728 (a second edition followed in 1731), with the title *The Dancing-Master: Or, the whole art and mystery of Dancing Explained.* The first edition by Essex did not utilize the illustrated plates used in Rameau's original text but rather replicated them nearly exactly, with translated captions. However, the human figures in the Essex translation were executed with greater artistry than Rameau's simple figures, and the etchings were drawn with additional detail in the surface of the dance floor, including the suggestion of perspective and the dancer's shadow on the floor surface, as well as shading on the dancer's clothes (fig. 5).

In Rameau's original text, a folded plate of somewhat abstract illustration also suggests the use of perspective: this image utilizes a grid on the dance floor that angles toward a vanishing point, with a male and a female dancer mid-dance (see fig. 6). These simple suggestions of perspectival representation begin to reflect (or prefigure, depending on whose narrative one believes) the work of Kellom Tomlinson, whose innovative illustration style utilizes figurative, diagrammatic, and perspectival representation simultaneously to present a more complete picture of Baroque dance than is presented by any other dancing master of the day.

Tomlinson's unique tome *The Art of Dancing* was published in 1735, though according to Tomlinson and sworn witnesses, his book was completed in 1724, one year prior to Rameau's publication of *Le Maître à Danser*, not to mention four years before the first translation of Rameau by John Essex. *The Art of Dancing* is, simply stated, a manual for solo and partner dancing in a formal setting. Comprising 182 leaves of text and 37 illustrated plates, the book represents Tomlinson's major

Figure 6. Oversized illustrated plate of male dancer and female dancer, from
Pierre Rameau's *Le Maître à Danser* (1725).

Figure 7. Musical score and dance notation of a portion of the saraband, in Kellom Tomlinson's
The Art of Dancing Explained (1735), Book I, Plate VI. Note the mirrored notation
for leading with the left foot or the right foot.

intellectual contribution to the written works of dance notation. The illustrated plates are divided into two books, the first of which addresses various dances and dance phrases for a man or a woman, and the second of which exclusively addresses the subject of the minuet, a highly important dance of the day. Nearly all of the illustrated plates are dedicated to a subscriber or one of Tomlinson's former students; after spending 11 years raising funds for publication, Tomlinson likely had a number of people to whom he needed to express gratitude.

The Art of Dancing is Tomlinson's best-known and most studied work, and it currently serves as a reference for scholars and performers of 18th century dance styles. Tomlinson composed the notational portions of his work in Feuillet notation, but several important enhancements should be noted. Tomlinson's notational innovation lies almost entirely in his conjoining of the dancing human figure with the path indications of Feuillet notation to present a simultaneous picture of the dancing figure, the dance floor, the steps of the dance, and the path of the dance's movement. Tomlinson also includes bars of the relevant music, with the corresponding movement phrases indicated by number. On occasion Tomlinson also includes mirrored images of the steps for either the right foot or the left foot leading (fig. 7).

Like Rameau, Tomlinson employs illustrations of the human figure to show the foot and body positions of the dance, but unlike Rameau, whose figural representations primarily showed static positions, Tomlinson's figures are meant to show a given moment in the performance of a dance, sometimes mid-movement. An image such as Book I, Plate XIII illustrates a shift of weight from one foot to the other during the dance. In Tomlinson's illustrated exposition of the minuet, we can glimpse something of the grace and formality of this dance.

Tomlinson's particular style of dance notation is remarkable due to its complexity and thoroughness. In her introduction to a recent reprint of a workbook by Tomlinson, Jennifer Shennan provides a contextual explanation of Tomlinson's notation style:

> Baroque dance notation features abstract step symbols placed on a stave which graphically represents the floor patterns of the dance; it is read in conjunction with a music stave on the same page. The notation thus operates two dimensionally, with the paper on which it is written representing the floor. In the illustrations for his books ... Tomlinson took the artistic license of drawing actual dancers onto the page and notating stop symbols in a trail beneath their dancing feet. His illustrations are thus an ingenious combination of the horizontal and the vertical, so that we look both at, and down onto, the images at the same time. (1992, 5)

The illustrations in *The Art of Dancing* were created by a team of some of the finest engravers of the day, working under Tomlinson's instruction. It can be presumed that Tomlinson would likely have made crude sketches of the desired images, perhaps adding or substituting verbal description of the particular postures to be depicted. The full roster of illustrators included George Bickham, Gerard Van der Gucht, George Vertue, and Henry Fletcher, who accounted for the better-known engravers, as well as R. W. Seale, J. Smith, and I. Clark. In addition to this, two plates (Plates I and XII of Book II) were delineated by Arnold Vanhaecken and engraved by G. King. Subtle differences in engraving style are visible throughout, namely in the depiction of the dancers' hands, altogether these stylistic differences are relatively easy to overlook when reading the images for movement instruction and content, rather than for traces of authorship.

The original cost of the book is stated by Tomlinson in the book itself, both in his preface and in the introductory plate to the first book of plates. Tomlinson notes the price of his book in comparison to Rameau's book, which cost half as much and, Tomlinson asserts (1735, 15), was correspondingly inferior. In the introductory plate to the plates correlating to Book I of the printed portion of the book, Tomlinson notes: "The Price of the cuts belonging to the first and second Books without ye Printed Part, is Two Guineas, and those who are willing also to purchase the latter, viz. the Printed Part, may have it of the author ... for Half a Guinea, pursuant to my Printed Proposals wherein I assured the Public, that the whole Work, except to Subscribers, should not be sold under Two Guineas and a Half" (125). The relatively high price of the book is likely due in large part to the expense of the artwork, the heavy paper stock used for the plates, and the overall quality of the work. As mentioned above, several of the engravers were among the recognized names of their day in the art of engraving; the expense incurred by Tomlinson to commission the production of the illustrated plates from these engravers might have been high. Beyond this, the cost of merely producing the textual portions of the book, or "the printed part," to use Tomlinson's words, could have been formidable to a dance instructor whose income was likely inconsistent and relied upon a form of patronage.

At a cost of two guineas, Tomlinson's masterwork would have seen sales restricted only to the very wealthy, since the average income in Britain at this time was approximately thirteen guineas per year.[2] Like other printed books of this era,

---

2. Historic income data is based on "The Annual RPI and Average Earnings for Britain, 1209 to Present (New Series)," https://www.measuringworth.com/datasets/ukearncpi/result2.php.

the binding of the printed pages would likely have been at the discretion of the purchaser, with the book sold as an unbound collation of gathered pages (i.e., in "signatures," to use historic bibliography terms), accompanied by a stack of printed plates. In his introduction to each of the two sections of the printed plates Tomlinson reveals that his intentions for the illustrated plates were not necessarily to see them bound with "the printed part." Tomlinson encourages the reader to consider that the engravings would serve as "proper Furniture for a Room or Closet, being of themselves an intire [sic] and independant [sic] Work, for if put in Frames with Glasses, they will [...] be very agreable [sic] & instructive Furniture" (1735, 125). Curiously, Tomlinson makes no specific suggestion to hang these images in a room where dancing or dance instruction would take place. If one regards the plates not as illustrations bound in a book but rather as independent artwork worthy of framing and display, perhaps the price of two guineas seems like a bargain.

Kellom Tomlinson was both a notator of his own dances and a firm proponent of inculcating dance literacy in the dancers he taught, most of whom were the children of English nobility and gentry. Most dancing masters of the time had professional scribes notate their compositions for publication, but Tomlinson was one of the few masters to prepare his own dancing notations. Tomlinson championed the cause of dance pupils learning to read dance notation or "characters" and expressed scorn for those who taught children to "dance without book" (17).

In the preface to *The Art of Dancing*, Tomlinson explains the relationship between his new work and the dance manuals and works in notation by Feuillet and others that preceded his book's publication:

This Undertaking [i.e., *The Art of Dancing*] must needs

have been attended with great Difficulty, because it was really the first of the Kind. For tho' Monsieur Beauchamp lay'd the first Foundation, upon which Monsieur Feuillet built, (as some more ingenious Person may perhaps improve upon mine); yet the Works of both relate only to the Characters of Dancing; which, like the Notes of Music, can be only useful to Masters, and cannot be understood by any other without their particular Instructions. But the Piece which I here offer to the World will be of general Use to all, who either have learned, or are learning to dance: the Words describing the Manner in which the Steps are to be taken; and the Figures representing Persons as actually taking them; both which together will make the Learning more pleasant to the one, and serve as a continual Remembrancer to the other. (1735, 17)

As Tomlinson states in his preface to *The Art of Dancing*, "The Figures in each Plate are designed only to shew [sic] the Postures proper in Dancing, but not to bear the least Resemblance to any Person to whom the Plate is inscribed; which it had been ridiculous to have attempted" (14). Tomlinson goes on to explain that gloves were deliberately omitted from the illustrations in order to best display the expressive gestures of the hands in the dances depicted, and he begs the forgiveness of the reader for any shortcomings: "The Faults, which may have happened in the Execution, either of the Printing, or Ingraving, will, I hope, be the more eafily execufed, if the Nicety of the Subject be considered, together with the Difficulty of the Performance, and the many Hands through which it has paffed: efpecially if it be remembered, that this is not only my firft Attempt, but likewife the firſt that has been made of the Kind" (14). Tomlinson conveys his own heightened awareness of the originality of his method of notation in his caption text to plate 7: "The figures to ye Music above & to ye characters or steps of Dancing below shew [sic], how they are connected or agree together; & ye Figures to ye Characters, which are some of them upright & others ye wrong End upwards, sideways, &c. shews [sic] to which part of ye Room ye Beginning of ye Steps is performed, & ye Steps or Characters are place upon ye Floor in a perspective Manner entirely new" (130). Throughout *The Art of Dancing*, Tomlinson repeatedly draws the reader's attention to the originality of his illustrated notation style. This highlighting is done both through textual assertions as well as through an inscribed signature in each illustration: "K. Tomlinson [or K.T.], inv."—that is, "K. Tomlinson, inventor." While the addition of "inv." in an engraving can mean simply the creator of an image, Tomlinson insists on a broader conceptual meaning. He refers to the concept of invention in his preface, noting "my invention" and expressing profound concern that any other dancing master should attempt to claim credit for his innovation in depiction style (15). Beyond this, Tomlinson devotes nearly one-third of the preface to *The Art of Dancing* to discussing the similarities between his work and that of Rameau. Tomlinson notes in his preface that his *The Art of Dancing* was completed by 1724, but financial hindrances did not allow publication until 11 years later. This unfortunate timeline appears to have vexed Tomlinson not only for the obvious financial reasons, but also because of the attention and privilege accorded to ensuing works on dance that came to publication while his ostensibly completed work lay fallow. As historian Wendy Hilton describes, "Kellom Tomlinson suffered the agonizing experience of writing a book and, before it could be printed, witnessing the publication of another similar in content. *The Art of Dancing* was completed in 1724, but it was not until 1735 that a total of one hundred and sixty-nine subscribers had donated sufficient funds to support its publication in London." While this unfortunate publishing timeline might bring to mind the publication controversy surrounding the development of calculus independently by Isaac Newton and Gottfried Leibniz, neither Tomlinson nor Rameau accused the other of plagiarism.

Thoroughly unraveling the connection between Pierre Rameau's 1725 dancing treatise and Tomlinson's 1735 master-work may not be feasible, but several pieces of information are quite clear. Beyond the similarities of title, the illustration styles of Tomlinson and Rameau are highly similar. Although nearly identical in content and composition, the engravings in Rameau's book are technically inferior to Tomlinson's engravings, with awkwardly proportioned human forms, clothing that appears unaffected by gravity, and feet and legs that appear to bear no weight. Tomlinson's illustrations show well-proportioned dancers whose clothing and bodies appear affected by gravity in a natural manner. In both works, the similar use of perspectival viewpoint and display of the dance floor is striking; however, this viewpoint should be regarded as common to its historic moment, since numerous other examples exist of early 18th-century prints depicting dance that bear similar composition and staging. Aside from any technical superiority, one notable difference between Rameau's illustrations and Tomlinson's lies precisely in what Tomlinson declares as his great innovation: the presentation of dancers, the dance floor with notated steps trailing after the dancers' feet, and the musical score for the dance. Whether Rameau's work was truly the original explanation of dance that Tomlinson improved upon, or whether Rameau was a lesser imitation of Tomlinson's long-completed, slowly published work, it is clear that Tomlinson's work is a greater achievement of visual art and representational innovation.

Tomlinson's depiction method was not only original and distinctive at its moment of production, but ultimately it proved to be wholly unique over time. While even Feuillet's early notation scores linked dance steps with musical scores, no other ensuing dance notation method has embraced the same approach as Tomlinson in dance notation depiction that displays a melding of the technical, the representational, and the illustrative in a simultaneous image. The notational style presented by Tomlinson in *The Art of Dancing* is more elegant than Rameau's, though less exhaustive in the roster of movements; it is more illustrative, though less thorough. The question arises as to whether Tomlinson's method was, perhaps, irreproducible, or whether, with the waning of the Baroque fashion of dance, notation was no longer suitable. As Ann Hutchinson Guest notes, "Though the [Feuillet] system served the 18th century so well, it offers nothing as a practical system for dance today. … The system was very much a product of, and suited to, the dance of its period" (1989, 21). As Guest indicates, a representational system and the thing represented bear upon each other a strong influence.

While analogies between music and architecture are abundant in scholarship and popular architectural dialogue, analogies between dance and architecture are frequently more appropriate, and this is particularly true in regard to dance notation. Notation was to dance what printing was to architecture: a means to broadcast the original works of an author to a wide audience, to establish the prominence and name recognition of the dancing master or the master builder, and to engender the professionalization of the field itself. The dancing masters of the 18th century contributed to discussions about the influence of representation in the field of dance; similar discussions are perennial in the field of architecture. In the case of dance, the spatial forms are fleeting, whereas in architecture the forms are durable. Both practices have spurred discussions within their respective fields about the implications of the mutually influential relationship between representation and the thing represented. As architectural historian and theorist Robin Evans states in his discussions of architectural projection, in architecture there is an inevitable concordance of building and representation: "In architectural drawings the projectors are not only perpendicular to the sheet of paper but also perpendicular to the major surfaces of the building drawn on it. Buildings are often rectangular, so aligning their surfaces with the surface of the drawing seems a sensible thing to do; yet this convention of imaginative vision also helps keep them that way. Whether it does so like some sort of butter paddle or like some sort of rolling pin—whether, in other words, it makes buildings into blocks or sheets—it is a powerful, conservative, forming agency" (Blau et al. 1989, 25). While rectilinearity clearly was not the issue in question for the dancing masters of the 18th century, the issue of constraints provided an important point for debate. Some dancing masters perceived a risk of fixity in choreography and composition when dances and specific movements were put to paper. In dance as in architecture, the selected tool or method of representation circumscribes the possibilities not only of depiction, but of form or action as well.

Irmgard Bartenieff (1963, 3–5) describes Jean-Georges Noverre, a French dancing master of the mid- to late 18th century who feared that the process of notating dances would result in a general stultifying effect within the field, whereby the only dances performed would be those that previously had been recorded, with movements limited to those that had found shorthand notation in books. If Bartenieff's assessment of Noverre's opinions is accurate, we can presume that as the grandfather of modern ballet, Noverre may have helped to marginalize the practice of dance notation. Presumably his opinions on the topic of notation would have permeated his teaching and borne an influence on later generations of dancers and dance instructors. Beyond any influence on the field wielded by Noverre's antipathy toward notation, it was Noverre's choreographic innovation of *ballet d'action* itself which helped to end the practice of Baroque dance notation. As a movement style, *ballet d'action* was marked by an increased use of gestural and emotive movements, in distinction to the precise and highly formalized movements in Baroque social and theater dance. To be more specific, the gestural and emotive movements of *ballet d'action* were situated in and performed by the arms and upper body, as opposed to the footwork-dominant dance of the Baroque. This shift in bodily emphasis would have presented a significant problem for the capacities of the dominant dance notation of the time. As Linda Tomko states (1999, 3), "Beauchamp-Feuillet notation was absolutely incapable of indicating arm gestures for ballroom and theatre choreographies alike." Tomko goes on to describe that "in practice, arm motions were almost never specified." As mentioned above, Feuillet hardly addressed the movement of the arms, and Rameau only later attempted to address the upper body. Tomlinson's addressing of the arms was done only through his illustrated figures, and his use of Feuillet's footwork notation precludes an effective incorporation of arm movements in notation. As Mark Franko (2011, 324) suggests, Baroque dance notation contributed to something of a closed loop in choreography: "These spatial relationships—the relations of the dance floor and the danced patterns upon it to notational script and the page—underlie the sense that baroque dance existed largely in relation to the conditions of possibility of its own notation."

While a limited system of notation such as that developed by Feuillet and expanded upon by Rameau and Tomlinson may impose particular constraints that ultimately create the disuse of such a system, the benefits of dance notation were numerous, and chief among them was posterity. The advantages gained by dance notation are described contemporaneously by Soame Jenyns in his 1729 poem *The Art of Dancing*:

> Long was the Dancing Art unfix'd and free;
> Hence lost in Error and Uncertainty:
> No Precepts did it mind, or rules obey,
> But ev'ry Master taught a diff'rent Way:
> Hence, ere each new-born Dance was fully try'd,
> The lovely Product, ev'n in blooming, dy'd:
> Thro' various Hands in wild Confusion toss'd,
> Its Steps were alter'd and its Beauties lost:
> Till feuillet at length, Great Name! Arose,
> And did the Dance in Characters compose:
> Each lovely Grace by certain Marks he taught,
> And ev'ry Step in lasting Volumes wrote.
> Hence o'er the World this pleasing Art shall spread,
> And ev'ry Dance in ev'ry Clime be read;
> By distant Masters shall each Step be seen,
> Tho' Mountains rise and Oceans roar between.
> Hence with her Sister Arts shall dancing claim
> An equal right to Universal Fame,
> And Isaac's Rigadoon shall last as long,
> As Raphael's Painting, or Virgil's Song. (Canto 2, p. 25)

Ultimately Baroque dance notation fell into disuse entirely, but the great age of Baroque dance documentation exerted a lasting effect on the field of European ballet. The standardization of the foot positions, jumps, and basic movements in the Baroque era contributed to a durable, recognizable ballet vocabulary that has carried through to the present day. Dance notation of the early 18th century helped to transform an art form formerly "unfix'd and free," taught by numerous masters in a range of stylistic and technical variations, into an art that relies on a specific fundamental vocabulary of technical movement.

Every technical drawing or representation presents a proposition about the world therein depicted. Even a superficially neutral drawing contains implicit instructions for viewing and suggests methods for interpretation. The privileging of a viewpoint, for example, or the choice between axonometric or perspectival, conveys cultural priorities and personal sensibilities. In the humanistic Renaissance, the use of perspective flourished; the eye of the viewer was the operative viewpoint. In Tomlinson's work, one can see the privileging of order and grace, and of dance literacy and proficiency. Tomlinson's illustration style truly is *The Art of Dancing*'s most remarkable feature, a unique representational method that continues to captivate modern readers much as it did nearly three hundred years ago.

THE ART OF THE PRINTED BOOK

When a digital surrogate of a book is created, the physical properties of that book can be obscured by the electronic version. While content, access, and readability are enhanced and the book itself is preserved from the ordinary damage caused by physical use, the tactile qualities of the original book are vaulted away. As a librarian committed to books as physical objects as well as digital entities, I find it vital to describe to the reader the physical characteristics of Kellom Tomlinson's *The Art of Dancing Explained by Reading and Figures*, so that this remarkable book can assume a more distinct physical form in the imagination of the reader of this new, digitally created edition.

There are just 16 copies of the 1735 first edition of *The Art of Dancing* identified by WorldCat, the union catalog of global libraries, and held by institutions throughout the world. Additional copies likely exist in private collections, but the details of such copies and collections remain private. To begin, we must first locate a suitable physical copy of the book; for the purposes of our description, this is the copy held by the Morgan Library and Museum in New York City.

The Morgan Library's copy is complete and near-perfect, consisting of 180 leaves (including preliminary leaves) and 42 plates of illustrations, bound in mottled calfskin with gilt panels on the spine. As I mention above, early printed books were sold as unbound gatherings of pages, and any formal binding was commissioned after purchase by book owners. The binding style of this copy would have been chosen by an early owner, probably in the 18th century. The spine is divided by five bands into six panels, the second of which bears a direct label imprinted with the book's title and year of publication, which suggests to me that the book was bound by a collector. The bound book measures 25 centimeters wide by 32 centimeters—about the width of my two hands side by side, with fingers slightly splayed, and roughly the height of my two hands, heel to fingertips, with the upper fingertips curled around the top edge of the book. The book is about two inches thick, altogether a sizable volume for the 21st century reader. The format of the book is *quarto*, a term derived from the dimensions of large sheets of laid paper, a type of handmade paper used in early printed books such as this one. To create quarto leaves, the full sheet of laid paper would be folded twice, into fourths; for *octavo*, the sheet would be folded a third time, into eighths, and so on. Laid paper bears a subtly ribbed texture due to the wire molds used in the papermaking process, a feature visible in the paper of the textual portion ("the printed part") of the Morgan Library's copy.

The book comprises several components: the dedication, a list of subscribers, preface, introduction, first book, second book, and plates. The pages of all textual portions are printed on laid paper, and the plates of illustration are printed on rag paper—a thick, supple paper that feels somewhat like fabric, and fittingly so, since the paper is made of reused cloth remnants. Rag paper was the preferred paper for etchings such as the plates in Tomlinson's book, partly due to the ability of the paper to accommodate the plate and hold the printed image. Though the paper of the illustrated plates is thick and fully opaque, there appears to be transfer of pigment or chemical seepage from the ink through to the back of each plate, as a pattern of yellowed discoloration on the verso transmits the mirrored image of the print on the recto of each plate. Platemarks – the impressions of the edges of the etched metal plate of illustration – are visible around each printed illustration. The leaves of the book are unevenly trimmed, with sometimes wide variation in the margins, particularly in margins of the plates. Tail margins are generally 5 cm at minimum, inner margins range from 1-3 cm, fore-edge margins range from 3-5 cm, and head margins range from 1 cm to 3 cm. The plates are almost always imperfectly aligned to leaf edges, or alternatively, binding and trimming are almost always imperfectly aligned to plate edges.

Watermarks are generally not visible on the leaves of the book, though a mere four leaves do bear a visible portion of a watermark; the only elements of the watermark design that are discernible are two parallel lines joined by a diagonal line, in the style of a capital letter N, with upward curlicues on each vertical, one of which extends further upward into an inverted capital G. The endpapers bear a clearly visible watermark – a unicorn with one forefoot raised – and countermark – a capital I encircled with a smaller O at the upper half of the I. The unicorn watermarks are applied to the pastedowns with the countermark on the free endpaper. On the back pastedown, the unicorn is inverted.

In the original printed book, catchwords appear throughout all textual portions as an aid to the person collating the pages. Catchwords, which typically appear at the bottom right corner, repeat the first word of the following page, and are used to match paragraphs between pages. While they would have been easily ignored by contemporary readers, to a modern reader they may be distracting and are unnecessary in reproductions.

The physicality of the book reveals its age, and its life: The mottled calfskin cover of Morgan Library's copy shows some surface deterioration in areas of darker coloration, which leads me to conjecture that the mottling was achieved through a chemical process, possibly through sprinkling of lye or copperas (Carter 153). Narrow turn-ins are executed on the front and back covers, with uneven edges of the pastedown endpapers (i.e. not parallel with the board edges). Stab-holes – traces of an earlier simple binding – are visible in some of the inner margins, particularly at the lower edge of the leaf.

Through bookplates, we can see the biography of this particular book as it passed through hands over the centuries before arriving at the Morgan Library in 1994. The earliest bookplate appears at the center of the pastedown, measuring roughly three inches wide by four inches tall. Engraved with a light hand and fine detail, this bookplate is a horizontally striped escutcheon topped with a dragon's head, set inside an oval frame and with an engraved ribbon that reads "ubi spiritus ibi libertas"—*where the spirit is, there is liberty.* Below the ribbon is the name "Wm. Constable, Esq." in an elegant and orderly cursive script. According to the Hull Collection, which now possesses the bulk of Constable's collection, William Constable lived from 1721 to 1791, and was "an avid collector" of all manner of objects, from specimens of the natural world to books and dolls. The next bookplate measures approximately two inches wide by three inches tall. Printed in black ink on white ground, it bears a coat of arms, topped with an open crown in the style of a British earl, set inside a looped garter that reads "Honi soit [qui m]al y pense"—*shamed be he who thinks evil of it.* The bookplate can be traced, by way of both its symbolism and by an identical bookplate that appears in the digital collection of the Folger Shakespeare Library, as belonging to A.P. Primrose, Earl of Rosebery (1847-1929). The third bookplate is pasted just below William Constable's bookplate, measuring approximately two inches tall by two and a half inches wide. This 20th century bookplate is embossed in gold on a white ground, and features the image of a hunt: three riders upon two horses are set amid trees and short shrubs, with two dogs chasing a rabbit in the foreground. Below the image is the name "Julia Parker Wightman."

The Morgan Library obtained its copy of *The Art of Dancing* through the bequest of Julia Parker Wightman (1909-1994), a New York-based book collector and bookbinder. Wightman was one of the first women elected to membership in the exclusive Grolier Club, a society of book collectors and dealers based in New York City. Upon her death, most of Wightman's collection was donated to the Morgan Library (Miniature 2003), including this copy of Tomlinson's book.

When reading this new edition, it may be easy to forget the grand physicality and life of *The Art of Dancing*—it is, after all, in part the purpose of this accessible version. However it is because of the book's grandness that it was able to survive the years since its publication in 1735. It bears remembrance that the faithful stewardship of the physical book, of which only 16 identified copies remain, is what allows our continued interest and scholarship.

ABOUT THE AUTHOR

Gabriella Karl-Johnson has directed the Architecture Library in the School of Architecture at Princeton University since 2015, following work in rare books cataloging, history research, choreography, and the architecture industry. She holds a Bachelor of Arts in Political Science from Beloit College, a Master of Architecture from the University of California, Berkeley, and a Master of Library Science from City University of New York. Her current scholarly interests include palimpsest building renovations, spatialized ritual practices, and built environment tourism ephemera.

NOTES

A portion of this article was originally published in *Signs and Society*, vol. 5, no. 2 (Fall 2017), by Semiosis Research Center at Hankuk University of Foreign Studies and University of Chicago Journals. https://doi.org/10.1086/693783

I gratefully acknowledge the generative critical comments offered by Richard Parmentier, editor emeritus of *Signs and Society*, who shepherded this article to its first publication. I also wish to thank Danielle Castronovo and J. Fernando Peña for their insights in the initial stages of research, and Hunter Johnson for perceptive reading in later stages of research and writing. The work of this article could not have been completed without access to the excellent research collections and knowledgeable staff of the Jerome Robbins Dance Division of the New York Public Library for the Performing Arts, where I first leafed through an imperfect copy of *The Art of Dancing* and browsed typewritten lecture notes by Irmgard Bartenieff. I am grateful for access to the reading room of the Morgan Library and Museum, a storied haven for rare books, where I became acquainted with the Tomlinson copy that I describe above. Lastly, I wish to thank Katherine Oktober Matthews for the generous invitation to join her as she revivifies this remarkable book for new audiences, in a new form.

Figure 1 is a public domain image sourced from Wikipedia. All other images are photographs by the author of the original books held by NYPL LPA.

REFERENCES

Bartenieff, I. 1963. "A Presentation of Movement Notation—a Means of Recording and of Studying Movement." Lecture given at the Thursday Afternoon Colloquium of the Center for Cognitive Studies, Harvard University, Cambridge, MA.

Blau, Eve, Edward Kaufman, and Robin Evans. 1989. *Architecture and Its Image: Four Centuries of Architectural Representation: Works from the Collection of the Canadian Centre for Architecture.* Montreal: Centre Canadien d'Architecture/ Canadian Centre for Architecture.

Carter, J., & Barker, N. (2006). *ABC for book collectors.* 8th ed. [with corrections] New Castle, DE: Oak Knoll Press.

Caroso, Fabritio. (1600) 1986. *"Nobiltà di dame": A Treatise on Courtly Dance, Together with the Choreography and Music of 49 Dances,* ed. Julia Sutton; music ed. F. Marian Walker. Oxford: Oxford University Press.

Feuillet, Raoul-Auger, and John Weaver. (1706) 1971. *Orchesography, translated from the French of Feuillet, and A small treatise of time and cadence in dancing.* Farnborough: Gregg International.

Franko, Mark. 2011. "Writing for the Body: Notation, Reconstruction, and Reinvention in Dance." *Common Knowledge* 17 (2): 321–34.

Guest, Ann Hutchinson. 1989. *Choreo-Graphics: A Comparison of Dance Notation Systems from the Fifteenth Century to the Present.* New York: Gordon & Breach.

———. 1990. "Dance Notation." *Perspecta* 26: 203–14.

Hilton, Wendy. 1997. *Dance and Music of Court and Theater: Selected Writings of Wendy Hilton.* Stuyvesant, NY: Pendragon.

Jenyns, Soame. 1729. *The Art of Dancing, a Poem, In Three Canto's.* London: printed by W. P. and sold by J. Roberts.

Miniature Book Society. Miniature Book Society Newsletter 2003 October. Ohio. UNT Digital Library. http://digital.library.unt.edu/ark:/67531/metadc9338/. Accessed May 6, 2021.

McKee, Eric J. 2011. *Musical Meaning and Interpretation: Decorum of the Minuet, Delirium of the Waltz: A Study of Dance-Music Relations in 3/4 Time.* Bloomington: Indiana University Press.

Pierce, Ken. 1998. "Dance Notation Systems in Late 17th-Century France." *Early Music* 26, no. 2 (May): 286–99.

Rameau, Pierre. (1725) 1967. *Le Maître à Danser.* New York: Broude.

———. (1725) 1970. *The Dancing Master.* [Brooklyn, NY]: Dance Horizons.

Thorp, Jennifer. 1992. "P. Siris: An Early Eighteenth-Century Dancing-Master." *Dance Research: The Journal of the Society for Dance Research* 10 (2): 71–92.

Tomko, L. J. 1999. "Dance Notation and Cultural Agency: A Meditation Spurred by Choreo-graphics." *Dance Research Journal* 31 (1): 1–4.

Tomlinson, Kellom. 1735. *The art of dancing explained by reading and figures: Whereby the manner of performing the steps is made easy by a new and familiar method.* London: Printed for the author.

———. 1992. *A Work Book by Kellom Tomlinson: Commonplace Book of an Eighteenth-Century English Dancing Master: A Facsimile Edition,* ed. Jennifer Shennan. Stuyvesant, NY: Pendragon.

THE
ART
OF
DANCING

Explained by

READING and FIGURES;

Whereby the

MANNER of Performing the STEPS

IS MADE EASY

By a NEW and FAMILIAR METHOD:

Being the

ORIGINAL WORK

First Design'd in the YEAR 1724,

by

KELLOM TOMLINSON, Dancing-Master.

In TWO BOOKS.

THE FIRST BOOK treats of the beautiful attitudes or postures of STANDING, the different positions from whence the STEPS of DANCING are to be taken and performed; and likewise of the manner of WALKING gracefully. The several sorts of BOWS and COURTESIES are also fully described, and all or most of the STEPS used in genteel DANCING, as well as many of those properly belonging to the STAGE: Illustrated with sixteen copper plates containing twenty-nine figures.

THE SECOND BOOK contains fourteen plates, consisting of twenty-eight figures of GENTLEMEN and LADIES, one of each in a plate, as dancing a MINUET; beginning from the REVERENCE or BOW, and proceeding regularly on till the whole is finished; showing the beautiful attitudes and graceful deportments of the performers, in the different figures and circles of that celebrated DANCE; together with the instructions for understanding and keeping time, and directions for the elevation, movement, and graceful fall of the arms in DANCING. To which are added at the request of some particular persons of quality, some instructions concerning COUNTRY DANCES.

The whole WORK is adorned with thirty copper plates, consisting of fifty-seven figures; with five other additional plates, marked A. E. I. O. U. containing all the STEPS described in this treatise, written in CHARACTERS; for the amusement of the curious, the further illustration of this work, and the instruction of such as are desirous to understand the CHARACTERS of DANCING.

THESE *are to certify, that the following work, entitled,* THE ART OF DANCING EXPLAIN'D, *was designed and composed by Mr.* Kellom Tomlinson *in the year 1726 in the same manner in which it now appears, we having seen the said work in the year above mentioned, which he told us be intended for the press as soon as his subscription was full; in witness whereof and in justice to the author we have hereunto set our hands this twelfth day of* February 1728.

JOSEPH SANDYS, *Gent.*
HENRY CAREY, *Master of Music.*

CATHERINE

Viſcounteſs FAUCONBERG.

MADAM,

HE work I here presume to offer your *ladyship*, treating of a subject in which you are not only well versed, but even excel; it was natural and obvious for me to *dedicate* it to you, confiding that, under so honourable a protection, it may at least be screened from such unjust censures as malice or envy ordinarily produce.

It may perhaps be expected that I should say something of the nobility and great endowments of your ancestors, as is usually done in *dedicatory epistles*; but the world is so well acquainted with your LADYSHIP's illustrious families, both that from which you came as well as that to which you are happily allied, that to mention anything of them would rather be derogating from their praise, seeing all I could relate would be inferior, both to their merit and to the opinion of all those who know them. All that I will venture to say is, that your candour, affability, sweetness and charity, joined to all your other great qualities, give as great a lustre to your family, as what you receive from it.

But of all your perfections what touches me the most, is your great talent in the ART of DANCING, which I can speak the more freely of, as I was not only a spectator, but had the honour to contribute to, for some time: Not that I pretend to arrogate to myself the glory of the great proficiency you made (for that was wholly due to your natural genius for that science) but only think myself happy in having had the good fortune to give lessons to a LADY that performed in a manner no less elegant than uncommon.

Nor do I so much wonder at the progress your LADYSHIP made in this science, when I consider your wonderful genius and exquisite taste for *music*, which is one of the greatest helps to a perfect performance in DANCING. All these rare talents give me a greater title to your LADYSHIP's gracious acceptance of this work; at least it gives me an occasion of assuring you how much I am, with all respect and esteem,

MADAM,
    Your LADYSHIP's
        most obliged,
            most obedient, and
                most humble servant,

                        KELLOM TOMLINSON.

A
LIST
OF THE
SUBSCRIBERS' NAMES.

N.B. This mark (†) shows that the subscriber, before whose name it is placed, died while this work has been carrying on.

A.

The Right Honourable the Lord Aston.
The Hon. Edward Aston, *Esq;*
The Hon. Mrs. Catherine Aston.
Sir Francis Andrews, *Bart.*
Sir John Astley *of* Patshull *in* Staffordshire *Bart.*
William Andrews *Esq;*
† *Mrs.* Eleanor Andrews.
Mr. A. Labbé, *Dancing-Master to their Royal Highnesses the young Princesses.*
Mr. Jonath. Ayleworth *Dancing-Master.*

B.

Sir Edward Blount, *of* Soddington *in the county* of Worcester, *Bart.*
The Lady Blount.
† *Sir* William Blacket, *of* Newcastle, *Bart.*
John Basket, *Esq; three Setts.*
B. Bagshaw *of* Wigwell *in* Derby Shire *Esq;*
Edward Brett: Bainbrigg *of* Derby *Esq;*
Ed. Bigland *of* Long W——n *near* Loughborough *Esq;*
† William Bourke, *Gent.*
Miss Bullar.

Mrs. Grace Brown, *of* Bentley *in* Darbyshire.
Mrs. Deborah Bowdler *of* Queen's-square.
Mrs. Catharine Bird.
Richard Bostock, *M. D.*
Capt. William Brooks, *of* Derby *Esq*;
Mrs. Margaret Butler, *of* Maryland.
Mrs. Booth *the celebrated dancer.*
Mrs. M. Bostock, *Paintress.*
Mr. John Brograve, *of* Rudgley, *Dancing-Master.*
Mrs. Bullock, *Dancer, at the theatre in* Goodman's-Fields.
Samuel Buck, *Engraver, for two Setts.*
Mr. Geo. Bickham *junior, Engraver.*

C.

The Right Honourable James, Earl *of* Castlehaven.
The Right Honourable Elizabeth, *Countess of Castlehaven.*
† *The Right Honourable* Ann, *Countess Dowager of* Clanrickard.
† *The Right Honourable the Lady* Frances Clifton.
Sir Richard Corbet, *Bart.*
The Lady Curzon *of* Kedleston *in* Derbyshire.
Mrs. Anna-Maria Calmady, *of* Devon.
† Francis Cottington, *of* Founthill-Giffard, *Esq*;
W— C—, *Esq*;
Mrs. Elizabeth Cannon, *Daughter to the late* Dean *of* Lincoln.
Richard Cresswell, *of* Bridgnorth *in* Shropshire *Esq*;
Rowland Cotton *of* Etwall *in the county of* Derby *Esq*;
Mr. Thomas Caverley, *of* Queen-Square *Dancing-Master.*
John Clark, *Engraver.*
Mr. Henry Carey *Master of Music.*
Mr. Ben. Cole, *Engraver.*
Mr. Thomas Cobb.

D.

Her Excellency the Marquess d'Aix, *Lady of Honour to the late* Queen *of* Sardinia.
F. D—ll *Esq*;
Kenelm Digby, *of* North-Luffingham *in the County of* Rutland, *Esq*;
Mrs. Ann Darnall, *of* Maryland.
John Dalton, *Gent.*
Mr. J. Dupree, *Dancing-Master at the Theatre Royal in* Covent Garden.
Mr. Lewis Duplessy, *Dancing-Master.*

E.

The Right Hon. Hannah-Sophia, *Countess of* Exeter.
The Right Hon. the Lady Mary E—.
Henry Every *of* Egginton *in the county of* Derby *Esq*;
Charles Edmonds *Esq*;
Mr. John Essex, *Dancing-Master.*
Miss Everet.

F.

The Right Hon. Thomas, *Viscount* Fauconberg.
The Right Hon. Catherine, *Viscountess* Fauconberg.
† *The Lady* Fust *of* Hill *near* Gloucester.
C. Fleetwood, *of* Gerards-Bromley *in* Staffordshire, *Esq*;
Mrs. Mary Fairbrother.

G.

Mrs. Giffard, *of* Chillington.
H. Gaylor, *M. D.*
Mr. Leech Glover, *Dancing-Master.*

H.

† *The Right Honourable the Lady* Mary Howard, *of* Worksop.

10

The Hon. Mrs. Winifrede Howard, *of* Norfolk.
The Lady Elizabeth Heathcote, *Daughter to the late* Earl *of* Macclesfield.
The Lady Hanmer.
Sir Arthur Hafelrigge, *of* Nosely *in* Leicestershire, *Bart.*
Thomas Heneage, *of* Cadeby *in the county of* Lincoln, *Esq*;
George Heneage, *of* Hainton, *in the same county, Esq*;
M. Hare *Esq*;
† Richard Holland, *Esq*;
William Herbert, *Gent.*
George Hills, *Gent.*
Mr. Henry Hargrave, *of* Newark, *Dancing-Master.*

J.

The Right Hon. Sir P. J—k, B.
The Lady Isham.
Mrs. Dorothy Jackfon.
Mrs. Elizabeth Jennens *of* Gopshall *in* Leicestershire.
Mr. Joseph Jackson, *Dancing-Master.*

K.

The Right Hon. the Lord Kingsale.
† *The Right Hon. the Lady* Frances Keightley.
Mr. Ascough Kirk, *of* Stamford, *Dancing-Master.*
Messieurs Knapton *Booksellers.*

L.

Sir William Lemon, *of* North-hall, Hertfordshire, *Bart.*
Richard Langley, *of* Grimston *in the county of* York, *Esq*;
George Legh, *of the* Temple *Esq*;
The Lady Lambard *of* Sevenoak *in* Kent.
Coke Littleton, *Esq*;

Miss Mary Lewis *of* Tarracoed *in* Carmarthenshire *South Wales.*
Mr. Tim. La Bufiere *Dancing-Master.*
Mr. Daniel Lewis *of* Bristoll *Dancing-Master.*
Mr. Henry Lintot *Bookseller, three Sets.*
Mr. Edward Langton *Dancing-Master of* Leicester.

M.

Sir Richard Moor *Bart.*
L. Masters, *of* Red-Lion-Square, *Esq*;
William Moore, *of* Fetcham *in* Surrey, *Esq*;
Mr. James Mechel *Printer.*
Mr. A. Moreau *Dancing-Master at the theatre in* Dublin.

N.

† *His Grace* Thomas *late Duke of* Norfolk.
His Grace Edward *Duke of* Norfolk.
The Right Hon. Francis *Lord* North *and* Guilford.
Mrs. Jane Needler, *of* Hollyland *in* Surrey.
John Newton of Gray's-Inn, *Gent.*
Mr. William Newton *of* Burton *upon* Trent, Staffordshire.

O.

Joseph Offley, *of* Norton-hall, Derby, *Esq*;
† Thomas O'Brien, *Esq*;

P.

His Grace William *Duke of* Powis.
Her Grace Margaret *Duchess of* Portland.
† J. Pearson, *M. D.*
Mr. P. P. *of* Litchfield.
Mrs. Parkhurst.
Mrs. Mary Peacock.
Mrs. Charlott Pigott.
† *Mr.* Edmond Pemberton *Dancing-Master.*

R.

Aymor Rich, *of* Bullhouse, Yorkshire *Esq;*
Mrs. Catherine Rolf, *of* Lynn.
John Rich, *Esq; Master of the Theatres Royal in* Lincoln's-Inn-Fields, *and* Covent-Garden.
Mrs. Mary Ricardy.
Richard Ruffel *Gent.*

S.

† *The Right Hon.* William *Earl of* Stafford.
† *The Right Hon.* Ann *Countess of* Stafford.
The Right Hon. Mary, *Countess of* Shrewsbury.
The Right Hon. the Lady Frances Shirley.
The Right Hon. the Lady Ann Shirley.
The Hon. John Stafford, *Esq;*
Sir Thomas Samwell, *of* Upton *in* Northamptonshire, *Bart.*
Robert Sutton, *Esq;*
Samuel Sanders *of* Caldwell *in the county of* Derby *Esq;*
Miss Elizabeth Stanley *Daughter to Sir* Edward Stanley, *Bart.*
† *Mrs.* Elizabeth Smith *of* Great James Street.
Thomas Southcote, *Esq;*
John Southcote, *of* Blyborough *in* Lincolnshire, *Esq;*
J. Strickland, *Gent.*
† William Somerset, *Gent.*
Richard Stanley, *Gent.*
William Stukeley, *M. D.*
Mr. P. Siris, *Dancing-Master.*
Mr. William Sawyer, *of* Rudgley *in* Staffordshire, *Dancing-Master.*
Mr. Robert Smith, *Dancing-Master.*

T.

The Hon. Mrs. Talbot, *of* Longford.
The Hon. Mrs. Ann Thompson.
Wilbraham Tufton, *Esq;*
† John Tufton, *Esq;*
Mr. James Tully, *Dancing-Master.*
Mr. John Topham, *Dancing-Master.*
John Tayleur *of* Roddington *in the county of* Salop *Esq;*
Mr. W. H. Toms *Engraver.*

W.

The Hon. Lady Webb, *of* Canford.
Mrs. Webb, of Hadthorp.
Mrs. Mary Wingfield
William Woolfe, *of* Queen's-square, *Esq;*
Edward Walpole, *of* Dunston *in the county of* Lincoln, *Esq;*
Mrs. Alethea Walpole.
† *Mrs.* Mary Walpole.
Ernle Washbourne, *of* Washbourne, *in* Worcestershire, *Esq;*
Thomas Wollescot, *of* Gray's-Inn, *Gent.*
John Walkinshaw, *Gent.*
Ayliffe White, *Gent.*
Edward Wright, *Gent.*
Mrs. Jane Williams.
John Woolley *of* Darley *in the county of* Derby *Esq;*
Mr. John Weaver *Dancing-Master.*

Y.

Charles Young *of the* Friers *in* Shrewsbury *Gent.*

THE
PREFACE.

I now at last have the pleasure of presenting to the world a work, which has been long promised; but which, through the difficulty of the undertaking itself, and the many obstacles to the execution of it, I was not able to finish before.

This undertaking must needs have been attended with great difficulty, because it was really the first of the kind. For though Monsieur Beauchamp *laid the first foundation, upon which Monsieur* Feuillet *built, (as some more ingenious person may perhaps improve upon mine); yet the works of both relate only to the characters of dancing; which, like the notes of music, can be only useful to masters, and cannot be understood by any other without their particular instructions. But the piece which I here offer to the world will be of general use to all, who either have learned, or are learning to dance: the words describing the manner in which the steps are to be taken; and the figures representing persons as actually taking them; both which together will make the learning more pleasant to the one, and serve as a continual remembrancer to the other.*

As most other arts and sciences, reduced to certain rules, have been now long since taught in books, I have often wondered no one should have hitherto paid the same regard to the Art of Dancing. *This is what I have endeavoured to do in the following work: wherein I have not pretended to advance any new laws for dancing unknown before; but only to collect and submit to view those principles and rules, which I had seen taught with the greatest success by the most eminent masters in the genteel way. As the notes of the music are placed on the top of every plate, the characters of the steps marked below, and the figures represent two persons in the very action of dancing; whoever has made any progress in the knowledge of musical notes and of the characters of dancing, will be able by intently viewing one of these plates, at one and at the same time, to call to mind the tune, to know the order of the steps, and to put the body into the proper attitude to take them. And though this book, like all others which treat of any art or science, cannot be perfectly understood without some study and application; yet by a little assistance from the author, or others of the profession properly qualified, all the difficulties will be soon surmounted. The figures in each plate are designed only to show the postures proper in dancing, but not to bear the least resemblance to any person to whom the plate is inscribed; which it would have been ridiculous to have attempted: The sole intent of the inscription being to do honour to myself, by this small testimony of my gratitude to some honourable persons. The continual change of the fashion will afford, I presume, a sufficient excuse for the drapery of the figures: and gloves were designedly omitted, on purpose, to show the beautiful shape of the hands. The faults, which may have happened in the execution, either of the printing, or engraving, will, I hope, be the more easily excused, if the nicety of the subject be considered, together with the difficulty of the performance, and the many hands through which it has passed: especially if it be remembered, that this is not only my first attempt, but likewise the first that has been made of the kind.*

It may seem a little strange, that I should claim the honour of having first treated of the Art of Dancing; *when a book upon the same subject was published in France as long ago as in* 1725. *But the following account will, I hope, clear up all doubt in relation to the justice of my pretensions.*

In Mist's Journal Sat. Jan. 13 1728, *appeared this advertisement,* "*Next Week will be published* The Dancing-Master *or* The Art of Dancing explain'd *by Monsieur* Rameau". *This gave me no small surprise, having never before heard of either any such book, or author. Had it been my fortune to have known, either before, or after I undertook to write on this art, that such a book was extant, my curiosity would certainly have led me to have consulted it; and had I approved it, it is highly probable I should have given the world a translation of it, with some additional observations of my own. This would have been a much easier task, than to compose a work entirely new upon the same subject: which I had actually finished in 1724 ready for the press, as it is now published, without any material alteration, a full year before the publication of Monsieur Rameau's book, and near four years before this advertisement appeared; the truth whereof several credible witnesses have testified under their own hands.*

I advertised this work of mine the first time, as ready for the press, and that it only waited for a sufficient number of subscribers to defray the expense, in Berington's Evening Post, Oct. 15, 1726, *and again in the same paper* Oct. 22. *This advertisement was repeated in* The White-Hall Evening Post, Nov. 12. *and in* The London Journal, Dec. 3. *In* Mist's Journal *of* March 4, 1727, *I gave notice of the publication of my* proposals, *together with some plates done by way of specimen; and renewed that notice on the* 18th, *in* Berington's Evening Post, *and again on* Oct. 28. *in the same paper. From this particular account it appears, that I had published seven advertisements concerning my work; the first of which was two years and three months before ever the translation of Monsieur Rameau's book was advertised in* Mist's Journal Jan. 13, 1728.

To secure myself in some measure from the damage I might receive by this advertisement; I thought it necessary to publish one myself a few days after, in Mist's Journal Jan. 27. *To which I prefixed this motto from* Virgil, —Tulit alter Honores; *intimating that another person had attempted to bear away the honour of my invention; and I may justly add, the profit of it too. That this was his intention is very plain from two circumstances: the addition to the title; and the alteration of the form of Monsieur Rameau's book. The title of his in the original is only* The Dancing Master; *to which the ingenious translator, or perhaps bookseller, thought proper to add that of mine,* The Art of Dancing explain'd: *The French oiginal was published in* octavo; *but the translation was magnified to a* quarto, *almost the size of mine, and yet proposed to be sold at half the price. The assuming thus the very title and form of the book proposed to the public by me, seems to have been done with no better view than to raise an advantage by anticipating my design; and to obstruct the success of it by making it seem to be only a servile imitation of the original invention of Monsieur Rameau. This contrivance was the more likely to have the desired effect, from the unfavourable situation in which the* proposals *for the subscription to my book might at the time appear. It was above two years since it had been advertised as ready for the press: and this delay in the publication, the not fixing any certain time for it, and the difficulty in procuring subscriptions, upon the number of which the publication must depend, might probably induce many persons to suspect that it would never be published at all. And this difficulty would be much increased, by offering to the public a book on the same subject, with the same title, and of almost the same size, which yet should cost no more than half the price of mine. To make which book appear still more perfect and complete, and mine less necessary, or useful, the gentleman who published it was not satisfied to present it to the world merely as a translation of Monsieur Rameau's work, approved by Monsieur Pécour, the greatest master in France; but was prompted by his ingenuity and generosity to make such surprising improvements in the figures, as will be a lasting monument of his great abilities in the* Art of Dancing.

Before I conclude this preface, it seems necessary to say something more particularly of myself, for the satisfaction of those to whom I may not have the honour to be known; who will naturally expect, before they encourage a piece of such an extraordinary nature, to receive some evidence, that the person who undertakes it is in some measure qualified for the performance.

In April 1707, *I was placed as an apprentice with Mr. Thomas Caverley, now living in Queen's-Square, St. George the Martyr, with whom I continued till the year* 1714. *During which time, I had likewise the good fortune to be further instructed in the theatrical way by that great performer Mr. Cherreir, once contemporary with the inimitable Mr. L'Abbé, with whom also I have had the happiness of a personal acquaintance. Mr. Cherreir's great merit, after he quitted the stage, was supported a long time by the late Mr. John Shaw, who was justly esteemed not only one of the finest theatrical dancers, but one of the most beautiful performers in the gentleman-like way: the acquisition of both which excellencies in practice, must be chiefly owing to those admirable instructions in the theory, which he received from Mr. Caverley, when he and I were fellow apprentices to that great master.*

I beg leave to mention in the next place two of my scholars, who have appeared upon the stage with no small applause. The one was Mr. John Topham, who danced upon both theatres under the name of Mr. Kellom's scholar, *when he had been with me no longer than betwixt two and three years. The other was Miss Frances, who, on the Theatre Royal in Little Lincoln's-Inn-Fields, performed the* Passacaille de Scilla, *consisting of above a thousand measures or steps, without making the least mistake; but she left me in the midst of her improvement.*

To this I hope it will not be thought improper to subjoin a short account of some of my compositions, which have been well received by the world. The Passepied Round O *in* 1715 *dedicated to Mr.* Caverley; *the* Shepherdess *in* 1716; *the* Submission *in* 1717, *which, by the name of* Mr. Kellom's New Dance, *was performed by Monsieur and Mademoiselle Salle, the two French children, on the theatre in Lincoln's-Inn-Fields, to very considerable audiences, every night, for a whole week together. To which I beg leave to add the* Prince Eugene *in* 1728; *the* Address *the next year; the* Gavot *in* 1720; *and the* Passacaille Diana *the year following, dedicated to Mr. L'Abbé. All which I composed, wrote in characters, and published, for the improvement of the* Art of Dancing.

I might here add a long account of the honour done me by many of the nobility and gentry in employing me to teach their children; and in permitting me to publish it to the world by the dedication of my plates. But I have perhaps dwelt too long upon this subject already, which I hope the candid reader will excuse; and not impute this account of myself to vanity or conceit, but to an earnest desire in me to give the utmost satisfaction to my subscribers, and to remove all suspicion of my want of talents proper for the execution of this new undertaking. And this was the more necessary to be done, because of the disadvantage to which I have been exposed by going accidentally under two different names, Kellom *and* Tomlinson; *being known formerly by the first, but of late only by the last; the occasion of which it may not be thought improper to relate.*

During the time of my apprenticeship I went generally by the name of Kellom, *a corruption of* Kenelm, *my true Christian name; as it is very common for young persons to be called Mr. John, Mr. William, and the like, without the addition of their surname. At the expiration of my apprenticeship, several of my friends out of respect called me by my surname of* Tomlinson; *but, being unwilling to decline the advantage I might probably receive from the reputation of having learned the* Art of Dancing *under so great a master as Mr. Caverley, I chose rather to retain the name of* Kellom, *by which I had been so universally known to have been under his instruction. This duplicity of appellation turned afterwards to my great dis-advantage: many of the nobility and gentry, who would have had their children taught by Mr.* Kellom, *refusing to employ Mr.* Tomlinson *though recommended to them; and many, who would have employed Mr.* Tomlinson, *rejecting Mr.* Kellom. *To prevent which confusion for the future, I shall acknowledge myself obliged to those, who, instead of either singly, shall be pleased to call me by both conjunctly,* Kellom Tomlinson.

THE
ART of DANCING
EXPLAIN'D.

BOOK THE FIRST.

CHAP. I.
Of STANDING.

BEFORE I proceed to treat on *motion*, I apprehend it to be necessary to consider that grace and air so highly requisite in our position, when we *stand* in company; for, having formed a true notion of this, there remains nothing further to be observed when we enter upon the stage of life, either in walking or dancing, than to preserve the same.

And, for the better understanding of this important point, let us imagine ourselves, as so many living pictures drawn by the most excellent masters, exquisitely designed to afford the utmost pleasure to the beholders: And, indeed, we ought to set our bodies in such a disposition, when we stand in conversation, that, were our actions or postures delineated, they might bear the strictest examination of the most critical judges.

Let us, therefore, to draw nearer to the subject in hand, inquire into the nature of those positions that must be observed, in order to attain this fine and becoming presence: And that our readers may be furnished with proper directions to arrive at the same, though perhaps, our rules may not be so perfect as could have been wished, we flatter ourselves they will be of no small use and advantage; wherefore, without further apology, I shall enter upon the description of *position* in general.

Position, then, is the different placing or setting our feet on the floor, whether in conversation or dancing; and those for conversation, or when we *stand* in company, are when the weight rests as much on one foot as the other, the feet being considerably separated or open, the knees straight, the hands placed by the side in a genteel fall or natural bend of the wrists, and being in an agreeable fashion or shape about the joint or bend of the hip, with the head gracefully turning to the right or left, which completes a most heroic posture; and, though it may be improper in the presence of superiors, among familiars it is a bold and graceful attitude, called the *second position*[†]: Or, when the heel of the right or left foot is enclosed or placed, without weight, before the ankle of that foot by which the poise is supported, the hands being put between the folds or flaps of the coat, or waistcoat, if the coat is unbuttoned, with a natural and easy fall of the arms from the shoulders, this produces a very modest and agreeable posture, named the *third position enclosed*[‡]:

---

† See Plate III.   ‡ See the feet in Plate IV.

Or, if the enclosed foot be moved open from the other, sideways, to the right or left, about the distance of half a foot, or as far as, in setting it down to the floor, the weight of the body resting on the contrary foot is not disordered by it, with the toes handsomely turning out, the hat under one arm, and the other in some agreeable action, the head also turning a little from the foot on which the poise rests, this we style the fourth position open, and it may be very justly esteemed a most genteel and becoming posture[*].

The positions, from which dancing dates its original, consist of five principles: As, first, when the toes turning outwards, the two heels are equally placed together[◊]. Secondly, when both heels are considerably separated or open[§]. Thirdly, when the poise rests upon one foot, the other being enclosed or placed before the ankle of that foot by which the weight is supported[ƒ]. Fourthly, when the enclosed foot is advanced upon a right line, about the length of a step in walking[Δ]. And, fifthly, when the heel of the advanced foot is so crossed and placed before the toe of that foot on which the body rests, as that the turning may be made, and yet one foot not, in the least, interrupt the other[▽]. Having briefly described the most agreeable postures of *standing* in conversation, and laid down the rudiments of the whole ART of DANCING, I shall now proceed to treat on *motion*, the result of position, and first begin with *walking*.

---

[*] See Plate VIII.   [◊] See Plate II.   [§] See Plate III.   [ƒ] See Plate IV.   [Δ] See Plate IX.
[▽] See Plate XI.   [∂] See Plate I.

CHAP. II.
Of WALKING.

WALKING consists of motion and a change of place, by transferring the weight or poise of the body from one foot to the other, by stepping or advancing the disengaged foot (whichsoever it be) from the first position$^\partial$ to the fourth advanced$^\Delta$, and so alternately, concluding as at first$^\partial$, but always on the contrary foot. In order to walk gracefully, it is to be observed, that, during the step or motion made by the disengaged foot, as above$^\Delta$, the whole weight of the body must rest on the same foot as at commencing it[†], until the stepping foot is advanced its due length of step[‡]; and, on its receiving the poise or weight on the ball or full part of the heel, upon setting it to the ground or floor, the now disengaged foot, which at first supported the weight, becoming by this means released, attends the poise in a gentle and easy motion, until it arrive in its former position[†]; but on the contrary foot for the step next ensuing, which is made in like manner, and so on; for if, instead of the body's waiting or attending the motion of the stepping foot, as above described[‡], it should either go before or along with it, the grace that ought to accompany our steps, in walking, is lost, because the foot must constantly go before the body[‡], to receive it, otherwise it will always represent the body in a falling posture.

And it is further to be noted, that, in walking with a good grace, time and harmony must be observed as well as in

---

Δ See Plate IX. ∂ See Plate I.   † See Plate I.   ‡ See Plate IX.

dancing: For example, the setting down or receiving the poise, at the end of the step, is upon *one*; the taking up the disengaged foot, by a gentle and easy raising the heel and pointing the toe, in one entire motion, which is the manner of taking up the foot to step, is upon *three*†; and *two* is in the coming up of the disengaged foot, after the step has been made†, which may be continued faster or slower, but must always be in one certain time, counting *one*, *two*, and *three*, as in music. And, by this method, the body with a good grace resting or standing, till two-thirds of the three we count, must necessarily add great beauty to our walking, which is the case under consideration; for the step is made upon *one*‡, the preparation or taking up the foot, to make the step, *three*†, and *two* is in the coming up of the released foot, to continue our walking.

And, as to the motion of the arms in walking, they will naturally have their due course or swing, in a continual contrast or opposition to the feet; for, when the right foot steps forwards*, the left arm advances, in contradiction, as the right arm does, when the left foot steps forwards◊, and so alternately; and the like in walking backwards, in relation to the contrast, but not with respect to the arms, because, in walking backwards, the contradiction is between the same arm and foot; for, when the right foot steps back◊, the right arm advances in opposition, as, when the left foot steps backwards*, the left arm advances, as aforesaid, and so on, if continued. Having, I hope, offered what will prove satisfactory, on this head[1], I shall next inquire into the different sorts of *bows* and *curtsies*[2] in conversation.

---

* See the second figure or woman's side in Plate IX.   ◊ See the first figure in Plate IX.

Editor's notes: 1. *On this head* - archaic phrase meaning on this subject.   2. The archaic spellings of *courtesy* and *courtesies* have been changed to *curtsy* and *curtsies*.

CHAP. III.

Of BOWING, or
the different sorts of HONOURS.

BOWS or *curtsies* are the outward marks of respect we pay to others, which, in one sex, are shown by bowing the body, but, in the other, by bending the knees; and, if made in a regular manner, they are indeed very grand, noble, and highly ornamental. They accompany our conversation, as well in standing as walking; in the former, on breaking off a conversation, as in taking leave, or by way of acknowledgment for some favour or obliging thing spoken in our praise; and in the latter, when we enter a room, or meet a person passing either on the right or left. These are the two different classes or sorts of *bows* and *curtsies*, which are, as it were, founded on the two preceding chapters of *standing* and *walking*; and, to begin with leaving a room, which relates to the first of the said orders, I shall observe, that taking leave in conversation consists in stepping aside, bowing, and leaving the disengaged foot pointed, sideways, in one entire motion to the first division of the bow or counting of *one*[△], during which it remains the respect or counting of *two*[△]; and, in the graceful raising of the body upon *three*, it is drawn pointed, with the knees straight till it crosses behind the foot on which the poise rests, and stands erect on the foot that it crosses behind[▽], to be repeated as often as occasion

---

[△] See Plates II and IV in Book II.   [▽] See Plate III in Book II.

requires; and it is to be noted that the respect, if repeated, is always made to the same hand; if the leave be taken to the right, the stepping aside is always with the right foot$^\partial$, as it is always to the left, if taken the contrary way♦.

In conversation with a gentleman or lady standing, the very same bow is made as in leaving a room, the receiving the poise on the foot drawn behind excepted$^\triangledown$; but, instead thereof, it remains, on conclusion of the bow, in the third position, upon the point, without weight, behind the foremost foot which here supports the poise, in readiness to repeat the respect, if necessary$^\diamondsuit$, because, in this bow of repetition, it always steps first to one hand$^\triangle$, and then to the other$^\triangle$, in order to preserve the same ground; otherwise, if made as leaving a room$^\wp$, it would have the contrary effect and cause the persons to retire, instead of resting in the same place; and it is a very genteel and becoming bow, if the stepping aside, bow, and point of the disengaged foot, be made at once$^\triangle$, and a pause or counting of *two* is observed between the stepping aside and bowing$^\triangle$, and the graceful rising up again from thence, in drawing of the pointed foot up, at the same time, into the abovementioned position$^\diamondsuit$, be also in one entire motion. As to the reverence or curtsy of a lady on the present occasion, with regard to the feet, it is much the same, but not so in relation to the body; because, as I have already said, the respect the former shows to any is by bending the body, but the curtsy or respect, which a lady pays to those of either sex, is by a graceful bending of the knees†, accompanied with a becoming and suitable disposition of the different parts of the body: As, having the hands before them, in some agreeable posture supporting, as it were, the slanting or falling shoulders, which,

---

∂ See Plate II in Book II. ♦ See Plate IV in Book II. $\diamondsuit$ See the feet in Plate V.
$\wp$ See Plate III in Book II.

at the same time, lengthen and more gracefully expose a fine
neck, as well as a beautiful face composed of so many delicate
and charming features, with which they are usually adorned by
the bounty of nature; and, though it may be, in some measure,
presumptuous to attempt any addition to the natural charms of
the fair sex, I flatter myself they will forgive me, if I acquaint
them, that a modest look or direction of the eye, an agreeable
smile or a lively and pleasant aspect, with a chin neither poked
out nor curbed in, but the whole countenance erect and graceful,
will add a lustre to the whole, where any of these are wanting,
whether in one sex or the other; and, together with the easy
situation or posture of the whole head, neck, and arms, with the
handsome turn of the feet, they complete the entire fashion or
agreeable disposition of a fine accomplished lady, as well in
conversation in general, as the curtsy[†], or walking, from its
being thus disposed, from top to toe, is only to preserve the
graceful position of the body, as above described.

It only now remains to inquire, whether a lady steps
aside and makes her honour, in the manner we have shown a
gentleman leaves a room, after stepping aside[‡], by drawing
the disengaged or pointed foot[†] into the first position, equal to
the foot, which stepped aside[*], instead of drawing it crossing
behind, as aforesaid[◊]; or that curtsying, without stepping aside
at all[*], as some do, is only to let the weight or graceful fashion
of the body, as just described, fall, or rather seat itself, as on a
chair or stool, without disorder, upon that foot which is
drawn or crossed behind[◊], as in leaving company, or on both
legs equally alike[*], if the pointed foot be drawn into the first
position[*]; and the like, if made on both legs, without moving
from the same place[*], only with this difference, in relation to

---

† See Plates II and IV in Book II.   ‡ See Plate II in Book II.   * See Plate II.
◊ See Plates IV and XI.

the weight's coming upon the pointed foot[†] or that which is crossed behind[◊], after touching the heel of the foot on which the poise rests[▽], in like manner as when the gentleman takes leave[†], and retires back, as it were a seat for the weight to rest upon[◊], whilst the curtsy or lady's respect is paid upon the beginning or first division; whereas, in a bow for the man, it does not receive the weight, till the third division[Δ], resting the counting of *two* for the respect, as we have observed, in the contrary sex; and, upon counting of *three* or completing the curtsy, it rises in the same slow, graceful, and deliberate manner, till it stands upright on the crossing behind foot[∂], as at first it seated itself thereon, in the curtsy or bending of the knees[†], completing the respect or curtsy, on a lady's leaving a room, in the disengaged or foremost foot's being at liberty to renew the respect, as occasion requires[∂].

As to which foot the stepping aside begins with, in relation to taking of leave, it is altogether the same, as was described for the other sex; but, as this curtsy or respect has the like effect, as I observed, in treating of the bow in conversation with another, *viz.* retiring from each other, it is to be evaded in rising, by transferring the poise from the hindmost foot to the foremost, which, being then at liberty, is ready to repeat the complaisance on the contrary side, and so to preserve the same ground. And the like may be said, in relation to concluding the curtsy on the stepping aside foot, when the pointed foot is drawn into the first position[*]; or the like, without stepping at all, by swaying or waving the principal part of the body, as occasion offers, either upon the right[◇] or left foot[℘], as will be most to advantage, in the

---

▽ See the feet in Plate V.   ∂ See Plate III in Book II.   ◇ See the second figure or woman's side in Plate I.   ℘ See the first figure in Plate I.

graceful bending or sinking down upon the knees[⅋]; which wave or sway of the body not a little contributes to the beauty of the curtsy, as does also the handsome position of the waist, neither too much forwards nor backwards, the whole poise of the body being beautiful and upright, as before described, directly perpendicular or right down over the heel or heels, on which the poise rests[ƒ]; and this, I think, concludes all that is necessary to be said, concerning the *reverence* or *curtsy* made by persons of either sex, according to the first class, relating to *position* or *standing*, at leaving a room, or in conversation with others.

I now proceed to the *second* sort of honours, *viz.* those which are introduced by *motion*, as in walking, etc. and I shall, first, finish what concerns the ladies, before I return to the gentlemen, who are to observe, that, at the end of the last step, after their entrance into a room, before they pay their respect or honour, they are to make a graceful pause or stand upon the foot that made the last step, which, as has been already said, in walking, is completed upon counting of *one*; so that the whole person rests the counting of *two*, in the coming up of the disengaged foot into the first position, equal to the foot which made the last step preparatory for the curtsy[⊕]; and *three* is the rest it makes, when thus joined in the graceful disposition of the whole fashion, or upon taking it up, if afterwards stepping aside[+], and thus erect from head to foot, it is duly prepared to make the curtsy in that smooth manner of bending the knees we have described, directing the eye, as occasion requires; or the like, if the curtsy be made in stepping aside, as in taking leave[⅋], for there is no other difference between the honour or respect, on leaving company and coming

---

[⅋] See Plates II and IV in Book II. [ƒ] See Plate II in Book II. [⊕] See Plates I and II. [+] See Plate I.

up to them, than that, as I have observed, the former proceeds from *position* or *standing*[‡], and the latter is introduced by *motion* or *walking*[+]; but, having shown what that *preparation* is, there is no occasion for any further enlargement.

If a lady makes an *honour passing*, either on the right or left, or in meeting anyone in conversation, walking, or the like, at the end of the step preceding the complaisance or respect, she turns about halfway towards the person, upon conclusion of the said preparatory step or counting of *one*; and, upon counting of *two*, she lets the disengaged or coming up foot touch the heel of that foot which stepped, crossways, before the said coming up foot[◊], which now attends the poise, in order to make the honour; and, upon *three*, she sets it down, somewhat obliquely or slanting off from the person to whom the respect is paid, without weight[§], and thus becomes duly prepared to make the curtsy[∾]; I mean, when the head is beautifully turned to the right or left, according to the side on which the respect is made, in a graceful contrast of the whole fashion; and, being so disposed, she makes the honour by a smooth and easy bending of the knees. The whole poise of the body, during the counting of *one* or bending, as aforesaid, rests the counting of *two*[∾], or, as we have already said, the respect in a fine contrast; and, upon the *third division* or completing the curtsy, it rises gracefully from the foot on which it rested, all the while, in this becoming twist, passing on, till it stands erect upon the foot which was placed or advanced for that purpose[§], by transferring the poise from the foot that made the preparatory step for this respect, which, being now at liberty, is ready to repeat the same, as often as occasion requires[+]; and from hence it becomes a kind of *walking curtsy*, changing the poise from

---

‡ See Plates IV, V, and VIII.   ◊ See the feet in Plate V.   § See the feet in Plate X.

one foot to the other. And it is to be noted, that it must always be the foot next the person, which makes the last step in walking before the respect: For instance, if the person be on the right, the right foot makes the step; and the left, if the honour be paid to the other side, turning, as before described, towards the person or foot which made the step in preparation for the curtsy, and directing the eye, sideways, upon the person to whom the respect is paid, instead of right forwards, as when entering a room, or meeting one, which is the only difference. And it is to be further observed, that, though this complaisance may be repeated, once or more, after passing a person, it must never be made before we come parallel to the person to whom we pay this respect; and if occasion requires its being transferred to the other side, which often falls out[3], as when company are seated or standing, on both sides of a room or gallery, etc. we continue walking on, till we arrive at the next occasion of paying this respect, as when company are scattered, at some distance, and then make the pause or stand, at the end of the step next the person or persons, by turning, etc. as before; or if the change or transferring may be soonest performed, as when company are thick on both sides, it must be divided by two steps made between the preceding curtsies, the second step preparing to pay the respect, as I have already shown, which will be the left foot, the foregoing honour being supposed to the right; and the right foot, if the complaisance be first paid to the left. And, in these *passing honours*, it must be noted, that no regard is to be observed with respect to the quality of the person, but only conveniency, in relation to the right or left, as the company first present themselves, as we pass along; nor, indeed, can it well be otherwise, because they are all to receive it, in their turns. As what has been said is all that I apprehend to be

---

Editor's notes: 3. *Fall out* - archaic or arcane phrase meaning to happen, to occur.

material, relating to the *ladies*, I flatter myself that they will not be wanting in putting these rules into practice, since I have been at so great pains in composing them for their service.

I shall now proceed to the conclusion of what I have to offer to the *gentlemen*, on this head, which is much to the like effect with what was observed to the ladies; for, when a gentleman enters a room, the graceful stand or rest he makes, as already described in the curtsy for a lady on this occasion, must be always made on the last step before bowing, which may be on the left foot; whilst the right, in coming up, as aforesaid, in its attendance on the poise, instead of ending in the first position†, as in walking, is placed considerably more open, sideways, without weight, the heel being somewhat raised, the ball or instep pointed or pressing lightly on the floor, the knee straight, and the whole weight of the body, in a gentleman-like manner, resting on the left foot‡, bows, as occasion requires, by bending the body and scraping the open foot, at the same time, in one entire motion forwards; upon the counting of *one**, remains the respect or counting of *two*, in this respectful posture, with the knee on which the body rests bended, to prevent its being awry, which otherwise would be the consequence, and the arms naturally hanging under the shoulders; and, upon *three*, it rises from this humble posture in one entire slow motion, till it stands erect on the right or scraping foot; and the left, at the same time, being released from the weight of the body, falls into the first position, as in walking◊, to repeat it, if it be necessary.

The *bow passing* differs in no respect from that advancing or coming into a room, except in the situation of the person: For instance, in entering a room, the person is before us, but only upon one side, on the present occasion. From hence it appears that, after the step preceding the bow and pause, placing the

---

† See Plate I.　　‡ See the feet in the second figure or woman's side of Plate VI.　　* See the feet of the second figure in Plate IX.　　◊ See the second figure in Plate I.

contrary foot or preparative, is made[§], the respect is paid in the very same method, as forwards, only that the body is turned in a beautiful and agreeable twist or contrast, sideways, looking upon the person to whom we pay the respect; if the bow be made upon the right, the antecedent step is made with the left foot, and the right, during the pause, is placed for the scrape in bowing[§]; as, if it be made on the contrary side, the right foot makes the preparatory step, and the left will be placed, as aforesaid, to pay the respect[ƒ]; and, if repeated, it will always begin and end with the same foot, till changed by adding a second step, which transfers the bow to the other side, as occasion offers. This bow is also made, in walking with a gentleman or lady, upon some obliging expression in conversation, once or oftener, as necessity requires, with the right foot scraping, if the person be on the right, but the contrary foot, if the person be on the left. It must also be noted, that the step made, before placing the foot for the bow, is to be made with the contrary foot to the side the person is on, to whom the respect is paid, and the placed foot is that next the person; though it is the reverse in the ladies, because the step preparatory for this respect is made with the foot next the person, and the contrary is the placed foot.

It will not be improper, before I conclude with the *gentlemen*, to take some further notice of a difficulty that may arise in the application of the *bow passing*; I mean, the changing or transferring it from one side to the other, because, in passing through a lane or room full of company, we cannot, as I have already observed to the *ladies*, bow on both sides at once; and therefore the rule is, to pay this respect to those that first fall in our way, and, if possible, conclude on that side, and then,

---

§ See the feet of the second figure in Plate VI.   ƒ See the feet of the first figure in Plate VI.

by walking two steps or more, to make the like compliments on the other; which will be, by bowing and scraping the left foot$^\oint$, if the first respect be paid to the right, and the contrary foot, if it be first paid to the left§. And if it should fall out, as in St. James's Park, or other public places, where you may walk perhaps a considerable way before you find an occasion for paying this respect, you are to note that these bows, as we said in relation to the ladies' curtsies, are never made before you come equal to those you salute; and, if it be a person of nobility or extraordinary fashion, an additional bow, sideways, as when leaving a room, may be added, with the contrary foot to that which made the scrape, turning full to the person to whom you pay this uncommon respect, in *passing*; nor must you forget that, in entering a room, or meeting anyone, it is always to be added to the *bow forwards*, as being of singular use, in paying respect to the company in general, as the former is to the person we salute in particular, by a cast of our eye round the company, omitting none, for an omission may, many times, be esteemed an affront and ill manners. It will be likewise expedient to observe, that some ladies make the *passing honour* the very same as that I have described for the gentlemen; the only difference is, that, after placing the foot$^\partial$, instead of *bowing*, in the scrape of the foot$^\blacklozenge$, they *curtsy* to the right§ or left$^\oint$, as occasion requires, in the graceful contrast described for the other sex's bowing, concluding on the scraping foot$^\blacklozenge$; which, if on the right, will be the right foot$^\lozenge$, and left at liberty to step and place the preparatory foot; as, on the contrary side, it will conclude on the left foot$^\wp$, and the right will then be in readiness to make the step, and place the foot, in order to its being repeated, according to the various occasions

---

∂ See Plate VI.　◆ See the feet in Plate IX.　◇ See the second figure in Plates IX and I.　$\wp$ See the first figure in Plates IX and I.

before mentioned. Some also use this method of curtsying when they enter a room, or meet a person, which is, in all respects, agreeable to the gentleman's bow, as above described, except in the scrape or sliding of the prepared foot forwards[†], *viz.* to bend both knees, at the same time, and to let the poise fall gracefully upon the hind foot, during the first and second divisions; and afterwards the body rises beautifully, as aforesaid, till it stands on the advanced foot[†], by transferring the weight from the hind foot, which, being released, is ready to walk[‡], and place the contrary foot, in order to repeat it, in like manner, if necessary: Or, if the curtsy used, at leaving a room, be added[*], it will then, in all respects, be answerable to the gentleman's bow, at coming into a room. But in fine[4], let the bow or curtsy, notwithstanding all the various methods, and the several occasions, here described, be made in which of those forms we please, they cannot fail of being performed to advantage, but must necessarily produce a good effect, provided they be made in the manner already shown, upon counting of *one*[*], the pause or rest *two*[*], and the rising upon *three*[◊]. Having, therefore, in this discourse upon honours in general, endeavoured to take notice of every particular that might prove useful or instructive, so as to omit nothing material, I flatter myself, that, if it be not, in all respects, accomplished according to my intentions, the difficulty of the subject will plead my excuse; and, as I have, in the preceding chapters, regularly gone through what I apprehended necessary, upon *standing*, *walking*, and *honours* in general, under the last of which heads, as the reader will easily perceive, it was scarce possible to avoid some repetitions, in my treating distinctly on bows and curtsies, I shall now proceed to the various *steps of dancing.*

---

† See the feet in Plate IX. ‡ See Plate I. * See Plates II and IV in Book II.
◊ See Plate III in Book II.

Editor's notes: 4. *In fine* - archaic phrase meaning finally, ultimately, or in sum.

C H A P. IV.
Of the DANCING ROOM.

BEFORE I enter upon the various *steps of dancing*, it will be necessary to describe the room in which the dancing or steps are to be performed; which indeed seems to claim our more immediate notice, since it will greatly assist us in forming clear and distinct notions of the ensuing work.

First then, you are to observe, that the shape and figure of rooms differ exceedingly; for some are of a direct square, others not square but oblong or longish, namely, when the two sides are somewhat longer than the top or bottom, and various others that, in reality, are of no form at all; which renders dancing extremely difficult and confused to those who have not a just and true idea of the room in its different situations; because, if this be wanting, although they may perform very handsomely at their own houses, or in school with a master, yet, in *assemblies* or *rooms abroad*, they are as much disordered and at a stand as if in an *uninhabited island*. I therefore conclude, that the crime, if it should by any be esteemed such, of dwelling somewhat longer than I intended on this subject, will the more easily be pardoned by the ladies and gentlemen, when I acquaint them, that it entirely proceeded from the earnest desire I have of rendering them service, by endeavouring to remove the above-mentioned causes of disorder and confusion; which I cannot but persuade myself will meet with a favourable reception, especially from the hands of those who, by this means, shall receive improvement.

Encouraged by such a pleasing prospect, I proceed to inform the gentlemen and ladies that, when they are about to dance in a room of the first sort, *viz.* a direct square[†], the dance may be begun, at any of the four sides or parts of the square or room; but then they are to note, that the side or part, on which the dance begins, is always called the *bottom* or *lower end*[‡]; the side or part which they face, the *presence* or *upper end*[*]; and the two remaining parts or sides of the room receive their names according to the hand they are on: For instance, the side to which the right shoulder points is called the *right side*[◊], and the other the *left*[§]; from whence it is to be understood, that the back is to the lower end of the room, and the face to the upper, so that, if, instead of beginning, as aforesaid, you were to commence, either upon the right or left sides, they would not be then *sides*, as before, but the *upper* and *lower ends* of the room; that is to say, if upon the right side[ƒ] the left would be the *presence* or *upper end*[Δ], and if upon the left[∀] the right[∂], and consequently the parts or sides, which at first were the *lower*[‡] and *upper ends*[*], now are the sides; but all this is subservient to, and depends upon the company, who must always be seated at the *presence* or *upper end.*

As to the *longish* or second sort of rooms, they differ from the *square*, in the sides being longer than the ends[♦]; and it of course follows that the dance must begin at one of the said ends[◇], which is likewise decided by the company; or, if the door be hung near the end of one of the sides, as usually it is, the dance commonly begins, at the end next

---

† See the square or room marked 1 in Character Plate A.   ‡ See the letters A B in the said square. * See the letters C D.   ◊ See the Letters E F.   § See the letters G H.   ƒ See the letters A B in the square marked 2.   Δ See the letters C D in the said square.   ∀ See the letters A B in the room or square marked 3.   ∂ See the letters C D in the said square.   ♦ See the letters E F G H in the rooms marked 4, 5, 6.   ◇ See the letters A B in the rooms marked 4, 5, 6.

the door[℘]. However that be, the dancers must have a particular regard to the *presence* and *bottom of the room*, where they began, otherwise it is no wonder that those who are of a timorous and bashful nature, with the fears of being out together with the various turnings and windings of some dances, should be perplexed and nonplussed; and this I have perceived to be the case, when I have seen a minuet begin at the *bottom* of the room, and ended at the *upper end*; which could not possibly have happened, had they observed the preceding rules.

I shall, for the more fully clearing of this point, add an observation or two more that may be of service: Supposing one page or leaf of the book you now read, or any other, to be the room or floor in which the dances or practise of the steps contained in the following work are to be performed, lay it flat and open upon a window or table, at the upper end of the room; and if, when the book is open, the two pages make a square, it will be agreeable to the *first* room, and the one half or single page to the *longish* or *second*; but you are to take special notice, as to the part or end of the room intended for the *presence*, that the title or page of the book be so placed or laid upon the table or ground, as that, when you stand at the bottom facing the upper part of the room, to perform the foresaid steps or dances, you can read the said book: Or, supposing the whole floor to be the same book, and to contain the matter written in the page or half page, the book lying fixed and immoveable upon the table or ground, let the turn be made to the right or left, in a quarter, half, or three-quarter turn, and you cannot possibly make the least mistake; for though the book, by which you are directed in compliance therewith, turns along with you, yet any other you shall lay upon

---

[℘] See the following mark † in the rooms aforesaid. [*Editor's note:* This mark does not appear in Character Plate A as described.]

the ground will remain fixed; so that from what has been said upon this head, I think it plainly appears that the lower end of the page or leaf is the bottom of the room, and the title above the presence or upper end; the beginning of the lines, as you read these in dancing, is the left side, and the breaking off of the lines the right[†], though the sides of the book are not so termed. The reason of this may be understood, by placing a person at the upper end of the room facing the bottom, holding a printed book or written paper perpendicular in his hands, so as that you can read it; for you will find it the reverse to *dancing*, in that the right hand will hold the part of the paper from whence the lines begin, and the left that where they break off. It is further to be noted, that, supposing the dance for *one* person alone in the square room or two pages of the book, as just mentioned, the dancer places him or herself in the center, or upon the joining of the two pages, which, when open, is directly in the middle[‡]; or, to practise any step of this book, the case is the same; but, if the dance be of *two*, the lady takes the right side of the said center or line[*], and the gentleman the left[◊], so that the joining or preventing of hands, if necessary, would fall upon the line or center upon which the single dancer began[‡]; in which it is to be noted, as on other occasions, that the lady takes the right of the gentleman.

And as I have now said what, I hope, will prove sufficient to remove all the difficulties that may arise, in dancing, on account of the *room*, or in relation to the *steps* I am about to explain, I shall no longer detain those who are ambitious of attaining to perfection in a science, of which I have the honour of being a professor; but, having prepared and made them

---

† See the 7th example room in Plate A.　　　‡ See the letter S in the said 7th example.
* See the letter W.　　◊ See the letter M.

thoroughly acquainted with the room, in which the steps of dancing are to be performed, I shall invite them into the same; but, before I describe the various steps of dancing, I shall, in a few words, endeavour to prepare their minds to form a clearer and more distinct idea of the following descriptions.

As the *human structure* is composed of different parts, *viz.* head, neck, body, arms, legs, feet, etc. so likewise is dancing of positions, steps, sinking, rising, springing, capering, falling, sliding, turning, figures, cadence or time, etc. And as the *head* consists of eyes, ears, nose, mouth, etc. the *arms*, of the shoulders, elbows, wrists, hands, fingers, and joints of the fingers, the *body*, as it were, remaining in the center or middle of the human frame, supporting the said arms, as the legs, which support them both, are composed of the hips, knees, ankles, feet, toes, and joints[§] of the said toes, on the first of which the rising upon the instep is always made; and as all these different parts have their peculiar excellencies, to adorn the whole, so the eyes give life to the face, as well as direct the steps; the ears mark time to the tune; the nose, as it were, points out the graceful twists or turns the head makes, in opposition to the other parts of the body, whilst the mouth, at the same time, adds those becoming smiles, which, together with the brightness and lustre of the eyes, complete a most agreeable and pleasing countenance. The neck too, in its graceful compliance with the turn of the head; the shoulders, in their natural rising, falling, or hanging down[ɸ]; the elbows, in their easy bendings, according to the occasion[Δ]; the wrists, in their pliable correspondence with the elbows and shoulders, as the handsome shaping or bending of the thumbs and fingers produces beautiful hands completing the arms[▽]; which, in their respective opposing the head, in

---

§ See the figure in Plate III.   ɸ See the different parts, as described above, in the ladies' figures in Book II.
Δ See the figures in Plate X.   ▽ See the abovementioned parts in the arms and fingers in Plate XIII.

conjunction with the body, is a further and large addition to the whole†; the legs, in the gracefully supporting the frame of the body, head, neck, and arms‡; and the hips or joints, which unite the legs and body, agree with the various movements or bendings and risings of the knees or insteps*, the positions or handsome turn of the feet completing the beauty of the legs, on the neat management of which the perfection of dancing so much depends◊; and these together, in confederacy with the head, oppose the body and arms, rendering the whole body complete and capable of dancing, in all its various attitudes or postures§.

Having, by the foregoing simile or comparison, given an account of the outward form of the *human structure*, so far as it relates to, or corresponds with *dancing*, or may, in any respect, conduce to the better understanding of the ensuing subject, by running over the different parts of the body, from the head to the feet, which compose the positions, with a short explanation of the said parts, showing how they agree in forming the most pleasing object, to grace the ART of DANCING⨍, before I proceed to treat on its various steps, I shall, by the way, observe that the foresaid particulars, from whence the whole BODY or ART of DANCING is produced, namely, position, sinking, stepping, rising, springing, etc. are of the very same use, in *dancing*, as the *alphabet* in the *composition of words*; for as words vary and are produced, according to the different placing of the letters; and different subjects, languages, etc. according to the different composition of words; or, as in *music*, by the different placing of the notes, that compose the gamut

---

† See the turn of the head, body, and arms of the figures in Plate VI or Plates IV, V, VII, IX, XI, XII and XIV.   ‡ See the figures in Plates III, VI, and VIII.   * See the figures in Plates III and X.   ◊ See the feet of the figures in general.   § See the figures in Plates IV, VI, IX, XI, XII, and XIV.   ⨍ See the figures in Plate XIII, etc. [*Editor's note:* Unclear which plates are included in "etc."]

upon the scale or spaces between the lines, are produced different sounds, which, as they ascend or descend, compose various bars or measures, that may be compared to words, and the various bars and measures compose the various pieces of music, in different keys and movements; so the different steps of dancing are produced, according to the various placings of the sinks, risings, bounds, etc. upon the step, whether consisting of one, two, three or more steps to the measure, and the different steps produce a variety of dances, according to the composer's fancy, upon all sorts of movements in music, whether *grave* or *brisk*.

We are, next, to show how these actions or motions of the body, which, as we said above, compose the whole ART of DANCING, correspond with the positions and various motions and steppings of the feet, in composing the following steps and movements; and the manner, in which they are made, will fully appear from the description I am about to give of the said steps, beginning with the *half coupee*, the movement that first occurs in dancing.

C H A P. V.

Of the COUPEE of one step, or HALF COUPEE.

IT is, first of all, to be observed that the *half coupee*, though a very agreeable step in dancing, as well as one of the most difficult to be performed well, by reason of its plainness, is originally nothing more than a single step, made with either foot, from one place to another with the additional ornament of a movement or bending or rising of the knees in time to music; and it is most amiable, when executed in that gentle and graceful manner it ought to be, whether upon the toe or heel.

The half coupee may be performed various ways, as by sinking, rising, and stepping forwards; and the like backwards, sideways, to either hand, or in turning a quarter or half turn†, etc. It usually takes up a time or measure of the tune, and, being continued, transfers the weight, as in walking, from one foot to the other; and, in distinction from the rest, the dancing-masters have named it a *half coupee*, though I think it may rather be called a *coupee of one step*, as the title above specifies: But, as I shall have occasion to give a further account of this step, when, in treating of the bouree or fleuret, I carry on a comparison between the step and the half coupee, I shall, in the meantime, proceed to the *coupee*, the movement that next occurs in dancing.

---

† See the explanation and table of this step in Character Plate E.

CHAP. VI.
Of the COUPEE.

THE *coupee*, on the other hand, is a compound step; that is to say, it is formed of two steps joined together, which, however, are to be accounted but as a single step: The first movement of which begins in a sink and rise. If the tune, to which it is performed, be of triple time (as a saraband, for instance, which admits only of three notes in a bar) then the first step takes up one of the three notes, and the other two notes are counted in the remaining step. The weight of the body must always rest on the contrary foot to that, on which you begin; so that, if you begin your coupee with the right foot, the poise must be on the left[‡] and continue so to be, till you have completed the first step of the two, which, as I said, compose the coupee. The first part being finished, the right foot immediately receives the weight[*], in the rising from the sink which is made, at commencing the step, and in the same instant beats time, as we call it, to the first of the three notes contained in the bar; supporting the body[◊], whilst the left foot, to complete this compound step, slides with a slow and gentle motion, filling up the remaining two notes of the bar or measure[§], and the whole step is completed, at the instant when the left foot a second time receives the weight[‡]. This step, like the half coupee, admits of being variously performed, as forwards, backwards, sideways,

---

‡ See the first figure or man's side of Plate I.   * See the second figure or woman's side in Plate IX.
◊ See the second figure or woman's side in Plate I.   § See the first figure or man's side in Plate IX.

and circularly§. It differs, indeed, from the half coupee, in the continuance of performing it; for whereas the half coupee, as in walking, transfers the weight, every time, from one foot to the other, the coupee does the very reverse, in that it always begins with the same foot: For, if you begin it with the left foot, it will end with the right; and, if with the right, it concludes on the left§; and so mutually, as often as ever it is repeated, and until it is changed by some other step. It is called a *coupee*[5], from its containing two steps instead of one, which is all that the *half coupee* employs.

---

§ See the explanation and table of the coupee in Character Plate E.

Editor's notes: 5. *Coupée,* French past participle of *couper,* meaning to cut.

CHAP. VII.

Of the COUPEE with two movements.

THE *coupee with two movements* is composed, as the coupee I have already explained, of two steps; but it differs in this, that whereas the coupee treated of before consists only of one movement, that is to say, of one sink and rise, which is what we call *movement,* and made to the first step; so it consequently follows, that there must be another movement added to the second, though different from the first; for in that the sink is made before the foot moves; and the rise, after the foot has moved, that is to say, when you have made a step, as I have already observed, as in walking either forwards, backwards, or sideways, etc. but, in this additional movement, the sink and rise are together in the midst of the motion the leg makes, in stepping, as in the preceding; and supposing the step is to a *loure*[5], or suchlike slow air, it is performed in the manner following, *viz.* to make the first step which is to sink, before the foot moves†, and rise in moving, or immediately after it has moved‡; which said rising and receiving of the weight upon the foot, that made the first step†, marks time to the first note of the three, which each bar or measure contains. The second note is taken up with the sink of the second movement; and the rise from it takes up the third note of the same measure, and completes the step; so that the first movement and step are made to the first note of the three, and the

---

† See Plate I.   ‡ See Plate IX.   * See the explanation and table of this step in Plate E.

Editor's notes: 6. Original text refers here to a *Louvre,* but it's understood to be the *loure,* a slow jig, also known as the gigue lourée or gigue lente (slow gigue).

second to the remaining two, and may be performed the different ways aforesaid, as forwards, backwards, sideways before, or sideways behind, etc.* and, as to its continuance in dancing, it is the same as the *coupee of one movement*, that is, always beginning with the same foot, whether right or left: It is named a *coupee of two movements*, from its having the addition of a second added to the former; which second movement is made sometimes smooth upon the floor, and sometimes by bounding off.

---

* See the explanation and table of this step in Character Plate E.

C H A P. VIII.
Of the BOUREE STEP or FLEURET.

THE *bouree* is composed of three plain straight steps or walks, except the first, which begins in a movement, and is to be performed in the same method, as the *half coupee* or *coupee with two movements*, that is to say, must always sink at the beginning of the step or walk, and rise at, or gradually before the end of it; which is the manner in which the first step is usually taken, in the performance of all steps, except springs, bounds, hops, or chassees, etc. wherefore, for the future, I need not say any more of the method of beginning these sorts of steps in dancing, otherwise than to make a movement, without mentioning how the sink and rise are to be made, since they have been already explained.

A bouree or fleuret, as I have observed, consists only of three plain straight steps; but a movement is added to the first of them, the rise of which movement, as has been said, always strikes the cadence or time; and, if this step is done to a tune of three notes in a measure, the first step answers to the first note, the second step to the same note, and the third step to the last note of the measure, concluding together.

You are also to note, that though in the bouree there are three distinct walks or steps, yet nevertheless, these three steps are to be esteemed but as one step, in regard of its being a composed step; as will appear by the half coupee, which, though no more than a single step, is, however, a step, because it generally takes up a measure, but more especially in tunes of triple time;

and it is made by a smooth and easy bending of the knees, rising in a slow and gentle motion from thence; which rising, as I have said, is upon the first note of the measure, the weight of the body being supported by the foot that made the step, during the counting of the second and third notes of the bar.

The graceful posture of the dancer's standing adds not a little to the beauty of this step, who, till the time be expired, is to wait or rest; by which it is evident, that the half coupee, though a single step, is equal in value to any compound step whatsoever, whether of two, three, four, or more steps in a measure.

But to return, the bouree step may be performed various ways, as forwards, backwards, sideways, crossing before, the same behind, before and behind, behind and before, etc.[†] the explanation of which, I think, may not be improper in this place; and therefore I shall proceed to show the method of their performance, one after the other, in the order above set down, except the *fleurets forwards and backwards*; which being so intelligible of themselves, and having occasion hereafter to speak of this step, by way of grace to the minuet, instead of saying anything further of them here, I shall begin with the *bouree step crossing before, sideways*; which is to be performed, as follows, either with the right or left foot: For instance, provided you begin with the latter, the weight must be on the right[‡]; and the left foot, which is at liberty, commences by making a movement and step, to the right side of the room, crossing before the foot on which the body rests[*], the face being to the upper part of the room, and it receives the weight[◊]. The second is the right foot, which steps the same way[§]; and the third and last, which is with the left, crosses before, as at first[*], only without a movement[◊]. The *bouree crossing behind, sideways,* differs from the former in

---

† See the explanation and table of the bouree in Character Plate E.   ‡ See the second figure or woman's side in Plate I.   * See the first figure in Plate IV, and the second figure or woman's side of Plate XI.   ◊ See the first figure or man's side in Plate V.   § See the second figure in Plate VI.

this, that whereas that was *before*, this is *behind*; that is to say, the weight being, as aforesaid‡, the left foot, instead of making the movement and first step crossing before the right, it now is made crossing behind it; and the next step, which is with the right foot, moves the same way, after which the third and last step with the left foot is drawn behind the right, and concludes. The *bouree before and behind* is when the first movement and step are made crossing before the foot on which the weight is, whether right or left, the second step moving sideways, the same way, and the third drawn behind it, facing upwards, as before. *The bouree behind and before* is done in the like manner, only the first step is not crossed before but behind, the second stepping sideways, and the third drawn crossing before. The bouree, which I call *twice behind*, is made as follows: Suppose, for example, you make a movement, stepping backwards with the right foot$, into the third position enclosed behind the left on which the weight is, and releasing it$^\Delta$; upon which it makes the second step of the bouree, in a plain step backwards, receiving the weight enclosed in the third position behind the right$^\triangledown$, which then performs the third step of the bouree, in a plain step forwards$^\partial$.

There are many other ways of performing this step, which would be too tedious to be mentioned here; and, as they are not to my present purpose, omitting them, I shall only observe that this step, continued several measures, changes the foot every step, as has been taken notice of in the half coupee; but with this difference, that whereas the half coupee changes the weight every single step, as in walking, the bouree or fleuret only changes it at the end of every third step.

$ See the first figure in Plate I.   Δ See the first figure in Plate IV.   ▽ See the second figure in Plate IV.   ∂ See the second figure in Plate IX.

C H A P. IX.

Of the BOUREE with two movements.

THE *bouree with two movements* consists of the same number of steps as the former; but as that was of *one movement,* this is of *two*; which second movement is added to the last of the three steps of which the *bouree* is composed. This step, in effect, contains in itself two distinct steps, namely, the *whole* and *half coupee*; only it is not the same in the manner of its performance; for they, as was already observed, in treating of them, are both equal to a measure of themselves, but, in this step, they are both to be performed to a time or measure, and must be accounted only as one step: For example, to a tune of three notes in a bar, admitting it begins with the right foot†, it is to be likewise granted, that the weight must be on the left†, which supports the body, till the first step and movement are made‡; the rise of which step is to the first of the three notes belonging to the measure, on which the weight rests, until the second step is performed, that answers the same note* and ends the coupee; whereas the second step of the coupee to a measure takes up the second and third notes, and consequently is as slow again, in its performance, as this; which third note of the coupee to a measure is taken up in this step with the rise from the half coupee, and is the third and last step on which the second movement falls‡, from whence this step derives its name.

---

† See the first figure in Plate I.   ‡ See the second figure in Plate IX.   * See the first figure in Plate IX.

From what has been observed, we may see in what this step differs from the two said steps before described. In the continuance of this step the weight changes[◊], as in the *bouree with one movement*, and may be performed forwards, backwards, sideways, circularly, etc. Note, this step may be done with a bound, that is to say, on the last step upon which the second movement is made, with a spring from the ground, which is what we call a *bound*; and of this I shall take occasion to say something in its proper place, and give it the name of *bouree with a bound*, as not being made on the floor, as the *bouree with two movements*.

◊ See the second figure in Plate I.

CHAP. X.
Of the PASGRAVE or MARCH.

THE *march* is originally a single or plain step, as the half coupee, but different in the manner of its performance, in that the half coupee bends or sinks before the step is performed, and rises after it has been made; whereas, on the contrary, in this step, the movement or bending and rising are made together, as in the second movement of the *coupee with two movements* after which commences a slide; and the sink, rise, and slide compose this step, which, in its performance, is as follows: For example, if forwards, the foot you design to begin with, is to be entirely disengaged from the weight behind the foot on which the body rests in the third position, that is to say, the ankle of the beginning foot must touch the heel of the foot that supports the weight[§]; from which position this step always begins and is performed by making a sink and rise; but instead of stepping forwards, as in the half coupee, you rise and point the right or left toe sideways, according to the foot you commence with, about the distance from the foot the body is upon, as half the step you take in walking[†].

After this the foot moves slowly forwards[‡], pressing the floor, as it passes along, about the length of a step in walking[‡]; which pressing of the toe or instep to the ground, as it moves[‡], is what we call a *slide* in dancing. And as to its agreement with the notes of triple time, as mentioned before,

---

§ See the first and second figures in Plate V.   † See the first and second figures in Plate VI.   ‡ See Plate IX.

you are to observe, that the rise or point* marks time to the first note; the march or sliding forwards of the foot‡ takes up the second and third notes, on the expiration of which it receives the weight, concluding in the third position, as at first, but on the contrary foot◊. This is one of the most agreeable steps in dancing; and it may be performed either forwards, backwards, or sideways, etc. and in performance, when continued, it transfers the weight from one foot to another, as in the half coupee.

---

* See Plate VI.   ◊ See Plate V.

CHAP. XI.
Of the POINT and MARCH.

THE *point and march* is so called from having a *point* more added to the *march,* which *point* is equal, as to its time, with a *march,* and in its performance the same, except that, instead of the second and third notes being taken up in the marching or sliding of the foot forwards or backwards[‡] etc. they are counted, during the time you stand or rest, in the graceful manner before observed in the half coupee; only with this difference, that the disengaged foot, instead of being in the first position, as in *that,* is upon the point *here,* as may be seen by the beginning or first movement of the foresaid march[§]. The point is made with either foot, as has been observed in the march[§], which point is performed with a soft easy rising from the foregoing sink[ϕ], made to the first note[§]; in which posture it remains the counting of the second and third notes of the measure, concluding what we call the *point*[§], the body all the while resting upon the same foot as at commencing; after which follows the march[Δ]; as it has been before described, and the point[§] and march[Δ] generally fill up two measures of the tune, though sometimes they are both performed to a measure.

It will not, I think, be here improper to take some notice, how the point[§] and march[Δ] agree with the notes of the measure: For instance, if you make a movement and point, sideways, the rise of the point answers to the first note[§]; the rise of the

---

§ See the figures in Plate VI.   ϕ See Plate V.   Δ See Plate IX.

second point or movement, which immediately ensues upon the same place, on which the first point was made, marks the second note[§], and the third is counted in the march or progress of the foot, either forwards or backwards from thence[Δ]; which are two methods, in which this step is usually performed. But when this step is performed to two measures of the tune, the point[§] and time you rest upon it, that is to say, the counting of the second and third notes, whilst you are beautifully standing[§], takes up the first measure. The second is in the march or slide[Δ], and, if continued, transfers the weight every other step, as in the half coupee; and in fine, as to the manner of performing this step, it is fully shown in the march, since it is no more than the first movement, or sink and rise thereof, on which rising and pointing of the toe or instep[§], you pause or rest, until the measure is expired[∇].

[∇] See the explanation and table of this step in Character Plate E.

CHAP. XII.
Of the SPRING *or* BOUND.

THE *spring* or *bound* is produced from a plain and single step, as the *half coupee* or *march*, but it very much differs from them in performance; for, as they are both made on the ground, the *bound* springs off from thence. For example, suppose you were about to perform a march, then, instead of sinking and rising on the floor, you are to sink, and, in the spring or rise from the said sink, throw the body into the air, off from the foot on which the weight was, when you began, and light upon the contrary foot; that is to say, if the bound is on the right, the weight is to come from the left†, where it was upon commencing this step. And in like manner, if performed with the left foot‡. One bound alone rarely, if ever, answers to a measure; but, in tunes of common time, or of four in a measure, as in rigadoons, marches, etc. two bounds answer a time; and, in sarabands or slow tunes of triple time, three of them may be done in one bar.

This step may be performed various ways, as forwards, backwards, sideways before, or sideways behind, as also in turning either to the right or left, etc.* And it is further to be noted, that the foot, on which the bound is to be made, commences from the third position behind the foot upon which the weight rests, as in the march, and advances, much in the same manner, from the third to the third position; only that it bounds off from the ground, and if continued to a tune of common time, as above, changes the weight twice in every measure, and in triple thrice.

---

† See the first and second figures in Plate V.   ‡ See the second and first figures of Plate V.   * See the explanation and table of this step in Character Plate E.

C H A P. XIII.
Of the CLOSE or JUMP.

WHAT we call a *close* in dancing is, when, the weight being upon one foot, we sink, and in the rise *jump* or *close* both feet equal one to the other, in the first position$^\lozenge$, or the feet are enclosed either before or behind, in the third position§; and this step generally concludes in the said positions or postures. It may be performed two different ways, *viz.* on the ground, and off from the ground, as in the bound; but it differs in its method of performance, for as *that* advances forwards or backwards, about the length of the half coupee or march, this never proceeds further than from behind the foot which supports the body, either to the first position even, or to the third enclosed before or behind, as aforesaid.

I shall, in the first place, begin with the description of the *close* in the first position, which is as follows: For instance, the foot that is free from weight begins whether it be the right or left, in making a movement, or sink and rise from the third position behind$^\oint$, as when you begin the march; that is to say, so far as the point$^\Lambda$; but, instead of pointing the toe to the ground as in that here, in rising from the sink aforesaid, preparing for the close ensuing, you give a kind of a spring upon the toe or instep of the foot the weight is on, and the same time or instant both heels come to the floor together, and receive the weight equal alike$^\triangledown$; but you are to observe, that the body is thus

---

$\lozenge$ See the figures in Plates I and II. $\S$ See the figures in Plate IV. $\oint$ See the figures in Plate V.
Δ See Plate VI. $\triangledown$ See Plate II.

thrown into the air by the spring of the instep, I mean no higher than you can rise without quitting the ground with your instep or toe, and from hence it is called a *close on the ground.*

To close in the third position is performed entirely in the same manner, except that, in lighting on both feet in the first position as before▽, the fall or coming down is in the third; that is to say, the feet are enclosed one before the other, the heel of the foremost foot touching the ankle of the hind foot∂. In the performance of this step backwards it is the very same, only, instead of beginning from behind the foot on which the weight is, it commences from before the same, or fourth position open in the air♦; so that what we have described forwards is to be accomplished backwards in the same method: For example to *close* backwards in the first position◇, or *enclose* backwards into the third∂, when this step is performed off from the ground, the difference is only in this, that you sink, in order to spring, as before; but, instead of rising to the extremity or point of the toe you only spring quite off from the floor, lighting on both feet in any of the before mentioned positions, whether forwards or backwards, and it is called a *close* or *jump.*

You are also to observe, that this step never advances either forwards, backwards, or sideways, as is usual in others, but is always performed upon the same place; for, although the disengaged foot moves from behind or before that on which you stand, the weight always comes down in the same place: For instance, suppose you were to be in the third position on the left foot℘ and to perform this step to the first position even from behind, the right foot is brought equal to that on which the weight is, the very instant the close or jump is made*f*; and, if the fall or coming down be enclosed in the third position

---

▽ See Plate II.   ∂ See the figures in Plate IV.   ♦ See the figures of Plate IV, IX, XI, XIV, or XV.
◇ See the figures in Plates I and II.   ℘ See the first figure or man's side in Plate V.   *f* See the first figure or left side in Plate I.

before the foot℞, instead of joining even to the foot on which the weight is*f*, the heel of the right foot is enclosed or joined before the ankle of the left℞, and the same backwards from before.

This step in dancing much resembles a period or full-stop in letters; for, as that *closes* or shuts up a *sentence*, the *close* in dancing does the very same in *music,* since nothing is more frequent than, at the end of a strain in the tune, to find the strain or couplet of the dance to conclude in this step, as also at other remarkable places of the music. Besides, this close gives great life and variety in the composition of dances; for whereas most other steps lead the dancers a regular figure, and consequently render a change thereof more difficult, in this step, the body being as much upon one foot as the other, the change is more familiar, since it is as easy to take up one foot as the other. This step generally takes up a measure, that is to say, with the time you rest or stand still: For instance, to a tune of triple time the close is performed to the first of the three notes, and the second and third are counted, during the time you rest; but to tunes of common time, as marches, gavots, rigadoons, etc. this step and time it is to rest sometimes are a measure, and at others not, as having a plain step or walk added thereto, which said close and step together fill up the time.

℞ See the second figure or woman's side in Plate IV.

C H A P. XIV.
Of the SPRING or LEAP.

THE *spring* or *leap* is the same as the latter end of the foregoing *close* or *spring* from one foot upon both, except that the close or jump always begins from one foot[†], the weight constantly coming down in the same place[‡], whereas this step begins and ends upon both feet[*], whether in the first or third position[◊] and may be performed several ways, *viz.* forwards, backwards, sideways, to the right or left, upright and circularly[§]; but, when it is performed either of the two latter ways, the weight comes down in the place from whence the spring was made, as in the close aforesaid, though in any of the former, as forwards, backwards, etc. they *spring* or *leap*, about the length of the half coupee or march, and light on both feet, as in leaping.

As to the agreement of this step with the notes of the tune, it is uncertain; for to a tune of three it sometimes takes up a measure, and at others not: For example, if you *spring upright* in this step, the fall marks what we call the *time* or *cadence* upon the first note, whilst the other two are counted during the time you rest; and in the like manner, when it is performed *circularly* upon the same place. *Upright* and *circularly* are the two ways in which this step is performed, when it singly answers to a bar, as it frequently happens on the ending of a strain or other remarkable part of the tune; and when it does not, as it rarely, if ever, does in the other ways of performing it, we often meet,

---

† See the figures in Plate V.   ‡ See the figures in Plate I.   * See the figure in Plate II.   ◊ See the figures in Plate IV.   § See the steps in Plate II and the explanation and table of this step in Character Plate E.

instead thereof, two leaps and a plain straight step in a measure, which together with the two springs agree with the notes of the music; and many times we find a third spring added, instead of the plain straight step; which three springs agree with the notes, as before, though they are seldom used except in *comic dancing* and tunes of common time, that is to say, of four in the bar, as in gavots, marches, rigadoons, etc. in which this spring or leap on both feet is the same, in its answering with the notes of the tune, except that, instead of two springs and the plain straight step to a measure, or the three springs, as in triple time, in these of common there is but one close and the straight step; and also, instead of three springs or leaps, here are but two, which steps agree with the notes, as follows: The fall or coming down of the weight from the first spring beats time to the first note of the bar; and the second and third notes are counted, during the performing of the plain step. The fourth note is always taken up with the sink which prepares for the succeeding step; and consequently it is very necessary to take notice that the two leaps are performed in the same method. The coming down of the first spring, as I said before, marks the time or first note; the sinking or bending of the knees, in order for the second rise or spring, answers the same note; and the third is in the coming down of the weight in the sink, etc. as was just observed, which step, if continued, is a sort of harmonious leaping to music either forwards or backwards, etc.$^{\oint}$ It is to be likewise noted, that the *upright spring* or *close* affords the dancer the like opportunity of changing the foot, during the time of resting as in the foregoing close, the difference being only in its beginning and ending on both feet; and, if performed on the ground, it is entirely in the same manner, as we have already described it in the jump or close from one foot.

$\oint$ See the table of the leap or jump in Character Plate E.

CHAP. XV.

Of the RIGADOON STEP of one spring open in the same place and close.

THE *rigadoon step of one spring open upon the same place* is composed of two plain steps or motions of the feet, except that the first commences with a *spring* or *hop*; which said spring and plain step is to a measure, and introduces the *upright spring* or *close* on both feet, before treated of, to another measure in its attendance on the former, from which it is almost inseperable; insomuch that the said *rigadoon step* is seldom, if ever, without this *close* following it, as adding the greatest grace and beauty thereto, and being from thence so strictly united that, although in themselves they are two distinct steps, the first never appears but concludes in the latter which in its performance is as follows, *viz.* commencing from the first position, or the feet joined even one with the other, from whence the sink or preparative for the hop is taken, and may be done with either foot. However, for the better understanding thereof I shall describe it, with the right foot: Therefore, as has been already observed, the weight being on both feet in the first position†, you sink and give a rise or spring, either off from the ground, or upon it, as you shall think most agreeable, since it may be performed both ways; which said spring is made upon the left foot, in rising from the aforesaid sink, by taking the right foot up from the floor, the very same instant the

---

† See the figure in Plate II, only instead of facing down the room you may suppose it looking to the presence.

spring or hop is made, and moves open off to the right side of the room, if to the upper end, or otherwise according to what part of the room the body is directed in the air, about the length of a step in dancing‡; and then it returns to the first position from whence it came receiving the weight; upon which the left foot, being now disengaged, moves open sideways in the like manner[*], and, in returning, receives one half of the weight in the same position as at first[†]; after which comes the close on both feet◊ which sometimes is to a measure, and at others not, in that there often follows in rigadoon movements, a plain step or walk in the time or measure, as for example, you'll find in this movement of the bretagne; that is to say, the beginning of the second part is the very same step I have here described.

As to the agreement of this step with the notes of the tune, which is of four in the measure, the spring or hop that is made upon the left foot, on the taking up of the right, marks the time or first note; the setting of it down the second; the third is in the setting down of the left foot; and the fourth and last note, in the sink for the ensuing close that attends this step, which together compose one of the most agreeable steps in dancing.

There are, besides these already described, many other ways of performing this step, as in the third position forwards, and the same backwards; but, for the better understanding of this, suppose you are standing in the first position, or the feet are joined even to each other§, you perform this step into the third position, that is, you make the first step which is with a spring, and enclose it before the foot on which the weight rests⨍, and the second before that△ in the like manner.

To perform this step backwards differs in this, that as the foregoing was enclosed before, after the spring, this is enclosed

---

‡ See in some measure the feet in the second figure of Plate XV.   * See the feet in the first figure of Plate XV.   ◊ See Plate II.   § See the figure in Plate II, supposed to be looking up the room.   ⨍ See the second figure of Plate IV.   △ See the first figure of Plate IV.

behind the foot that supports the weight$^\Delta$, and the second step behind that$^\phi$; or else the first of the said two steps, namely, the spring, may be done in the third position before$^\nabla$, and the second behind$^\partial$; or the first with a spring behind$^\partial$, and the second step before$^\nabla$, and are to be performed from either of the said positions, whether the first or third, as is also the spring or close that follows them, whether upright or changing of the position; that is, instead of coming down in the first, or in the third, as at beginning, the feet are changed, for instance, the first last, and the last first$^\blacklozenge$.

ϕ See the second figure of Plate IV. Δ See the first figure of Plate IV. ∇ See the fore or enclosed feet of Plate IV. ∂ See the hind feet of Plate IV. $\blacklozenge$ See the table and explanation of this step in Character Plate E.

C H A P. XVI.

Of the RIGADOON STEP of two springs or SISSONNE.

THE *rigadoon step with two springs* differs from the former of *one* in this, that whereas the aforesaid is performed in the same place, and only with one spring, this is of two; the first of which advances or retires, about the length of a march, whilst the second spring is in the same place upon one foot.

This step may also be performed sideways crossing before, or sideways crossing behind, either to the right or left, or turning[†], etc. the difference of which, in the manner of performance, I shall describe in their order. For example, first *forwards*, which may be done with one foot as well as the other; yet, for the more easy comprehending thereof, I intend to explain it, beginning with the right foot, which is as follows, *viz.* the weight is on the left in the third position, and the right behind; that is to say, the ankle of the right foot rests against the heel of the left, but is entirely free from any weight of the body[‡]; from whence you make the first spring which is upon the left foot, whilst the right, at the same instant, moves directly the same way, as in the march, except that the march is performed on the ground from a bend and rise only, but this off from thence, by an upright spring into the air from the sink you make upon your left foot, on which the weight falls in the same place, the right advancing, as has been

---

† See the explanation and table of this step in Character Plate E.   ‡ See the first figure of Plate V.

already observed, about the length of a march; but it does not receive the whole weight of the body, as in that, by reason of its continuing principally on the same foot on which it was, at commencing; so that, although the right foot is advanced before the other, it receives no more than its own weight, the whole being to follow on making the second spring[*]. Having thus far only concluded the first spring or movement, the second is made from the aforesaid position divided; that is to say, the right foot is, near the length of a step in dancing, before the left; in which position or posture both knees bend, the right to receive the body, and the left to be disengaged from it, as it entirely is on giving the hop or spring; for, at the instant the foot on which the weight was, is taken from the floor, the other receives it, ending the step in the third position upon the right foot, the left being behind but free from any weight; the ankle of which rests against the heel of the foot that supports the body, in the same position in which it began, only with the contrary foot[◊], and may be continued from one foot to the other, as in the march, etc.

This step *backwards* is performed in the like manner as *forwards* except that *forwards* it is taken from the third position behind, but in this begins from the same position before; that is, the heel of the right foot touches the ankle of the left on which the body rests[§], from whence you make the spring in the same method already described in this step *forwards, viz.* the right and foremost foot, at the same moment the spring is given upon the left, moves backwards, as in the march, much about the like distance, and receives half the weight, at the same time the other half comes down upon the left, leaving the weight divided to the first spring or hop[ϕ]; and the second is made on the right foot, in

---

[*] See the second figure in Plate IX.   [◊] See the second figure in Plate V.   [§] See the second figure in Plate IV.   [ϕ] See in some measure the first figure in Plate IX or second figure in Plate XI.

the taking up of the left, which falls enclosed in the third position as at beginning except that the contrary foot is foremost[Δ], and the left is ready to commence, as before. This step, *sideways crossing before*, is so called from its being crossed before the foot on which the weight of the body rests, and it chiefly differs from the two ways already described namely, *forwards* and *backwards*, in that it begins from the third position behind, as aforesaid[▽], but instead of the right foot's moving, as in them, you in this give the spring and fall in the fifth position, the right or beginning foot crossing before the left, the weight being divided, as before; that is, the heel of the right foot is equal to the toe of the left[∂], which manner of placing the feet we call the *fifth position*. The second spring or hop is made upon the right foot on the taking up the left, which is then brought into the third position behind, and the right foot into the same position as the beginning but contrary foot[◊]; which said foot is ready to perform the same thing either *sideways crossing before* the right on which the body is, or *sideways crossing behind*, the latter of which I shall explain in the next place, and it is as follows.

Sideways crossing behind varies from the former only in this, that, instead of commencing from the third position behind, it begins from before: For example, the weight being upon the left foot[§] you sink and make the first spring with the right, falling in the fifth position crossing behind; that is, the toe of the right foot is equal to the heel of the left, the weight being divided, as has been already explained[℘]. The second spring is performed upon the right, on the left's being taken up from the ground, as aforesaid, which falls enclosed in the third position before; that is, the heel of the left foot is joined to the ankle of the right, and, being disengaged from weight, is at liberty to perform the

---

Δ See the first figure in Plate IV.   ▽ See the first figure in Plate V.   ∂ See the feet of the first figure in Plate XI.   ℘ See the feet of the second figure in Plate XI.

same with the left foot, as we have described with the right[Δ].

Having now shown, how this step is performed *sideways crossing before,* as also the same *behind,* it is unnecessary here to take any further notice of this step *sideways to the right,* than that it differs in nothing from what we have described *to the left* but in the contrary foot; nor likewise of the manner of its performance in *turning,* otherwise than that it may be performed several ways, as to the right or left, in a quarter turn, half turn, or three quarter turn, etc. since I shall take occasion hereafter, in the ensuing steps, to treat more particularly on that head. I shall only observe at present, that those who learn to dance, and are acquainted with the rigadoon of the late Mr. Isaac, will meet with this step, *turning* in all or most of the ways abovementioned, in the different parts thereof; and it is here, for distinction sake, named of *two springs.*

There is still another way in which this step is often made, and not as yet observed, which is the reverse in the second spring to the foregoing; for, instead of taking up, in the second spring, the foot on which the body was when you began, the contrary foot or that foot which advances or retires is taken up: For instance, admitting this step to begin with the right foot, of consequence the weight must then be upon the left, from whence you make the first spring, as is usual, upon both feet; but, instead of the left foot's being taken from the floor, as in the aforesaid, the right or beginning foot is taken up on making the second spring; which choice of feet in this step renders it of equal use, in the composition of dances, as the *close,* in that the change of figure is to be effected in this, as well as in the aforesaid.

Having described most of the different manners of performing this step in dancing, I shall proceed to show its agreement with

---

Δ See the first figure in Plate IV.

the notes of this movement, which, as we have already said, is of four in the bar, and it agrees as follows: The first spring is made upon the time or first note; the sink for the second is in the second note, which second spring is performed to the third note; and the fourth is in the sink preparing for the succeeding step. And, when it is done to a saraband or tune of triple time, it is in all respects the same, except that, instead of four notes in a bar, in this you have only three, which are, in their performance, much slower than the before mentioned of four to the measure; and it is further to be observed, that one half of the third note is borrowed for the sink that prepares for the ensuing step, in which it chiefly differs from the foregoing of common time, but that it is not so brisk.

CHAP. XVII.

Of the GALLIARD *and* FALLING STEP.

THE *galliard* step is in a manner the same as the before described *close* from one foot to both, except that in this, the weight of the body, after making the spring or movement for the close, remains on the same foot upon which it was at the beginning; from whence it follows, that the foot which, in the foregoing close, received one half of the weight, is here to be disengaged, and at liberty to perform the succeeding one which is a plain straight step or walk; which step could not have been performed with the commencing foot, had it received one half of the weight, as in the close from one foot. And you are to note, that this step always ends with the same foot it begins, whether it be the right or left, and is various, as to its performance in dancing. I shall describe the most usual of these ways, which are as follows *viz.* forwards, backwards, sideways to the right or left, and also in turning a quarter turn, half turn, etc.† and, in all the aforesaid methods of performing the *galliard* step, the *falling* step rarely, if ever, fails to accompany it, in that they are inseparable in their performance, as the rigadoon step open in the same place of one spring and upright close upon both feet we have before described, though they are two distinct steps in themselves. However, sometimes, instead of the galliard step, we find the coupee crossing before sideways introducing the falling step; which it does very naturally, their endings being

---

† See the explanation and table of this step in Character Plate E; see also Plate VII.

directly alike.

Now, as to the method of performing the galliard step which, as I have said in the description thereof, is compounded of a close and plain straight step or walk, I shall begin with the right foot advancing forwards, in the following manner, *viz.* the weight of the body is upon the left foot in the third position, and the right disengaged behind‡; from whence you sink and give an upright spring upon the left foot, closing the right or hindmost foot equal to it directly the same way as has been described in the close from one foot to both, except with this difference that, as I have said, the before mentioned lights on both feet, but this comes down only upon one, namely the left; and it varies from the aforesaid, the right foot being in the first position, joined even with the left, and at liberty to perform the following plain straight step*, which together with the foregoing close completes the *galliard step*; that is to say, after the plain straight step has been made forwards with the right foot, about the length of a step in walking, it does not bring up the left equal to it, as in that, but leaves it in the same place, whilst the weight of the body advances forwards with the stepping of the right foot, the end or setting to the floor of which receives the weight; so that, as I have just observed, the left foot is upon the point behind, the like distance, and the right advanced from it, in which posture the galliard step concludes◊. Upon this commences the *falling step*, which is performed in the following manner, *viz.* the weight of the body ending in the *galliard step* upon the right, the left foot is pointed behind; at the same time the body bends or bows forwards, in order to the ensuing *fall* which is backwards, but is prevented in it by the left foot, which was planted for that purpose upon the point behind; and, at the very instant the weight of the body

---

‡ See the first figure in Plate V.　　*See the first figure in Plate I.　　◊ See the second figure in Plate VII.

inclines forwards preparing for the fall, the left is advancing up to prevent it; which it does by receiving the falling weight in a sink or bend of the knee, in the third position enclosed behind, releasing the right foot[§], which is then ready to receive the weight, on the spring that is given from the left, immediately after its receiving the aforesaid falling weight, and comes down upon the right foot again, in the nature of a latter part of the *balonne,* of which more hereafter; concluding in the same position from whence the foregoing galliard step was taken, with the contrary foot[ð] and, in continuance together with the galliard step, it changes the foot, as in the half coupee, or march, etc.

In performing this step *sideways,* either to the right or left, it only differs from the former in the plain step, which, instead of being made, as in the aforesaid *forwards,* is here performed *sideways;* and it may easily be understood by comparing it with the foregoing described, advancing to the upper part of the room: for instance, supposing the close to be made in the first position, as before, the right foot, instead of making the plain straight step as in that, here makes it *sideways* to the right hand, in like manner as *forwards.* That is, the end or setting down of the plain straight step receives the body; leaving the left toe upon the point sideways the like distance from the right on which the weight is, as has been shown in this step *forwards,* when the said toe was left pointed behind, as it now is *sideways;* from whence commences the falling step, which, instead of forwards, as before, is made as follows, *viz.* the weight being on the right foot, and the left toe upon the point[Δ], as was already observed, the weight of the body falls to the right hand, but, as I have said, is prevented; for, at the same time the weight falls, the left foot which was upon the point is brought with a swift motion to its

---

§ See the second figure in Plates IV and XIV.   φ See the second figure in Plate V.
Δ See the first figure in Plates VI and XV.   ⱴ See the first figure in Plate XI.
ð See the second figure in Plate XIV.

relief, crossing behind the right on which the falling weight is in the fifth position, receiving the body$^\nabla$ which must otherwise have fallen, and releases the right foot$^\partial$ which immediately receives the weight again, in a *bound* or *balonne* sideways to the hand the fall was on, in that the left no sooner receives the falling weight in a sink or bended knee, than it gives a spring, in rising, and throws the body, as in bounding back, upon the right foot, concluding the falling step in the third position, with the left upon the point behind, instead of the right, as at first[†]; from whence the said galliard and falling step may be performed to the left being only in the contrary foot, examples of which with both feet begin the second strain of the rigadoon part of a dance, named the *bretagne*, the first time of its playing over, for they are the very same steps here treated of.

These steps may also be made with a quarter turn, or a half turn, etc. which, to give a more perfect idea thereof, I shall explain with the left foot, as follows, *viz.* the weight being upon the right in the third position, the left upon the point behind[†] begins, in making the spring or close in the first position as aforesaid only, instead of the presence looking up the room after the close, it now faces to the right side, which is a quarter of a turn, and in this it differs from the two ways last described; but the remaining part of the step is entirely the same, stepping the beginning foot sideways to the left hand, and facing to the right side of the room, as before to the upper. The falling step is also the same as before except, as I have said, in not facing to the same part of the room; and turning a half turn only differs in this, that the first spring or close, instead of ending in a quarter of a turn to the right, as before, continues a quarter turn more, facing to the bottom of the room, the left foot stepping sideways

---

† See the second figure in Plate V.

to the same hand, as aforesaid, etc.

As to the agreement of these steps with the notes of the music, it is much the same as in the others: For example, in the following tunes, as forlanes, jigs, etc. the close is made to the first note; the second and third are counted in the straight step of the galliard, that is to say, the second note, at the beginning of said step, and the third, at its ending or receiving the weight of the body. And, suppose instead of performing this step with a plain straight step, as in walking, you add thereto a sink and a rise, the sink then answers the second note, and the rise the third; and in the succeeding step the fall of the body marks the first note, the pause or rest the weight makes upon the knees bent the second, and the third is in the contrary foot's receiving the body upon the spring or bound given from the foot which preserved the weight from falling, where ends the second measure or time. When these steps are performed to tunes of common time, as they for the most part are in galliards, bourees, rigadoons, etc. they are entirely the same as in triple, only, instead of borrowing half the third note for the sink in common time, the sink or preparative for beating the time is upon the fourth note, as has been shown in the rigadoon step of two springs; and the most usual manner of performing this step is in a soft and gentle movement upon the floor, though it may be done to advantage either way, *viz.* off from the ground, or upon it.

C H A P. XVIII.
Of the BOUREE with a BOUND.

THE *bouree with a bound,* so called from its having a *bound* added to the *bouree,* is a compound step consisting of four plain steps and two movements, the first whereof is made upon the ground, but the other not: For instance, you make a movement or sink and rise to the first of the four steps, the second and third completing the bouree or fleuret; and the fourth and last is a bound which is always performed off from the floor, as we have already shown, in treating of that step.

I shall now proceed to show how these four steps are to be reduced to agree with the notes of triple time or of three in the measure, which may be accomplished as follows, *viz.* the left foot, with which we shall for example begin, and the right are to be performed in a motion as swift again, as the remaining two steps, by reason they are both to be accounted but as one note, and are made to the first of the measure. The third step, which is with the left foot, is to the second note, upon which the bouree concludes; and the fourth step is a bound with the right foot to the third note, and completes the bouree with a bound. This step continued in dancing, whether it be the right or the left, always begins with the same foot, as has been already observed in the coupee, and may be performed forwards, backwards, sideways to either hand, crossing before, crossing behind, or crossing before and behind in the same measure, or twice behind; and they are all of them directly the same in their manner of performance, as was shown in the *bouree of one movement,* only, as that was but of three steps and one movement to a bar, this is of four and two movements; and consequently, instead of performing the first two steps equally slow, as in them, they must be quick here, in that they are both to be accounted as no more than one step, as I have said; and as the bouree or fleuret breaks off, at the end of the third step which is upon the left foot, the bound must be added thereto with the right, which is the only difference from the bouree aforesaid. It is unnecessary to say anything further of these steps in this place, since they will be understood by what has been said in the *bouree* or *fleuret of one movement,* having in that described all the different ways mentioned here; but only to observe, that the first two steps, as above, and the bounds must be added.

CHAP. XIX.

Of the SLIP before and then behind, or SLIP behind and afterwards behind, and HALF COUPEE sideways.

THE *slip before and then behind* is a step composed of four plain steps, in a measure, and two movements; which said movements may be done upon the ground, or off from thence; but it differs from the bouree with a bound in this, that, whereas, in the *bouree* aforesaid, the first movement is always to be made on the floor, and the second off, in this step both are performed alike, either springing from the ground, or upon it; and it is also to be noted, that these steps seldom, if ever, are performed any otherwise than sideways to the right or left hand, or with a quarter turn, half turn, etc.

These are the ways this step is usually made, as either *slipping before and afterwards behind*, or *slipping behind and then before*; the first of which I shall describe, beginning with the right foot. For example, the weight of the body is upon the left foot in the third position, the right being entirely disengaged from the weight, so that it may be at liberty to begin[†]; which it does by making the first movement or bend and rise from behind the left foot to the first of the four steps, stepping open off sideways to the right hand[‡], and the second step, which is with the left foot, is drawn crossing before it[*], after which the right foot makes

---

† See the first figure in Plate V.   ‡ See the point or second figure in Plate VI.
* See the point or first figure in Plate VI, and the second figure in Plate XI.

the second movement the same way, which is the third step; but, instead of the left and last foot's being drawn before, as in the first *slip*◊, it must now be drawn behind where it concludes receiving the weight in the fifth position§.

To slip behind and then before is when the right foot has made the first movement and step sideways in the manner just described; and the second step, which is with the left foot⨍, instead of being drawn crossing before, as in the former, is drawn behind§. The second movement is also with the right foot, stepping to the same side△, which is the third step; and the fourth and last, which is with the left foot⨍, is drawn crossing before the right into the position aforesaid◊.

To perform this step with a quarter of a turn, either to the right or left hand, is only turning a quarter turn to one of the said hands, as it shall fall out; in dancing however, as an example, I shall explain it sideways to the right hand, facing to the left side of the room, *viz. before and behind,* and *behind and before,* which are both to be performed as follows: For instance, these *slips,* as before described, were sideways, facing the upper end of the room to the right hand; whereas, in a quarter turn to the left side of the room, in the sink of the first movement, you prepare for the rise or beating time; but instead performing it, facing to the upper end of the room, as in the foregoing, in the rising, it makes a quarter of a turn to the left hand, which then will face to the left side of the room; yet in the performance of the rest of the step to the right, it is entirely in the same manner as I have explained it, to the upper part of the room, there being no difference except in the turn.

A half turn is the same as the quarter; only that, in the rise of the first movement, which is made with the right foot, instead

---

◊ See the second figure in Plate XI. § See the first figure in Plate XI. ⨍ See the first figure in Plate VI. △ See the the second figure in Plate VI.

of turning a quarter turn as before, that is, facing the left side of the room, in this you make a half turn, which then faces the bottom of the room, performing the rest of the step to the right hand, in the same manner we have described it to the upper end.

These steps may likewise be done both *slipping behind* or both *slipping before*; the former is, when, in making the movement to the right or left side, the second step, which is the slip, is drawn crossing behind the first or beginning foot; and the second movement and slip are performed in the like manner.

Both *slipping before* is, when, in performing the said movements, the foot, which makes the slips, is both times drawn crossing before the foot which begun, that is, the second and fourth steps; and the first of these steps, namely, *twice slipping behind*, is in the rigadoon of the late Mr. Isaac, where, in the beginning of the tune, the second time of playing over, it forms a perfect square, which is no small addition to the beauty of the said dance; and this step *slipping before* is no less remarkable, in that it is frequently met with in dancing.

This step, in all the different ways of performing it, as above described, is seldom, if ever, without the half coupee sideways following it, on the same hand to which the slips were made, which seem not to have received their utmost perfection without this step attending them; and as the slips, before explained, were to the right hand, this must be so likewise, and consists of one plain step, as has been observed, in treating of the half coupee; to which is added a movement or sink and rise, made with the right foot stepping open off, sideways, from the position in which the foregoing slips ended, receiving the weight on the setting of the toe or heel to the floor[Δ]; after which the left foot makes a motion in the air, in the form of a half circle, before the ankle of the right foot, opening to the left hand, and accomplishes the time or measure‡.

It still remains to show how these steps agree with the notes of common or triple time; for they are very different in their manner of performance, which we shall proceed to explain, and chiefly in this, that in tunes of triple time either the first or second slip, instead of being made quick as in tunes of common time, are as slow again; yet, for the further illustration of this point, I shall observe how these steps agree with the notes both of common and triple time; which is as follows: To common time or of four in the bar, as in rigadoons, bourees, etc. But having already described the motion or stepping of the feet, I shall wave the saying anything further of it here, and only show, that the first slip or first and second steps are to be performed in the same swift manner we have shown, in the beginning or two first steps of the bouree and a bound, and are both to be made upon the first of the four notes. The second note is counted in the sink which prepares for the second slip, which is the third and fourth steps; the rise which is made on the setting down of the third step, or beginning of the last slip, beats time to the third note, which said slip is completed in the sound of the third note, in the same manner as the first movement to the first note; and the fourth and last note is counted in the sink which prepares for the ensuing step.

When this step is performed to a tune of triple time or of three notes in the measure, as in sarabands, loures, passacailles, etc. sometimes the first slip is quick, as in the aforesaid, and the second not; and at other times the first is slow, and the second swift. When the movement is made quick, it is performed, as above, to the first of the three notes; the second, which is slow,

---

‡ See the first figures in Plates XIV and XV.

takes up the second and third notes. For instance, as was already said, the first slip or coupee being made with the first and second steps to the first note, the second slip, which begins with the third step, is to the second note; and the third is taken up in the gentle sliding or drawing of the fourth and last step, whether before or behind. Half the third note is borrowed, to mark the sink which is for the next step, as has been observed before; and, if the first slip is slow, the beginning step is to the first note, the slip or easy drawing of the second step behind or before to the second note, and the remaining slip is swift to the third note.

As to the half coupee, the first movement or stepping sideways marks time to the first note; the second and third are counted in the half circle the foot makes in the air; and the fourth in the sink, provided it be common time; but, if triple, half the third note is borrowed, as I have said.

CHAP. XX.
Of the HOP *or* CONTRETEMP.

THE *hop* or *contretemp* is a compound step consisting of two walks or steppings of the feet, as the coupee; and it may be performed various ways, as advancing, retiring, sideways to the right or left, turning, etc. There are also two different positions from whence this step is taken and performed, namely, the third and fourth; the first of which we shall explain forwards, beginning with the left foot, which is behind the right in the third position[*], but so disengaged from the weight of the body as to be ready to act; which it does in the sink that prepares for the spring or hop which is made upon the right foot, lighting in the same place; and at the instant the hop or rise from the ground is given, it leaves the aforesaid position where it rested, during the sink, and straightens the knee, pointing the toe directly sideways, as in the march[◊]; but it does not press upon the floor, as in that, by reason the march is performed upon the ground, and this off from thence which is the principal difference; for, instead of the progress made by the disengaged foot, as in the march, in this it must be performed in like manner off from thence in the air, the weight all the while continuing on the same foot upon which it was at commencing, till the left has advanced the length of a march or step in walking[§]; after which it receives the body, and releases the right foot that supported it, during its procession, as aforesaid, which then makes a plain step or walk forwards[ƒ],

---

* See the second figure in Plate V. ◊ See the first figure in Plate VI or Plate XV. § See the first figure in Plate IX. ƒ See the second figure in Plate IX.

which is the second step of the contretemp, and is completed on the setting down or receiving of the weight upon the said foot in the position as at first[Δ], being a sort of *hopping coupee.*

To perform this step *backwards* is entirely the same as *forwards,* only, instead of the left foot's being in the third position behind, the right is now enclosed before in the same or fourth position[∇], from whence it makes the spring or hop *backwards,* in the same manner as was described *forwards*[∂]; after which the right foot, instead of stepping forwards, as before, in this makes the second step backwards[♦].

When this step is done with a quarter or half turn, etc. the weight of the body, as has been observed, being on the right foot, the hop or contretemp is performed, as we have already explained, but not to the upper end of the room, instead of which it turns a quarter of a turn to the right hand; but the rest is the same, as in the foregoing, only you are to observe, that it is facing to the right side of the room to which it advances.

The half turn in no respect differs from the former, except in its not stopping at the right side of the room; but, instead of that, it adds a quarter more facing to the lower end of the room, to which it is performed in like manner, as above, to the upper; and if, instead of the right hand, it be performed to the left, as it equally is in turning, as aforesaid, it is much the same, except that the quarter or half turn, instead of being made to the right hand, as in the foregoing, are now advancing to the left side or bottom of the room; of which the *Royal George* affords us an example, in that the said dance begins with this step, both to the right and left hands, *viz.* the *gentleman* performs it to the left hand here spoken of, whilst the *lady* does the same to the right.

Δ See the second figure in Plate V, as aforesaid.   ∇ See the first figure in Plates IV or IX.   ∂ See the first figure in Plates VI or XV.   ♦ See the second figure in Plate IX, and for the second step of the contretemp the first figure in the same Plate concluding as at first; See also the first figure in Plate IV.

There are, besides, other ways of performing this step from the said third position, as sideways crossing to the right hand, and in a hop, step, and draw behind sideways to the left; which steps differ from the foregoing in this, that whereas they were made either forwards or backwards, facing to the upper part of the room, or the same turning to the sides or lower end of it, these, on the contrary, are always sideways, though they are performed turning all the ways aforesaid: For instance, to the right hand sideways, the face or presence being to the upper end of the room, and the weight in the position already explained[†], the hop is performed in like manner excepting that, instead of the left foot's advancing as in that, or retiring from the hop or spring which is made on the right, it is here cast crossways before the right upon which the body rests, about the length of a march, and then receives the weight[‡]; after which the right foot makes the second step of the contretemp open off sideways, in the manner above described in forwards[*].

When it is performed turning with a quarter turn, or a half turn, etc. it only varies in its not advancing to the sides or lower end of the room, as in the other, but, instead of that, it is made sideways to the right hand, facing to the right side of the room in a quarter turn, in the same manner as to the upper end; the half turn the like, only not facing to the right side of room, but instead thereof to the lower part of it, which is a quarter of a turn more.

The second of the ways aforesaid is the hop, step, and draw behind sideways, which is as follows, *viz.* to the right or left hand, the last of which begins from the same position treated of in this step, namely, the third, the disengaged foot being upon the point behind the right[†], from whence this step commences by

---

† See the second figure in Plate V.   ‡ See the second figure in Plate XI.   * See in some degree the second figure in Plate VI.

making a sink and upright spring or hop, falling in the same place and posture, as at first, only the knees are bent; after which the left foot upon the point steps open off sideways to the same hand, and receives the weight of the body from the right, either placing the heel to the ground or upon the toe[§]; and the right foot, being then released, after the hop and step are made, as aforesaid, is drawn behind the left, the toe pressing the floor[ƒ]; as it is brought behind, and receives the weight of the body, as at commencing in the third position, except that, instead of the left foot's being pointed behind, it is now enclosed before and concludes[Δ].

This step with a quarter turn differs from the hop crossways to the right, only in the latter's not being made to the same hand; for the quarter turn, instead thereof, is performed, as above described, stepping to the left hand, facing full to the right side of room, as in the other, and the half turn, facing the lower part of the room, is, in its performance to the left hand, the same as the quarter to the right.

Having explained the foregoing hop's beginning with the left foot from the third position, I shall now describe it sideways with the same foot, from what I call the *fourth position*; that is to say, the weight of the body is upon the right, the left being directly the same sideways as the beginning or first movement in a march, only the toe is not pointed to the ground, as in that, but the heel placed without any weight[§]; from which posture of standing this step is taken and performed: For instance, the weight being upon the right foot, and the left heel placed, as aforesaid, about the length of a step in walking, you make the sink or preparation for the spring or hop[▽] by transferring the weight from the right to the left foot, the very moment before

---

§ See the first figure in Plate VI.   ƒ See the second figure in Plate VI.   Δ See the first figure in Plate IV, or second figure in Plate XI.   ▽ See the first figure in Plate X.

the spring is made, in taking up the right foot from the ground, the left at the same instant receiving the body, upon which the hop is begun and completed, as follows: The right foot, being then at liberty[†], makes a plain step or walk sideways crossing before the left, that supports the weight, to the same hand[‡]; after which the left foot steps out the same way and places the heel, being ready to make the spring, as before[*], by reason you are now in the same position as at commencing, and concludes the step.

This *hop*, as just described, is to be found in the second strain of the rigadoon of the late Mr. Isaac, the first time of playing over, at the end of the third bouree of the woman's side; where the lady stands upon the second step of the said bouree, *viz.* the right foot, whilst the left, instead of receiving the body as it would otherwise have done, only sets down the heel to the ground. From this posture proceeds the hop or contretemp we are now treating of, which takes up the fourth bar or measure; and, as I have referred to this place for an example, I think it will not be improper to say something here of the hop that follows the foregoing: Which differs in this, that whereas in the former the heel is to be placed to the ground upon the last step, in this a bound is made instead thereof, which is the only difference, and the reason of its being called a *hop, step, and bound*; and it also remarkably varies from the aforesaid, in that it again conducts the dancer into the bourees, coupees, and half coupees, etc. as the other leads him out of these steps. To perform this contretemp or hop from the *fourth position forwards*, the left or beginning foot instead of being open sideways, as before, must be advanced, about the like distance before the right, as the other was upon one side of it; which manner of standing is what we call the

---

† See the second figure in Plates VI and XV.   ‡ See the first figure in Plate XI.   * See the first figure in Plate X.

fourth position, from whence the hop is to be made, being, in all respects, the same as *sideways to the left hand* only, as I have said, the left foot must be advanced up the room, which is done as follows: The weight of the body being upon the right foot, and the heel of the left to the ground, as aforesaid◊, the contretemp is made forwards upon the left foot, the right being taken up from the floor; which said right foot then makes a plain walk or step forwards§, that in the foregoing was made sideways crossing before the left; after which the left foot is advanced, the length of a step, and the heel placed in the fourth position, as at commencing this step, in readiness to repeat the same◊. But, instead of that, I shall proceed to show, how this step is performed from the said position *backwards, viz.* by the weight's not advancing *forwards* to the left foot, as before, but on the contrary the hop is made on the right foot *backwards* by taking up the left foot, in like manner as the other *forwards* in taking up of the right, except that the weight is not transferred, as in the former, and then it makes the step or walk backwards the same as before forwards§; after which the right foot makes the second and last step backwards also and receives the body, leaving the left heel to the floor, as at first, either to advance or retire◊; and these are the most usual ways of performing this step from the fourth position.

The method of performing the hop or contretemp, both from the third and fourth position, being now explained, I shall take some notice, how they agree with the notes of music, either of common or triple time, etc. as for example, from the third position forwards, beginning with the left or advancing foot to a tune of common time; which being accomplished will show the manner of the rest, whether

---

◊ See the first figure in Plate IX.   § See the second figure in Plate IX.

backwards, sideways, or round, in that the same method of counting will bear in them all, since the hop certainly marks the first note or what we call time, though it be upon the right foot, as in the third position, or on the left in the fourth as follows, *viz.* the spring or hop, that is made upon the right foot, beats time to the first of the four notes; the second note is counted in the setting down or receiving the weight of the body upon the left foot, after its having advanced the length of a step forwards; and the third note is counted, when the right foot receives the body, as before, and finishes. The remaining fourth note, as has been said, is in the sink which prepares for the succeeding step; and, to triple time or of the notes in three bar or measure, it is the very same, except that, as there are only three notes, half the third must be borrowed for the sink that prepares to mark the cadence of the succeeding step.

CHAP. XXI.

Of the CHASSEE or DRIVING STEP.

THE hop or contretemp last explained having introduced us to the position from whence the *chassee* or *driving step* is performed, namely, the *fourth*, since in that we took no further notice than of its being sideways or forwards in the said position, without explaining the particular manner in which the last step, whether of a bouree, coupee, half coupee, or march is to be performed, when introducing any of the aforesaid hops or driving steps; and as this step considerably varies, in its method of performance, from the way in which it would otherwise have been done, had a bouree, or coupee, etc. followed, I shall observe, that it is much the same as when, in *fencing*, we put ourselves in a posture of defence; but, this posture being probably unknown to the ladies, I shall endeavour to give an explanation of it, which take as follows: The posture of defence most usually is to the right hand, the whole weight of the body being upon the left foot, and the right stepped out sideways to the same side of the room, about the length of a step as in walking; the full part of the heel first comes to the ground, but afterwards the foot is flat, only free from weight, both the knees being bent†; from which position or posture the hop before treated of is taken, as well as the chassee we are now about to describe, or from whence the *lunge* or *pass* is made in *fencing*.

However it still remains to show the method, how the above-

---

† See the second figure in Plate X.

mentioned step is to be performed, when we put ourselves in the said position or posture, in which consists the perfection of it; and, for the greater variety, in describing the same we shall begin to the right hand, having already observed it to the left, in the hop aforesaid. But, for the better understanding of this, we must take notice, that in a *bouree* we are to make a stop or rest upon the second step, when any of this sort of steps follow; in the *coupee* upon the first, and in a *half coupee* or *march*, etc. we stand in one of the positions from whence it is to be taken, which differ according to the foregoing step's being performed forwards, backwards, or sideways; but, in all of them, it is generally taken from the first or third position either before or behind‡. We shall begin with the last: For example, the weight of the body being upon the left foot, the right at liberty behind it prepares for the *kick* or soft *stamp* sideways, for so I must name it, as not knowing what more properly to call it, by raising the heel of the hindmost foot, whether right or left, with a gentle and easy motion, the toe or ball of the instep pointing down to the ground, but not so as to bear upon it, by reason it will not be ready to perform the step aforesaid; which is exceeding swift, because, as I have said, the dancer makes a pause or rest, until the fourth note in common time is almost spent, and in triple the third; but, *before either of them expire*, the easy stamp or kick is given, and instead of the foot's being flat to the ground, as in fencing, in dancing the heel must first be placed thereto in order to receive the chassee or hop that succeeds*. How the latter of them is to be executed, we have shown in the hops; and, having just before observed the raising of the heel and pointing of the toe, I shall also take notice, that, just as the kick or stamp is about to be made, the toe, instead of pointing to the floor, as at

---

‡ See the first figure in Plate I, the second figure in Plate IV, or the first figure in Plate V.   * See the second figure in Plate X.

commencing, rises from thence; and the heel comes down, but does not receive the weight, till the hop or chassee is made, which, in dancing, is always immediately after this step, it being a preparation to that purpose; for, as I have said, the knees being bent, at the instant the right heel is struck against the floor, it only remains to perform the steps treated on; and whether forwards or backwards, the method is the same, as *sideways* above explained to the right hand.

Having now given some hints as to the manner how the step that introduces a hop or chassee is to be performed, I shall proceed to the explanation of the latter, which is a step composed sometimes of three, and at other times of four steps to the measure or bar; and the most usual way of their performance is *forwards* and *sideways*. I shall begin with the former of these, namely, the chassee or driving step of three steps in a measure, advancing to the upper part of the room, which is as follows, *viz.* the weight of the body being upon the left foot, and the right stepped forwards, as just explained, into the fourth position[◊] with the knees bent, in order to the performance of the chassee, it begins by transferring the weight; that is to say, before the rising from the said sink, the body, that was on the left foot, is conveyed upon the right and foremost foot, which then supports it, whilst the left, disengaged from the weight, advances the length of a step, in rising from the abovesaid sink into the third position enclosed behind the right, and again receives the body. The said rising beats time to the first note of the measure[§], upon which the right, being at liberty, makes the second of the three steps[Δ]; but it differs somewhat from that of the bouree, in its being stepped more open off to the right hand, whereas the bouree is directly advancing forwards upon which is counted the

---

◊ See the second figure in Plate IX.   § See the second figure in Plate IV, or the first figure of Plate XI.

Δ See the second figure in Plate IX, only the right or advanced foot is more open.

second note; and the last is reckoned in the kick or light stamp that prepares for the chassee following, which is the last of the three steps, and made with the left foot; for, as I have said, the body, being on the right, rests thereon, whilst the left moves slowly forwards, the toe pressing to the floor, as in the march; but not much above half its length, in that the remaining part is allowed to the light stamp the left foot gives forwards, on the expiration of the last note; upon which it is then in readiness to perform the same thing over again, as in the bouree[▽]; for this step, in continuance, changes the foot, every three steps, the same as a bouree. This step with the contrary foot differs only in the weight's being upon the right foot, instead of the left, as in the former; and the left, at the end of the second step of the foregoing chassee, being advanced into the fourth position, in the manner we have just observed, begins by transferring the weight, and taking up the right foot, as the other did by the left[∂], and so on if continued.

This step *sideways* is the same as above explained, except that, instead of forwards, it is made sideways, which is the principal difference; however, for the more easy comprehending of the same, I shall observe, that it begins from the fourth position sideways to the right side of the room, the face or presence of the body being to the upper end of the room, the weight upon the left foot as before, with the right placed, as described by the posture of defence, or step which introduces this sort of steps[♦]. The weight is transferred, as before; and, in rising, the left foot is taken from the ground, but instead of advancing up the room, is now brought sideways into the third position

---

▽ See the first figure in Plate IX.   ∂ See the first figure in Plate IV, or the second figure of Plate XI. For the second step only more open, as has been said, see the first figure in Plate IX and for the last step, see the second figure in the same Plate.   ♦ See the second figure in Plate X.

enclosed behind the right, and receives the weight in time to the music◇. The second step, with the right foot, is sideways, the same way, and receives the body℘, which it supports, till the third or fourth note is expired𝑓, according to the time in which it is done, that is, whether it be of triple or common; upon which the last step or *light stamp* is made, the same way crossing before the right𝄇, with the knees bent in readiness to proceed to the chassee following, which is performed in like manner, but on the contrary foot.

As we have now come to the chassee of four steps in a measure, the foregoing of three having been described commencing with the left foot, both *forwards sideways* and *to the right hand*, I shall, on the contrary, explain this beginning with the right foot, *to the left hand*; but, in the first place, I shall describe it *advancing* up the room, which is as follows: The weight being upon the right foot, the left advanced into the fourth position⊕, in the method already explained, begins, as before, by transferring the weight, but, as I have said, with the other foot; for, as the chassee of three in the bar transferred the weight from the left to the right, this does it from the right to the left, the right and hindmost foot advancing into the third position enclosed behind the left+, directly the same way as in that of three, except with this difference, that as the first note in that was counted in the rising and bringing of the foot into the third position, in this the two first steps of the four must be performed swift to the first note, as has been noted in the bouree and bound; and the second note is in the stepping forwards of the third step■, only, as I have observed, a little open; upon which

---

◇ See the second figure in Plate IV, or the first figure in Plate XI.   ℘ First upon the toe and afterwards upon the heel. See in some measure the second figure in Plates VI and X.   𝑓 See the point or first figure in Plate VI.   𝄇 See the second figure in Plate XI.   ⊕ See the first figure in Plate IX. + See the first figure in Plate IV, or the second figure of Plate XI. For the second step which is made quick at the same time, see the first figure of Plate IX.   ■ See the second figure in Plate IX.

the weight rests, till the third note in triple time is spent, or in common the fourth, in like manner as, in the driving step of three, it rested on the second, waiting for the expiration of the third or fourth last notes, at which instant the step or preparative for the next ensuing is made, and concludes[†].

In performing the chassee of four steps in a measure, above explained *forwards, to the left hand sideways,* the left foot, instead of being advanced, is open sideways in the fourth position, the like distance to the left hand, as in the point or beginning of a march, only the heel and foot are flat, as has been shown, in the hop or contretemp, to this side of the room[‡] and it commences by changing, as above, forwards, only the right foot, instead of advancing as in that, moves sideways and is brought, in the rising behind the left, into the third position[*], at which instant the left foot, which is the second of the four steps, is stepped with a swift motion, the same way, and marks time to the first note[◊]. Note the second is in the stepping and crossing of the right foot before the left[§], which is the third step; and the third is in the setting of the left heel down, in order to perform it again, as was illustrated by the posture in fencing, or in common time upon the fourth as has been said[‡].

This step may also be performed with a quarter turn, which only differs in this, that, after the rise or movement is made to the first two steps that mark time to the first note, the third step, which is with the right foot, instead of crossing before the left, as before, in the stepping of it, turns a quarter turn, which then faces full to the left side of the room to the music as above; the fourth and last step, which is with the left foot, steps sideways to the left hand, the same way as the foregoing to the presence, and, if continued one step further, the first two steps

---

† See the first figure in Plate IX.   ‡ See the first figure in Plate X.   * See the first figure in Plate IV or second figure of Plate XI.   ◊ See in some measure the first figure in Plate VI.   § See the second figure in Plate VI and the first figure in Plate XI.

face to the left side of the room, as the foregoing did to the upper part; and the third step, in which you turn the quarter, instead of stepping to the left side of the room, now faces to the lower end of it; the fourth step, with the left foot, steps sideways to the same hand, and so on, if you please, till arrived to the presence as at first. It is to be noted, that this step does not, in continuance, change the foot, as the chassee of three in the measure, or bouree, but always begins with the same foot, as in the bouree with a bound.

There is another way of performing this step, of which I shall take some notice, *viz.* two movements and steps to the measure, that is to say, the chassee of three steps in a bar already explained, to which is added a sort of a half coupee, in the nature of a driving step; which said step is the fourth of the last described chassee, except that it is made plain here with a movement or rise from the fourth position from whence it begun, and the released foot opens in the air, forming a quarter of a circle, or a half circle, etc.

As to the performance of this chassee or driving step of two movements, the most usual way is forwards, turning a quarter, half, three quarter, or a whole turn, the first of which is as follows, *viz.* beginning, as we will suppose, with the right foot, upon which the weight stands in the fourth position, and the left advanced, but without any weight$^{\oint}$, as has been said, except its own, commences by transferring the weight in the same manner as described in the chassee of four steps with one movement forwards to the upper part of the room, that is, the first two steps, namely, with the right foot and the left$^{\Delta}$; but not the third step with the right, for, although it steps a little open, as in the aforesaid, it does not receive any weight, by reason it prepares

---

$\oint$ See the first figure in Plate IX. Δ See the first figure in Plate IV. For the second step which is made quick at the same time, see the first figure in Plate IX.

for the half coupee, which is to be made in the manner of the chassee before mentioned. This step is made upon the second note of the three, as was explained by the posture in fencing, only instead of sideways it is forwards[†]; and, as was already shown, the knees being bent and weight upon the left foot, the half coupee, the second movement of the chassee, begins by conveying or transferring the body from the left to the right and foremost foot, immediately before rising, on which the left or hindmost foot advances, sliding the ball or instep flat to the ground into the third position behind the right[‡], which it releases; and, in its being taken up from the floor, it makes a quarter of a circle in the air, opening to the right side[*], facing the upper part of the room, or a quarter turn to the right side; or a half turn to the bottom, a three quarter turn to the left side, or a whole turn; which said coupee is performed to the third note, if to triple time; and in common to the fourth.

---

† See the second figure in Plate IX. ‡ See the second figure in Plate IV. * See the second figure in Plates XIV and XV.

C H A P. XXII.

Of the CHASSEE or DRIVING STEP of two movements or BOUNDING COUPEES.

THIS step is performed two different ways, *viz. advancing* and *retiring;* the former of which begins by transferring the weight resting on the right or left leg in the fourth position, and the latter by a sway or wave of the poise of the body, either on the right or left leg from the second position, which is the most usual method of performing this step; for, being in the second position, and the weight as much on one foot as the other, it is only waving or swaying the body, whether upon the right or left foot, during the sink, preparing for the *chassee* or *driving step*, that is made by the disengaged and pointed foot, whichsoever it be, always retiring to the right or left, or backwards. But, if it begin from the weight resting on the right or left foot, as advancing to make the contretemp, chassees, or the like, it begins by changing, otherwise directly, without changing, being duly prepared; though in its performance advancing, it much resembles the chassee to the left hand, of one movement to four steps, except that, instead of one movement made upon the ground, here are two movements or coupees off from thence; and it is a step frequently found in tunes of common time, not much unlike what we often see boys perform in play, when they run along, and, in rising from a sink, knock or beat one heel against the other, lighting in the fourth position with the knees bent, continuing the same, perhaps, the length of a street or field.

The *driving step* or *chassee of two movements* or *bounding coupees* is usually performed sideways, though sometimes to one part of the room, and sometimes to another, as it falls out, which is according as the foregoing step ended *to the right or left sides, or upper or lower ends* of the room; for the better understanding whereof I shall give an example of it to the left hand, facing up the room as follows, *viz.* the weight of the body being upon the right foot, the left in the fourth position sideways, as in the foregoing chassee or driving step of four steps, to the same side of the room, the knees bent[◊], etc. It begins by transferring the weight to the left foot, as in that, only in the rising, instead of the right foot's being brought behind the left in the third position as in that upon the ground, it is here made off from thence, in a sort of springing or bounding sideways, in which the right and commencing foot, in a manner, *drives* the left and second step of the coupee before it; for the spring or bound no sooner is given and the right foot brought into the first position even, or the third position behind the left[§], than the left being at liberty is driven the length of a step sideways[⨎] and then set down in the fourth position, the knees being bent, as in the posture of defence. This second step concludes the first of the two movements or coupees[◊], the bound or beginning of which is made upon the first of the four notes, in that they are both counted as no more than one step, as has been already shown, not only in the bouree and bound but also in the chassee of four steps; the second of the four notes is reckoned in the rest or pause the weight makes upon the sink that prepares for the second movement, *viz.* the third and fourth steps, performed in the same method as the first, by transferring the weight, as aforesaid, and being made upon the third note concludes the step; and the fourth, as I have said, is in

---

◊ See the first figure in Plate X.   § See the second figure in Plate I or the first figure in Plate IV.
⨎ See in some measure the first figure in Plate VI.

the sink or preparation for the succeeding step, whether it be of the same, or any other sort.

To perform this step *to the right hand* is only to transfer the weight: For example, instead of the body's resting upon the right foot, as before, it must be placed on the left, with the right disengaged from any weight except its own, as has been shown by the foregoing‡; the rest entirely, in the like manner, advancing sideways to the right side of the room, as the other to the left.

Having explained this step *advancing*, I will proceed to its method of *retiring*; and the difference between this and the former principally consists in the weight of the body's not being changed on its beginning now, as in the foregoing; but instead thereof it directly commences from the fourth position in which we stand: For instance, suppose you would perform it retiring, the same way we have described it advancing, *viz.* sideways to the left, then, instead of the body's resting upon the right foot, as in the aforesaid, it must now rest on the left, the right being in the fourth position sideways flat to the ground, without any other weight than its own, except the toe a little pointed or pressing to the floor, from whence it begins.

However, before I proceed in that, I shall explain it *retiring* down the room; which is from the same position, only the right foot is advanced, and not sideways, as here; and because a beaten coupee or hop, either forwards or sideways, generally introduces this step, it may likewise not be improper to take some notice of it, which I shall do, in the explanation of the said step's *advancing* up the room, since that will be sufficient for the comprehending of it both ways, in that the same manner of performance is to be observed in the one as in the other, only in the former the beat is made sideways, instead of backwards, as in the present.

---

‡ See the second figure in Plate X.

C H A P. XXIII.
Of the BEATEN COUPEE or HOP.

THE *beaten coupee* or *hop* forwards, beginning from the first position, the weight of the body being upon the left foot[*], makes a movement or sink and rise, as was shown in the half coupee up the room[◊] and receives the weight, as in that, upon the first note, supporting the body, whilst the left foot strikes or beats against the heel of the right[§], which beat is upon the second note; and then it steps back to the place from whence it came, in order to receive the weight again, which after the beat retires off from the foot upon which it was, in a slow motion, waiting for the expiration of the third note; upon which it comes down on the left foot, in the fourth position, much in the swift manner described in the preparation for a hop or chassee[ꝑ].

If you would perform this step with a hop you only need, instead of the movement as above, make a *spring* or *hop* upon the left foot, whilst the right advances, as was explained in the first spring of the rigadoon step of two; but though the weight there does not come upon the advancing foot, by reason a second spring is to be given first, here it must, as in the ending of a march, after which receiving of the body the beat is given, as above.

Having explained the beaten coupee or hop, which conducts us to the step we are treating of, and being in the position from whence it is taken, that is to say, in the fourth, with the weight upon the left foot, and the right advanced, or more properly

---

* See the first figure in Plate I.   ◊ See in some measure the second figure in Plate IX.   § See the second figure in Plate V.   ꝑ See the second figure in Plate IX.

speaking, where it was left, in finishing of the beaten hop or coupee; being I say in the fourth position, with the knees bent, the *flying chassee* or *driving step* of two movements commences backwards, by bringing the right and foremost pointed foot, in the nature of a spring or low bound in rising from the sink or bending aforesaid into the third position enclosed before the left[†]; which bound or coming down of the right foot marks time to the first note and relieves the left, which it drives backwards, the length of a step, receiving the weight in the fourth position[§], with the knees bent as at commencing, upon which the first movement is ended. The bound and step are both reckoned, on account of their swiftness, but as one; and the second movement is made to the third and fourth steps, which are, in their performance, entirely the same as the first. The second note is in the bending of the knees, after finishing of the first spring or coupee; the third in the bound upon the right foot, which begins the second movement; and the fourth is in the bending of the knees, as aforesaid.

As the method, in which this step is performed *retiring*, is now shown, I shall return to the place where I left off, and proceed in explaining it, as *retiring sideways* to the left side of the room and conclude what I shall further say on that head; and first of all it must be noted, that it is the reverse to the foregoing *advancing*, for as in that the foot, on which the body rests at beginning, pursues or drives before it the foot without weight, in this the disengaged foot drives or pursues the *retiring* foot that supports the body, much like retiring in fencing, as the first explained is a sort of advancing, which I think plainly appears from what has been said in the description of them.

The latter of the said steps being now fully described, it only remains to add that, instead of backwards, it must be made

---

† See the second figure of Plate IV.

retiring directly sideways, crossing the room to the left hand, in the same manner as retiring down it, which is all the difference; and consequently it is unnecessary to make a further repetition, except that, as where I left off*, it commences from the fourth position; and if performed retiring cross the room to the right side, it is taken from the same position as when advancing to the left, only as I have observed, it begins without transferring the weight; but, when taken from the second position, it is only swaying or waving the body to the side you would perform it, whether right or left.

It is to be noted, that the foregoing chassee or driving step of two springing movements, when performed in triple time, must have a *springing coupee* more added, to fill up the bar or measure; or instead thereof a *close*, which is nothing more than that instead of finishing the additional *coupee,* or in the bound's lighting upon one foot, as in that I described, it comes down upon both feet, at the same time, to the third note in triple time, completing the measure, as if the coupee had been finished. Examples of the latter are to be found in the *Chaconne de Phaeton* of Monsieur Pécour[7], twenty bars before the end; and the foregoing of two springs and a close is to be met with in the *Passacaille de Scilla* by the same master, twenty seven measures before the end, and in tunes of common time, as allemaignes[8], rigadoons, bourees, etc. but, instead of the chassee or driving step of two springs, we frequently meet with one of them put with the aforesaid close to a measure◊.

---

* See in some measure the second figure in Plate VI.   ◊ See the table of this step in Character Plate I.

Editor's notes: 7. Louis Pécour (also spelled Pecoor, Pecour, Pécourt; 1653 – 1729), a French dancer and choreographer.   8. *Allemaigne,* meaning German. Also called: *allemande, almain,* etc.

CHAP. XXIV.

Of the *CHASSEE or DRIVING STEP*
of three springs in the same place, from the third position.

THIS *chassee* or *driving step* differs from the aforesaid, in its not being taken from the fourth position, but from the third, in which position as an example we shall describe it, beginning with the right foot, as follows, *viz.* the weight is upon the left foot, and the right in the third position behind, being at liberty§, commences by bending both knees, and at the same time preparing for the close or drive, which is accomplished in the straightening of the right knee directly sideways$, in the rise or spring from the sinking aforesaid; in which it is brought into the third position before the left on which the body rests△, and drives the left off sideways, or rather obliquely, in the air▽, the length of a step. The said spring or drive with the right foot marks time to the first note of the three in a measure or triple time; and the second is in the spring or drive with the left foot now in the air, which together with the right knee that supports the body bends, in order for the second spring, which is made in a rise from the same by a spring or bound into the third position behind; then it releases the right by receiving the weight∂ and drives the right foot sideways into the air, the length of a step♦, from whence the third drive or close is made to the same

---

§ See the first figure in Plate V. $ See the second figure in Plate XV, or the second figure in Plate VI, only the toe does not touch the floor.   △ See the second figure in Plate IV.   ▽ See the first figure in Plate VI, only the foot is in the air.   ∂ See the second figure in Plate IV.   ♦ See the second figure in Plate XV.

note, by bending both knees, as before; and, in the spring or rising from thence, the right foot in the air *bounds* into the third position before the left† which it releases, though it is not *driven*, as in the others, but instead thereof remains in the third position behind the right on which the whole weight rests, concluding the step on the contrary foot‡, in readiness to perform the same step over again, and commencing with the left foot.

The second strain of the loure begins with this step, the last time of its playing over, with the same foot as here, that is to say, on the *man's* side, but with the contrary on the *woman's*; and in the dance it is performed facing to the right side of the room or lady, and not to the upper end of it, as here described.

In triple time this step transfers the weight and foot, every measure as in the half coupee, march, or bouree; but, when done to tunes of common time, instead of three drives or springs in a measure, as in triple aforesaid, there must be only two; and consequently, if continued, they will always commence with the same foot as the bouree and a bound, or coupee, etc. unless steps of a contrary nature, as the bouree, half coupee, or march be made between them.

The driving step of two springs agrees with the notes of common time, in the same manner as was described in the flying or driving step of two movements; and it makes no small figure, either in common or triple time, since in the latter it is rare to meet with a passacaille or chaconne without it; but, on the contrary it is sometimes found in three or four places of one dance, which demonstrates how greatly it is valued and esteemed by masters*.

---

† See the second figure in Plate IV.   ‡ See the second figure in Plate V.   * See the table of this step in Character Table I.

C H A P. XXV.

Of the *FLYING CHASSEE* or *DRIVING STEP backwards, with a CLOSE and COUPEE to a measure.*

THE step, which I am now about to explain, begins from the fourth position, as well as the hop or chassee; but, before I proceed, it must be observed, that it is composed of three different steps, and commences with the first movement of the *flying chassee* or *driving step* retiring down the room exactly in the same manner as was explained, in treating of that step[◊], ending in the fourth position to the first note, the weight being upon the left foot, and the right advanced, or rather, as I have said, left without weight, in readiness to begin the second movement of the said step[§]; which movement is made upon the second note of the saraband or passacaille, to which it is done by making a *close* from the position abovementioned, in rising from the sink or bending of the knees in which the chassee to the first note ended; which spring or close is made, in turning a quarter turn to the right side of the room, from the upper part thereof, into the third position, by taking up the right or advanced foot, at the instant the close is made upon the left, before which the right is enclosed[ƒ]. The third note is in the *coupee*, which is the third movement and concludes the step; and the said coupee, which must be performed swift to the last note, commences,

---

◊ See page 102.   § See the second figure in Plate IX.   ƒ See the second figure in Plate IV, only to be supposed facing the right side of the room.

by the right or enclosed foot's making a movement or sink and rise, stepping open off sideways to the right hand[Δ], facing, as aforesaid, to the right side of the room, rather inclining backwards than directly sideways, by reason of its making way for the left or hind foot's more easy and natural crossing before the right sideways into the fifth position, in the method shown in treating of the *slip before and then behind,* ending, as I have said, upon the third note, with the knees bent preparing for the following step, which most usually is a half coupee[▽]; and it begins by taking of the right or hind foot up, in rising from the aforesaid bending of the knees, which is brought behind the left into the third position[∂], turning a quarter turn back again, from the right side of the room to the upper end, upon the first note of the measure. The second and third notes are in the half circle or motion the left foot makes in the air, in its being taken from the floor[♦], which, as I have said, is upon the right foot's receiving the weight in the rise from the first step; and the left foot, being in the air, is ready to perform a pirouette, or any suchlike step.

If, instead of the right side of the room, you would perform it to the other hand, the left foot must be in the fourth position advanced before the right on which the body rests, in like manner as the right was before, without any weight except its own[◇], from whence it commences to the left side of the room, directly as the foregoing to the right; and the step here treated on is to be found in the *Passacaille d'Armide for a Woman,* composed by Monsieur L'Abbé, in the sixth measure, beginning with the right foot, as above explained[℘].

Δ See in some respects the second figure in Plate VI, only to be supposed to the right side of the room.
▽ See the second figure in Plate XI, and it also must be facing as aforesaid.   ∂ See the first figure in Plate IV.   ♦ See the first figure in Plate XV.   ◇ See the first figure in Plate IX.   ℘ See the table of this step in Character Plate I.

C H A P. XXVI.

Of the HOP of two movements, from the fifth position round in two half turns.

THIS step is much used in *stage dancing*, to which, indeed it properly belongs, as well as the foregoing; but as there are ladies who frequently arrive at such a perfection as to be capable of performing this sort of steps, it may not be improper here to give an explanation of some of the most remarkable of them, of which number that under consideration is one; which is often found in tunes of triple time, and sometimes in those of common, consisting of two movements, *viz.* a hop and a bound both made in turning, the first commencing either from the fourth or fifth position; from which last we shall explain it, beginning with the right foot that supports the body, as in the chassee or driving step, only the left, instead of being either open sideways or advanced in the fourth position, from whence the aforesaid steps are taken, must be a little more crossed, that is to say, the left heel towards the toe of the right foot, without the least weight bearing upon it, by reason the step begins by transferring the weight[†], which is accomplished in this manner: The body, as has been observed, being on the right foot, immediately before the *hop* or first movement is made, is conveyed upon the left and foremost foot, by transferring the weight, upon which the hop is given on the left foot, in the right's being taken up from the ground turning a half turn from the upper part of the room to the lower end

---

† See the second figure in Plate XI.

thereof, to the right hand, making a half circle in the air the same way behind the left foot where it arrives. At the same instant, the hop is made upon the first note of the measure; the second is in setting down the said right foot in the fourth position advanced before the left, on which the weight rests, in its being brought from behind the left foot, where it marked the first note[‡]. The third note is in the coming down of the bound,which is made, as aforesaid, in transferring the weight from the left to the right, the very moment before the spring or bound is made, by rising from the sink or bending of the knees, which was on the setting down of the right foot to the second note, and bringing the left foot on which the body rested in a low *bound* or *spring* into the third position behind the right; which being then released makes the remaining half circle in the air, by turning a half turn more to the same hand, as in the *hop* or first movement from the lower end of the room to the upper part, and finishes the step with the other foot in the air sideways[*]. To perform the same step with the other foot, we are only to set down the right foot into the fifth position before the left, on which the whole weight rests, which begins, as aforesaid, by transferring the weight[◊]; and the hop turns a half turn to the left, exactly as the foregoing was described to the right[§], etc. This step is to the third measure of the *Passacaille Diana,* beginning with the same foot, as above described[𝄆].

---

‡ See the first figure in Plate XII.   * See the second figure in Plate XV.   ◊ See the first figure in Plate XI.   § See the second figure in Plate XII.   𝄆 See the tables of this step in Character Plate I.

CHAP. XXVII.

Of the *CHACONNE* or *PASSACAILLE STEP.*

THE *chaconne* or *passacaille step* is composed of three movements, *viz.* first a *bound*, secondly a *hop*, and lastly a *bound* or *balonne*, and it is most usually taken from the third position. I shall, as an example, describe it commencing with the left foot which in its performance is as follows; that is to say, the left foot disengaged and at liberty behind the right, in the position aforesaid[Δ], begins the first movement by making a *bound*, in the manner already shown in treating of that step, which, as I have there said, is accomplished by a sink or bending of the knees; from whence the body is thrown into the air, in the spring from the sink or bending aforesaid, only turning a half turn to the right hand, and comes down upon the toe of the left foot to the first note; at which instant the right, on which the weight rested before the change was made, follows or rather attends the left foot, in the same swift manner as explained in the bouree and a bound, remaining behind the left up in the air, in order to perform the movement that next succeeds, facing to the lower end of the room[▽]; from which posture the *hop* or second movement is taken, and marks the second note, by sinking and making a spring or hop upon the left foot which supports the body, turning half a turn to the right hand, from the bottom to the upper part of the room. The right foot, which at the end of

---

Δ See the second figure in Plate V.   ▽ See the second figure in Plate XIII.

the bound was behind the left, about the length of a step in the air, is now the like distance before it$^{\partial}$, ready to make the *bound* or *balonné,* as the French call it, to the third note of the measure, which is in bending both knees; and, in springing from thence, the weight is transferred from the left foot, and lights upon the instep or toe of the right which was in the air, concluding in the third position, as at commencing[†].

This step, if continued, always begins with the same foot, as the coupee or bouree with a bound; and to perform it with the contrary foot only differs in this, that, instead of being in the third position just described, the weight must be upon the left foot, with the right at liberty behind[‡]; and, instead of turning to the right hand, it now turns to the left, beginning with the right foot, etc.[*] as the foregoing with the left.

This step, as above explained, is to the fifth measure of the *Passacaille Diana* aforesaid, and also in the same measure of the *Passacaille de Scilla* mentioned before, commencing with the right foot; and it is a most agreeable step in dancing, rarely missing to be found more than once in one of these sorts of dances[◊].

∂ See the second figure in Plate XIV.   † See the second figure in Plate V.   ‡ See the first figure in Plate V.   * See the first figure in Plates XIII, XIV, and V.   ◊ See the table of this step in Character Plate I, and also the list or explanation.

C H A P. XXVIII.

Of the HOP and two CHASSEES or DRIVES round in the same place.

THE *hop* and two *drives* or *chassees* is likewise a step composed of three movements, as the title above specifies, and is performed from the fourth position, in the manner described in the foregoing *hop* of two movements from the fifth position; which said step begins by transferring the weight in the like method as the present. Having explained the former, beginning with the right foot, I shall explain this with the contrary, and it is performed as follows, *viz.* the weight being upon the left foot, the right in the fourth position advanced and at liberty is prepared to receive the body§; which it does, the every instant before the *hop* or first movement is made to the first note, and from thence, I say, begins by sinking or bending of the knees, in order for the following *spring* or *hop*, which is made upon the right foot, in the left's being taken up from the floor, and marks time to the first note, as was before observed, turning a half turn from the upper end of the room to the left hand and leaving the left foot without weight, in the third position behind the right, facing the lower end𝆊; from whence the first of the two *drives* begins in bending of the knees, as already shown in the *chassee* or *driving step* of three movements, upon the same place, in preparation for the *spring* or *bound* made in straightening of the knees, turning

---

§ See the second figure in Plate IX. 𝆊 See the first figure in Plate XIII, only the left foot, instead of being in the air, must be supposed to rest against the heel of the right.

a quarter turn further to the left hand, facing full to the right side of the room, and lighting upon the left foot, on its being brought into the third position before the right, which is *drove* by it backwards, the length of a step in the air; which said coming down of the left foot is to the second note, and the third is in the spring or bound made upon the right; and, in the rise or spring from the sinking or bending of the knees, as aforesaid, the right foot advances into the third position behind the left, which being then released is drove the length of a step in the air, turning a quarter turn more, opening to the left from the right side of the room to the upper end, and concluding in the air[Δ].

To perform this step with the other foot only differs in this, that, instead of the right foot, the left foot must be advanced[∇] and, instead of turning the half turn to the left hand, as before described, it turns to the right, directly in the same manner as the aforesaid[∂]; Examples of both which are to be found in the *Chaconne de Phaeton* of Monsieur Pécour, in the eighty-seventh measure beginning with the right foot, and in the ninety-first of the same dance with the left, as above described[♦].

Δ See the first figure in Plate XV.   ∇ See the first figure in Plate IX.   ∂ See the second figure in Plates XIII and XV.   ♦ See the table of this step in Character Plate I, and also the list or explanation.

CHAP. XXIX.

Of the FALL, SPRING with both feet at the same time, and COUPEE to a measure.

THE foregoing step, ending in the air with the left foot, naturally introduces us to the present, which is of three movements, and taken from thence in *falling, springing* with both feet at the same time, and a *coupee*; all which steps are to be performed to a measure, and consequently accounted but as one step, which, in its performance, is as follows, *viz.* the face or presence of the body being, as in the foregoing, supposed with the weight upon the right foot◇, the step begins by falling much in the same manner, as explained in treating of this step, when introduced by the galliard sideways to the right hand, only this is backwards in a slow and easy motion, the very same as if you intended to fall quite to the floor; but, as I said before, it is prevented from that by the left foot which is in the air, with the toe pointed towards the ground, attending and watching the falling body so narrowly that, the very instant it is in a manner past recovery, it flies swift to its relief to save it from falling, by receiving half the weight in the fourth position behind the right foot†, with the knees bent upon the first note; from whence the spring is immediately made with both feet, acting at the same juncture upon the second note, that is, by changing the right foot backwards and the left forwards‡, the knees being bent, as

---

◇ See the first figure in Plate XV or XIV.   † See the second figure in Plate IX, only the weight must be equal between the two feet.   ‡ See the first figure in Plate IX.

aforesaid, in readiness to make the succeeding coupee; which is done by taking up the left or foremost foot from the floor and from the bending aforesaid rising upon the toe or instep, making an open step to the left side of the room to the third note, neither directly sideways nor forwards, but between both. The second step of the coupee, which is with the right foot, follows it, stepping the same way in the like swift manner, as the beginning of the bouree with a bound, into the fourth position before the left[*], with the knees bent as above.

In order to make the half coupee that usually follows this step, which is very slow in that, of itself, it answers to a bar, like the foregoing of three movements, upon the weight's being changed, the left foot, which before supported the body, being at liberty, advances, in rising from the sink or bending aforesaid into the third position behind the right[◊], which then is released, and makes a circle in the air to the second and third notes, the first being upon the left's receiving of the weight as aforesaid; and the half coupee, concluding thus with the right foot in the air, is ready to perform either a pirouette, or the same step over again with the contrary foot[§]; which only differs from the foregoing in its beginning with the right foot, and is found in the *Passacaille de Scilla*, twelve bars before the end, beginning with the last mentioned foot, and in other places of the same dance[ƒ].

---

[*] See the second figure in Plate IX.   [◊] See the second figure in Plate IV.   [§] See the second figure in Plate XV.   [ƒ] See the table of this step in Character Plate I, and also the list or explanation.

✿✿✿✿✿✿✿✿✿✿✿✿✿✿✿✿✿✿✿✿✿✿✿✿✿✿✿✿✿✿✿✿✿✿✿✿✿✿

C H A P. XXX.

Of the CLOSE beating before and falling behind in the third position, upright spring changing to the same before, and COUPEE to a measure.

THE *close beating before* etc. which we are now about to explain, differs from the before described step of this name, in its being done to the first note of the measure, and, instead of resting the remaining two notes, as in the aforesaid to the second, there are the *upright spring* and *coupee* to the third; and, instead of the close's ending either in the first or third position with the knees straight, as in the former, it here comes down behind with the knees bent, after its beating before. This step is to be performed as follows, *viz.* commencing either with the right or left foot from the third position[Δ], by sinking or bending not only the foremost foot on which the body rests, but likewise the hind foot without weight; or from thence it begins, by making the close in the like manner, as aforesaid, in treating of the step in the rise or spring from the above named sink; but, instead of the close's lighting in the first or third position, as in the foregoing, the beginning leg beats before against that on which the body rested at first[∀], and comes down in the third position, as at commencing, only the weight is equally upon both feet[∂], and the knees are bent, marking the first note. The second, as I have observed, is in coming down after the rise or *upright spring* from

---

Δ See the first and second figures in Plate V.   ∀ See the first or enclosed feet of the first and second figures in Plate IV.   ∂ See the hind feet of the two said figures in Plate IV.

thence into the air, in which the feet are changed, *viz.* the first last and the last first[†], the knees being bent, as aforesaid, upon the first note in preparation to make the following coupee, which is swift upon the third and last note of the measure, whether of a saraband or passacaille, etc. by rising in the step the first foot makes forwards, opening either to the right or left hand and receiving the weight[‡]; after which the hind foot and second step of the coupee move swift, the same way, into the fourth position before[*] it, with the knees bent, concluding in readiness for the coupee that usually attends these steps; which is, as I have said, in the last described step, as exceeding slow as the foregoing or its introducer was quick, and made in rising from the aforesaid after transferring the weight, and bringing the hind foot into the third position behind the foremost[◊], which being released makes a circle in the air, as aforesaid, either to the right or left hand, according to which foot the step begun with[§], and is ready to perform the step over again with the contrary foot to that with which you commence.

You are to take notice, that these two steps are in a manner inseperable, as I have already observed of some others in the beginning of this discourse, and are to the last measure excepting two and a half of the *Spanish Entree for Two Men,* composed by Monsieur Pécour, belonging to the *Opera de l'Europ Galante*; and also in the *Entree Espagnole for a Man and a Woman,* in the aforesaid opera, composed by the same master[ƒ].

The above described step is sometimes performed turning a whole turn round, that is to say, half a turn upon the close beating before and coming down behind in the third position, the other half being in the upright spring; and instead of the beat's

---

† See the change in the first and second and second and first figures in Plate IV.   ‡ See the two first or advanced feet in the figures in Plate IX.   * See the right or advanced foot in the second figure, and the left or advanced foot of the first figure, in Plate IX.   ◊ See the second and first figures in Plate IV. § See the figures in Plate XV.   ƒ See Table 21 in Character Plate I, and the list or explanation.

being made against the foot on which the weight rested, when facing the upper end of the room, it is here made to the lower part in a half turn, either to the right or left hand, lighting in the third position behind; from whence the upright spring is taken, in rising or springing from the floor, as aforesaid, only, instead of the feet being changed facing the bottom of the room, the remaining half turn is made to the same hand up it: For example, suppose it commences with the right foot from behind$^\Delta$, then the turn must be to the left, the close ending to the lower end in the third position, with the right foot behind$^\triangledown$; but in the half turn belonging to the upright spring, it is changed in the air, and comes down in the third position before the left, on which the body rested at first$^\partial$.

The coupee is entirely the same as described in the foregoing, beginning from the first or enclosed foot; and, if with the left foot, it begins in the same manner, by making a spring or close, etc. turning to the right, as above$^\blacklozenge$.

Δ See the first figure in Plate V. $\triangledown$ See the first figure in Plate IV and for the beat before see the second figure in the same plate, only the feet must be supposed in the third position down the room. ∂ See the second figure in Plate IV. $\blacklozenge$ See Table 22 in Character Plate E and the list or explanation.

C H A P. XXXI.
Of the PIROUETTE.

THE *pirouette* is a step that altogether consists of motion and turning. There are two different ways of performing it; either from a whole position, the weight resting on both feet; or a half position, when the weight only rests upon one foot, the other being in the air, from whence it begins, as will appear: For instead of performing it from the fifth position, directly as we stand, as in the former, in the latter it is made by adding a step with the foot in the air backwards into the abovementioned position behind, from whence they turn equally alike to either hand upon the same place, the weight of the body resting mostly upon the foot which at first supported the weight, the difference being only in the stepping of the foot which may as well be made forwards as backwards.

I shall now proceed to explain the method of performing this step, both these ways, beginning in the first place with the whole position, which is as follows, *viz.* being, as was already observed, in the fifth position, that is to say, when the heel of either the right or left foot, instead of being advanced right forwards, as in the fourth position, is, as I have before shown in the hop of two movements, round in two half turns from the position now treated on, and about the length of half a foot morc crossed before the hindmost foot; so as that the heel of the first in a manner touches the toe of the hind foot, the weight of the body bearing as much upon one foot, as the other, instead of the whole weight's being upon the foot which is behind, as in the hop of two movements[†].

Having shown the position or posture of standing, from whence this step is taken, I will continue its explanation, turning to either side of the room; and it is no more than making a sink or bending of the knees in the above explained position, the rise whereof is made upon both insteps to the first note, in binding or pressing them strong to the floor and raising the body into the air, during the turning or measure to which it is made: For instance, if to the right, the left foot is foremost[‡], if to the left the right[*]. From the last of these we shall describe it, as follows: The sink and rise being made, as aforesaid, to the first note, the second and third, if to triple time, are in the slow turning of the quarter turn, which is to the left side of the room, in which the feet are changed; namely, the right, which at commencing was first, is now last, and the left first, facing full the side of the room to which the turn was made; and, if a half turn, it is only adding a quarter turn more, which then will be full to the bottom of the room; and, if a three quarter turn, it continues on to the right side of the room a quarter turn further.

It is also to be observed, that, if a quarter turn be to a measure, the second and third notes are counted, during the turning or pirouette; the same, if a half or three quarter turn; or, if to common time, the same as already shown in many places of this discourse. And, if it be a whole turn, it is entirely the like in relation to the notes, but not in its method of performance; for, instead of the body's bearing equally upon both toes, as above, it now bears, in rising from the sink or preparative for the whole turn, upon the heel of one foot and toe of the other: For instance, in the rising, as aforesaid, or marking the time, the

---

† See the first and second figures in Plate XI.   ‡ See the second figure in Plate XI.   * See the first figure in the same plate.

weight bears half upon the heel of the right or foremost foot and the toe of the foot that is behind, in which manner it turns to the left, as before, as far as the bottom or lower end of the room; at which time the toe of the fore foot and heel of the hind come to the floor, continuing the turn, till you arrive to the upper end of the room or place of setting out, and finish in a readiness to perform the same to the other hand if occasion requires, by reason of the feet being changed, as I have said, in the middle of the turn or setting down the heel of the hind foot and toe of the foremost◊. Both the ways of performing this step, as above explained, turning a whole round, are to be found in the fourth bar of the saraband belonging the *Royal Galliard,* composed by the late Mr. Isaac and written by Mr. De la Gard, the second time of its playing; the foregoing three quarter turn, in the short *Saraband for a Man,* composed by Mr. Pécour in his collection of dances published at Paris in the year 1704, by Mr. Feuillet, the thirteenth and fifteenth bars before the end of the said dance; and the quarter and half turns are to be met with in most dances§. I shall now proceed to describe the second way in which this pirouette is taken and performed, *viz.* from a half position instead of a whole, as was, for example, the foregoing; that is to say, when the weight of the body is either upon the right or left foot, and the other open in the air pointed sideways, as in the march, or about an inch or two more forwards, only it does not touch the floor, as in that, by reason of its being the commencing foot; from whence it begins, by making a step backwards into the fourth position, if it be a quarter or half turn; but, if a three quarter or whole turn, it must be made into the fifth, as aforesaid, all of which are performed directly in the same manner, as the foregoing or whole position, by dividing the weight, at the end

---

◊ See the contrary figures in Plate XI, that is to say, for the first see the second, and for the second see the first figure.   § See Table 24 in Character Plate I, and also the list or explanation of the table.

of the stepping backwards of the foot that was in the air, which, upon setting it to the ground, receives so much of the weight as only serves to direct and assist the body in turning, as well as marking the time, as aforesaid, in rising from the sink made for that purpose, on the stepping of the foot backwards upon both toes, and turning either to the right or left hand, which is according to the foot that is in the air, for the turn must be made to the same side; for example, if the right foot be in the air, the turn is to that side[§]; and if the left, it is to the left[Δ].

Having explained the foregoing or whole position, turning to the left hand, the taking some notice of it to the right may not be improper, in this place, beginning with the quarter turn: For instance, the weight being upon the half position or left foot, the right, extended as aforesaid[§], begins in making a sink or bending of the knee of the left leg on which the body rests; at which instant the right is cast back, as was said above, into the fourth position behind the left[†], and preparing for the rise marks the first note, which is made on setting down or receiving a part of the poise of the body upon the foot that was in the air; from whence the turn takes its rise, turning in a slow and gentle turn to the right side of the room, and bearing or pressing the toes to the floor, as we have already shown in the foregoing, in which turning the second and third notes are spent; that is to say, the second note is counted in changing of the feet, which is in the turning, as I have said, for the right foot, which was in the fourth position behind, is about the second note in the same position before the left, facing full the right side of the room; and the third note is upon setting down the heel of the left foot, and taking up the right, which is extended open sideways, as at first, and concludes.

[§] See the second figure in Plate XV.   [Δ] See the first figure in Plate XV.   [†] See the first figure in Plate IX.

A pirouette with a half or three quarter turn only differs from the pirouette just explained, in not ending to the right side as in that; but, instead thereof, the half turn finishes to the lower part of the room, half a turn from the upper end‡. And the three quarter turn continues on, till it face full the left side; but the whole turn, as I have said in the pirouette, beginning from a whole or half position, on which the weight is equally divided, instead of rising upon both toes alike, at the end of the step made with the right foot, by sinking and stepping backwards, as before observed, into the fifth position behind the left foot*, in the rise or beginning of the turn the right toe or instep, being set down to the ground in the position just mentioned, receives one half of the weight, the other remaining upon the heel of the left on which the body rested at first. In the said manner half the turn is made to the bottom of the room, bearing equally upon the heel and toe; and, when it arrives there, the remaining half is continued, by putting down the right heel and toe of the left foot, which at first begun upon the heel, as the right did upon the toe, about which time the feet are changed, as we have observed; that is, the right, which was stepped or cast into the fifth position behind, is now first, and the left last, concluding with both feet flat on the floor, the presence of the body being to the upper end of the room, as at commencing◊.

As to the agreement of this step with the notes of common or triple time, it is the same as already explained in the pirouette beginning from the whole position; the only difference is that the weight in that, being equally on both feet, begins directly by making a sink and rise, the rise of which beats time to the first note of the tune, which is the same in this step, except that the body, being supported by a half position, before it can begin as

---

‡ See the first figure in Plate XII.   * See the second figure in Plate XI.   ◊ See the first figure in Plate XI. And, if beginning with the left foot, see the first figure in Plate XV, and the first and second figures in Plate XI.

in the whole position, the other foot which is in the air must be cast or set down in the fourth or fifth position; from whence this step is usually taken, in stepping either forwards or backwards, as the step is to be made. The remaining second and third notes of the measure, if to triple time, are counted, during the said turning, a whole round; or, if to common time, the fourth is included, as has been observed.

This step, in its performance *forwards*, is in all respects the same as the last described *backwards*, as to its agreement with the notes, or its rising, turning on the toes, etc. only whereas, in the two foregoing pirouettes, the manner of performing the whole turn is not the same as the quarter, half, or three quarter turn, in that the whole turn is done in the same method as the rest, except that the step is made *forwards* into the fourth or fifth position, instead of *backwards* as in the last explained; and, as I have already observed in the foregoing steps, if the turn be only a quarter or half turn, it commences from the fourth position[§], but if a three quarter or whole turn the fifth[ƒ]. This step forwards further varies from the foregoing backwards, in that, although it commences with the same foot, instead of turning to the right hand, as in the former, in this it turns to the left, as in the whole position; so that, comparing this with the pirouette first described, it will be easily understood, in that it is the same, except in not beginning directly, as in that; but if you suppose the stepping of the foot forwards to be made, and place your feet in the fourth or fifth position, as before observed from a whole position, there is then no other difference, except that the whole turn is performed in the same method as the other[Δ].

---

§ See the second figure in Plate IX, beginning from the second figure in Plate XV. And, if with the contrary, see the first figure in Plate XV, and the first figure in Plate IX.　ƒ See the first figure in Plate XI, commencing from the second figure in Plate XV; and, if with the other foot, see the first figure in Plate XV and it concludes in the second figure in Plate XI.　Δ See Table 25 in Character Plate E, the list or explanation of the table, and also the steps contained in Plate XV.

C H A P. XXXII.
Of the PIROUETTE introduced by a COUPEE.

THIS step is taken from a half position, as well as the two last described backwards and forwards; but, instead of the foot's being extended sideways in the air, as in them, the toe must here be pointed to the floor, as in the point or beginning of the march, from which position it commences.

However, before I proceed to a further explanation of this step, I shall take some notice of the *coupee* that introduces it, which is composed of a half coupee with one foot and a circular motion made in the air with the other, before its making the point; which step may be performed as follows, beginning with either foot, by sinking and making a half coupee or step forwards, marking time to the first note, in rising from thence.

If we suppose this step to be made with the right foot[*], the circular step or motion with the left must then be made inwards to the second and third notes, or the fourth, if common time; that is to say, the half coupee being made with the right foot, as aforesaid, the whole quarter of the left leg moving in the air, with the knee stiff and toe pointed, makes a circular motion, by moving directly off sideways, as in the point for a march[◊], only more round continuing on forwards, about that distance from the other, forming a sort of a circle in the air before the right foot on which the body rests all this time, in bringing the left

---

[*] See the first figure in Plate I.   [◊] See the first figure in Plate XV.

leg, as above directed, that is to say, the toe pointed and knee stiff into the third position, so as to touch the ankle of the right foot[§]; and then it passes on directly sideways to the left hand making a point, about the like distance from the foot you stand upon as the march[ƒ]; from whence proceeds the pirouette we are about to treat of, which is performed by making an easy sink or bending of both knees preparing for the rise or straightening of them, which resembles a spring, only it is not from the ground; for, in the rise or spring from the sink aforesaid preparing for the whole round, the left foot which was upon the point is taken up from the ground, turning quite round to the left hand in the air, with the leg or whole quarter extended in the air, the toe pointed, and knee stiff, as in the circular motion, about half a foot from the floor[Δ]. The body, at the very juncture the rise or spring is given, rises upon the toe or instep, as erect as a pyramid, and turns round along with it, finishing to the upper part of the room as at first, only with the toe in the air; from whence it may be continued as the half coupee, or bouree, etc.

This step usually takes up a measure, whether of three or four notes to the bar; the rise or spring to the pirouette marks the first note, and the rest are in the turning; but the coupee and pirouette, though frequently found together, are in themselves distinct steps[▽].

There are various other ways of performing this step, besides the described, as twice round, three times round, round in an upright spring beating before and behind during the turning, and many more; which, as they are foreign to my present purpose, I shall omit, and say something of the *bouree before and behind, turning*, etc.

---

§ See the first figure in Plate IV.　　ƒ See the first figure in Plate VI.　　Δ See the first figure in Plate XV; if with the other foot, see the second figure in Plate I, the second figure in Plate XV, the second figure in Plates IV and VI, and lastly the second figure again in Plate XV.　　▽ See Table 27 in Character Plate I, and the list or explanation of the table.

C H A P. XXXIII.

Of the BOUREE before and behind, and behind and before, advancing in a whole turn.

THIS step is composed of two bourees; but, though in dancing it may be performed to all parts of the room, or upon a circle, an explanation of it, commencing with the right foot advancing to the presence or upper part of the room, shall suffice, in that the rest will be comprehended thereby, since the difference is only instead of facing, as aforesaid. The presence or body, for example, must be directed to the part or side of the room, to which the step is made; whether to the right or left hand, lower end, or on a circular figure, it will be the very same, except that, advancing to the said parts, as before, upon a right or straight line, you must perform the said step circularly or round, commencing either with the right or left foot, as it shall fall out, from any of the aforesaid parts of the room. This will appear from the following, which, as I have above observed, is advancing to the upper end of the room with the right foot, in order to which the weight must be upon the left, with the right disengaged and at liberty in the first position‡, which begins in making a movement or bending of the knees; from whence the right makes the first step of the three that compose the first of the two bourees up the room*, in stepping crossways before the left, on which the body turns a quarter turn to the right side of

---

‡ See the first figure in Plate I.   * See in some measure the second figure in Plate IX, only it is to turn as directed.

the room, the rise of which, whether upon the toe or heel, marks the time or first note. The second note is in the next step with the left foot, on its receiving the weight, which it does, after making a step circularly before the right, in a quarter turn more, now facing full to the bottom of the room◊; and the third and last step with the right, which is now upon the point in the fourth position before the left, concludes the first bouree, in pressing or sliding the toe against the floor into the same position behind the left, receiving the weight upon the third note of the measure, and leaving the left foot upon the point in the like manner§.

The first bouree being thus ended, the second also begins with a movement or bending of the knees, as aforesaid; from whence the left is stepped or cast behind the right, in turning a quarter turn further, which will then be to the left side of the room, the rise of which is to the first note or time to a second measure; and the second step of this bouree is with the right foot, turning the fourth or last quarter turn from the left side of the room to the upper part or presence thereof, the setting down or receiving of the body upon which is to the second note. The third note is in the last step of the bouree made with the left, directly up the room; and upon its receiving the weight the second bouree is ended, concluding in the first position, as at commencing.

The foregoing step, as above described, consists of two plain bourees or fleurets of one movement only, whereas it frequently is performed with two; and if so, the second must be made upon the third step, whether on the ground or off from thence as in a bound, as has already been explained in treating of these steps.

But sometimes in dancing, instead of the second bouree, a coupee is found commencing with either foot, as it shall happen; but here it is with the left crossing before the right foot on

---

◊ See in some respects the first figure in Plate VIII, only the right toe must be, as directed, upon the point.　　§ See the second figure in Plate XII, except the left toe must be pointed as directed.

which the body rests[f], in a quarter turn from the lower end of the room to the left side, or in a half turn to the presence, the right foot or second step of which is set to the ground, in the method as when introducing a hop[Δ], or, instead of the coupee aforesaid, as in the seventh and eighth measures of the first couplet of a dance of my own composition, named the *Submission*, that is to say, on the *woman's* side. The left foot not coupeeing before the right, as above, instead thereof, in turning a half turn, receives the weight, in rising from the sink or bending of the knees in the third position behind the right[∇], which then is taken from the floor, making a circular motion in the air opening to the right[∂] and enclosed in the third position behind the left[♦], as in the two first measures of the second couplet of the aforesaid dance on the *man's* side; and if the said steps are with the other foot, as on the *woman's*, the same method of performance is to be observed to the left side of the room, as in the foregoing to the right[◇]. I have been the more particular in describing these steps, because they are of more than ordinary grace and variety to dancing; but I shall now proceed to the *minuet*, the subject of the SECOND BOOK of this work.

---

[f] See the second figure in Plate XII.   [Δ] See the second figure in Plate X.   [∇] See the second figure in Plate IV.   [∂] See the second figure in Plate XV.   [♦] See the first figure in Plate IV.   [◇] See the second figure in Plate I. See in some measure the first figure in Plate IX, only turning to the left. See in some respects the second figure in Plate VIII, only the left toe is pointed. See the first figure in Plate XII, the first figure in Plate X, the first figure in Plate IV, the first figure in Plate XV, and the second figure in Plate IV. See Table 29 in Character Table I, and also the list or explanation of the characters in this step.

The end of the FIRST BOOK.

T HESE *are to certify, that the foregoing book, entitled the* ART OF DANCING EXPLAIN'D, *was designed and composed long before the book entitled the* DANCING MASTER *appeared, as we believe; and that we have carefully examined the said book, and found it composed and written in the same manner it now is, on the twenty-seventh day of* January, 1727–8.

Witness our hands,

Alex. Jackson,
Joseph Jackson, } Dancing-Masters.

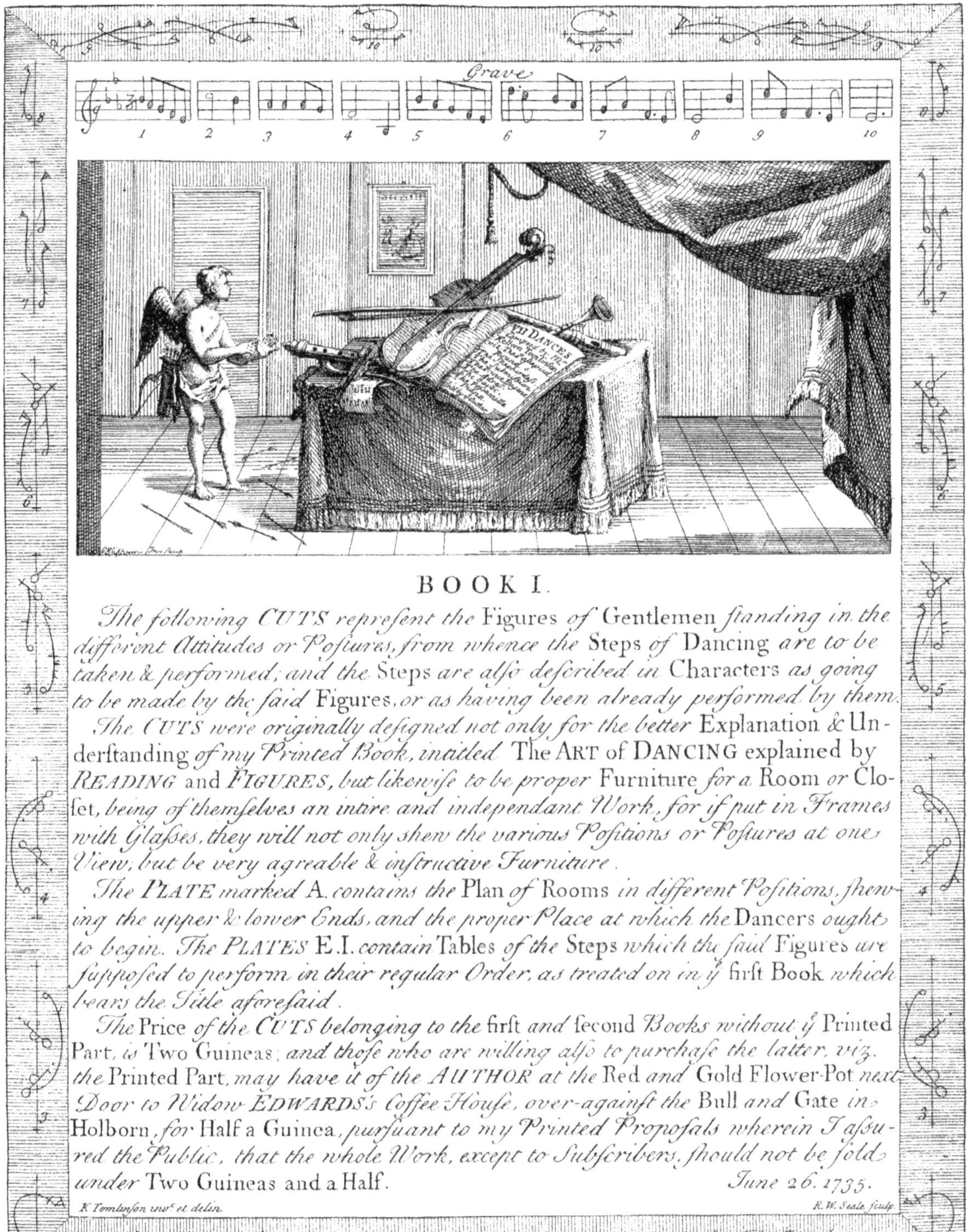

BOOK I.

The following CUTS represent the Figures *of* Gentlemen *standing in the different Attitudes or Postures, from whence the* Steps *of* Dancing *are to be taken & performed; and the* Steps *are also described in* Characters *as going to be made by the said* Figures, *or as having been already performed by them.*

The CUTS were originally designed not only for the better Explanation & Understanding *of my Printed Book, intitled* The ART of DANCING *explained by* READING *and* FIGURES, *but likewise to be proper* Furniture *for a* Room *or* Closet, *being of themselves an intire and independant Work, for if put in Frames with Glasses, they will not only shew the various Positions or Postures at one View, but be very agreable & instructive Furniture.*

The PLATE *marked A. contains the* Plan *of* Rooms *in different Positions, shewing the upper & lower* Ends, *and the proper* Place *at which the* Dancers *ought to begin. The* PLATES E. I. *contain* Tables *of the* Steps *which the said* Figures *are supposed to perform in their regular* Order, *as treated on in ẙ first Book which bears the Title aforesaid.*

The Price *of the* CUTS *belonging to the first and second Books without ẙ* Printed Part, *is* Two Guineas; *and those who are willing also to purchase the latter, viz. the* Printed Part, *may have it of the* AUTHOR *at the* Red *and* Gold Flower-Pot *next Door to Widow* EDWARDS's Coffee-House, *over-against the* Bull *and* Gate *in* Holborn, *for* Half a Guinea, *pursuant to my* Printed Proposals *wherein I assured the* Public, *that the whole* Work, *except to* Subscribers, *should not be sold under* Two Guineas *and a* Half.   *June 26. 1735.*

NB *Each Plate represents three things, viz. The Music, the Dance, and the Dancers. For the rest see Plates V. & VII.*

To my Ever respected Scholar George Heneage of HAINTON in the County of LINCOLN Esq.r
This PLATE is Gratefully inscribed by His very much obliged Serv.t   Kellom Tomlinson.

To my much Honoured Scholar the R.t Hon.ble the Lord Howard, Son to the Earl of Stafford;
This PLATE is humbly dedicated by his Lordships most obliged Servant
Kellom Tomlinson.

Saraband
Slow   1   2   3   4   5   6   7   8
K.T. Inv.
H. Fletcher Sculp.
To my Honoured Scholars, the Hon.ble THOMAS ASTON and the Hon.ble JAMES ASTON, Sons to the
LORD ASTON. This Plate is with all gratitude inscrib'd   By their most devoted Serv.t
Kellom Tomlinson.

Thofe who underftand Music and ỹ Characters of Dancing will hear the former by the fight of the Notes, & fee ỹ various Turnings and windings of ỹ latter in ỹ Characters below, & in ỹ Figures ỹ grace-ful Attitudes of ỹ Dancers, forming together not only a compleat entertainment of Music & Dancing but also a fine picture.

To my ever respected Scholars Nathaniel Curzon *and* Asheton Curzon *Esq.rs Sons to Sir* Nathaniel Curzon *of* Kedleston *in the County of* DERBY, *Bar.t This* PLATE *is most humbly inscrib'd by their very much obliged Servant,* Kellom Tomlinson—

The figures to y Music above & to y Characters or Steps of Dancing below shew, how they are connected or agree together, & y Figures to y Characters, which are some of them upright & others y wrong End upwards, sideways, &c. shew to which part of y Room y Beginning of y Steps is performed, & y Steps or Characters are placed upon y Floor in a perspective Manner intirely new.

To the *Honourable* Charles Talbot *and the Honourable* John Talbot, *Sons to the late* Earl *of* Shrewsbury, *this PLATE is humbly inscribed by their Honours most obliged Serv.* K. Tomlinson.

To my much respected Scholar Henry Hunloke Esq.r Son and Heir to Sir Windsor Hunloke of Wingerworth
in the County of Derby Bar.t and to master Windsor his Brother this Plate is most gratefully inscribed by their
ever obliged Servant.   Kellom Tomlinson

To my once Honoured Scholars the Marquiss de Seyssel, and the Count de Chattillion Sons of his Excellency the Marquiss d'Aix Envoy Extraordinary from ye KING of SARDINIA, to the Court of GREAT-BRITAIN in the years 1726, 1727, & 1728. This PLATE is most humbly Inscrib'd by, Their most obliged Servant

Kellom Tomlinson.

To Edward Blount *of Soddington in the County of Worcester Esq: Son & Heir to* Sr. Edward Blount Bart. *& to Master* Walter *his Brother. This* PLATE *is most humbly Inscribed by their most obliged Servant.* Kellom Tomlinson.

To Peter Giffard *Esq.* Son and Heir to Peter Giffard of Chillington *in the County of* STAFFORD *Esq.*
and to Master Thomas *his Brother this* PLATE *is most humbly inscribed by their much obliged Servant.*
Kellom Tomlinson.

To my ever respected Scholar Thomas Greasley Esq. Son and Heir to Sir Thomas Greasley of Dracklow in the County of DERBY Bar.t and to his Brother, this PLATE is most humbly inscribed by their much obliged Servant, Kellom Tomlinson

To my much respected Scholar James Mytton of Garth and Pontiscouerit in MONTGOMERYSHIRE Esq.r and Master Richard his Brother. This PLATE is most humbly Inscribed by their ever obliged Servant Kellom Tomlinson.

To Corbet Owen *of* Ynyfmaingynne *MERIONETHSHIRE, and* Riwfaifon *MONTGOMERYSHIRE Esq.* & *my much respected Scholar Master* Richard *his Brother. This* PLATE *is most humbly Inscribed by their most* Oblig'd Ser.
Kellom Tomlinson

To my once Honoured Scholar Mademoiselle de Seyssel, Daughter to his Excellency the Marquiss D'Aix. Envoy extraordinary from the KING of SARDINIA, to the Court of GREAT BRITAIN, in the years 1726, 1727 & 1728. This PLATE is humbly inscrib'd by Her most obliged Servant   Kellom Tomlinson.

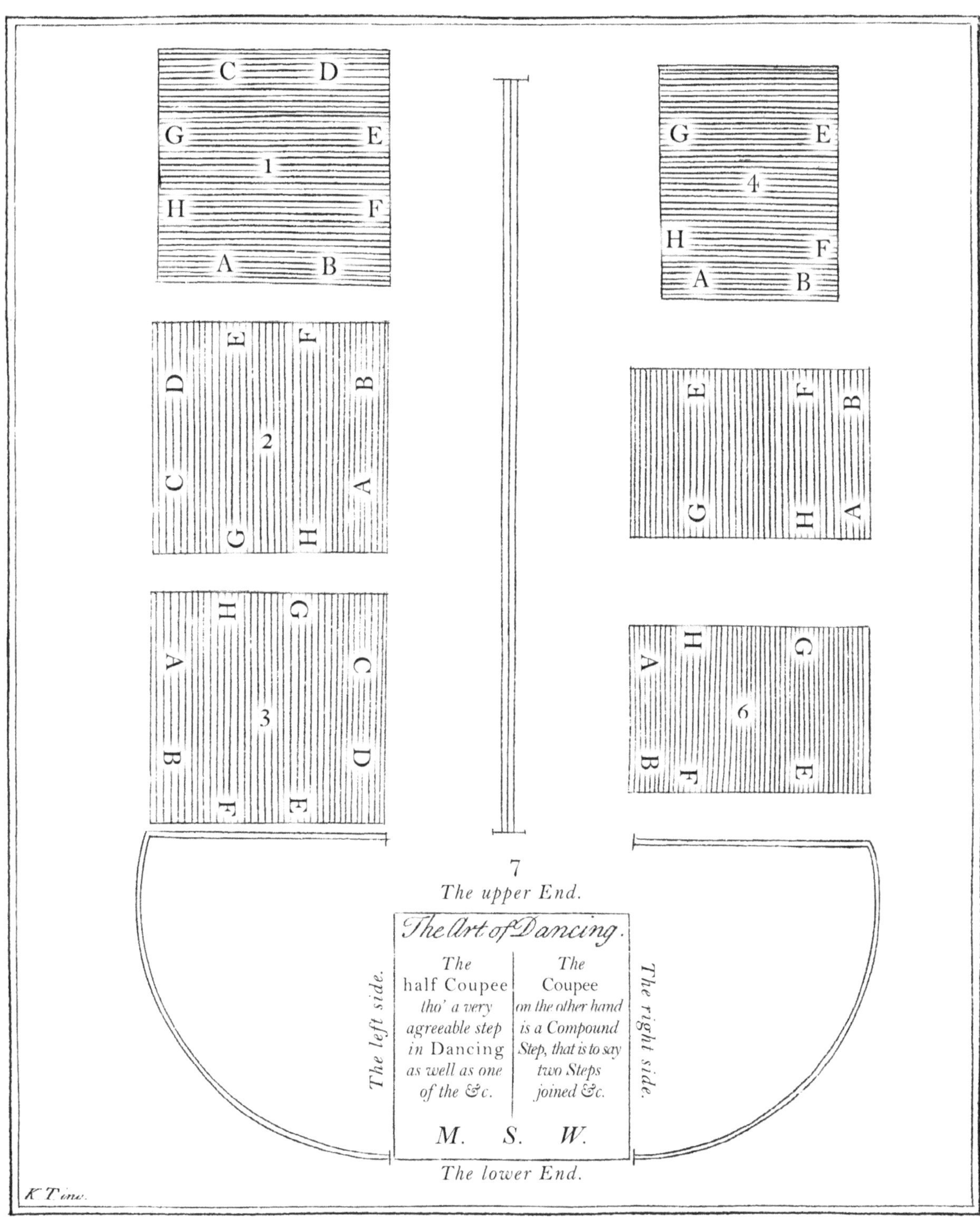

C   D
G   E
1
H   F
A   B
G   E
4
H   F
A   B
E   F
D   B
2
C   A
G   H
H   G
A   C
3
B   D
F   E
E   F
G   B
H   A
G   D
H   A
6
B   G
F   E
7
The upper End.
The Art of Dancing.
The   The
half Coupee   Coupee
tho' a very   on the other hand
agreeable step   is a Compound
in Dancing   Step, that is to say
as well as one   two Steps
of the &c.   joined &c.
The left side.
The right side.
M.   S.   W.
The lower End.
K T inv.

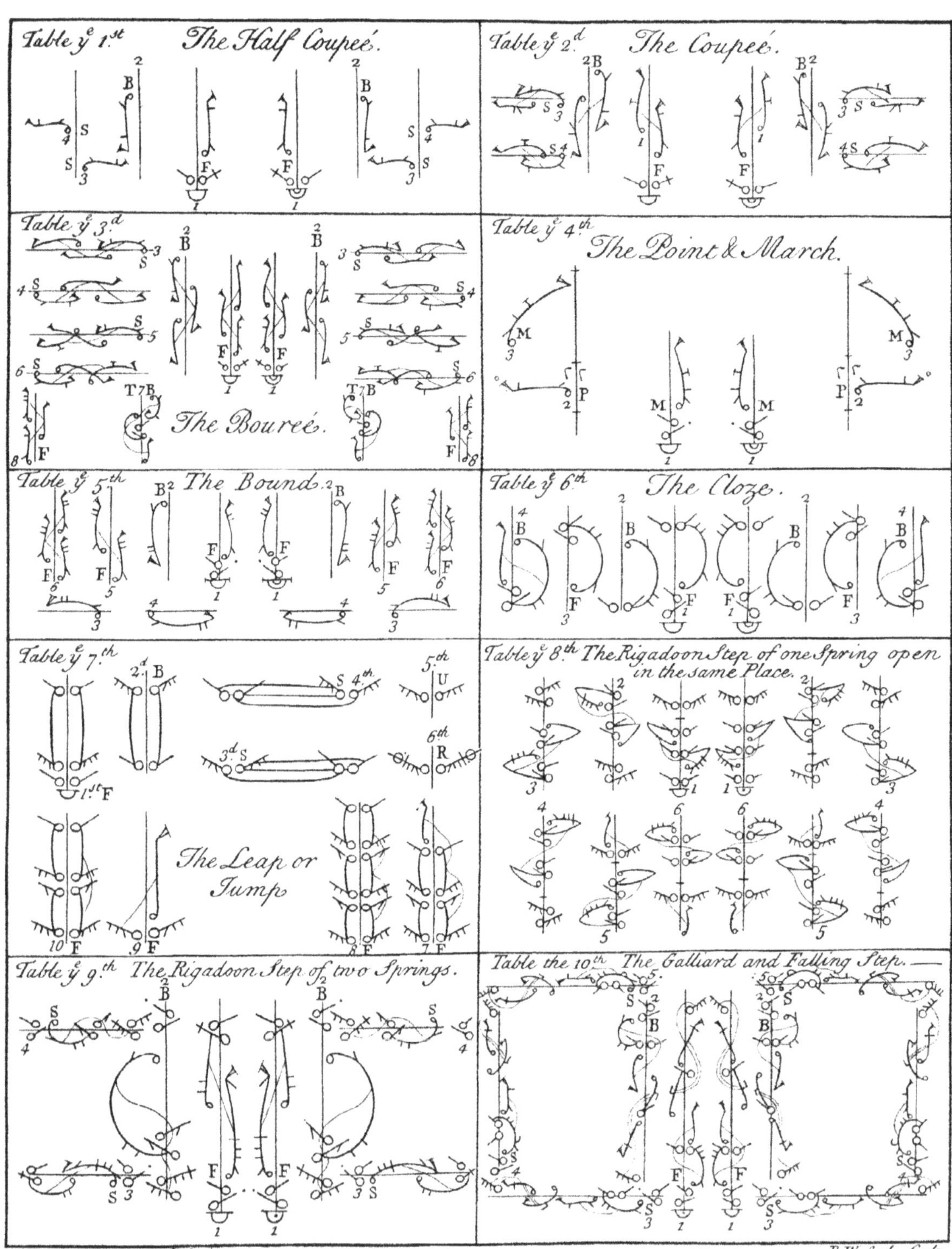

The Explanation of the Letters in the above Tables

F. Forwards.   B. Backwards.   S. Sideways.   T.B. Twice Behind.
M. March.   P. Point.   U. Upright.   R. Round.

THE STEPS TREATED OF IN BOOK I.

An explanation of the characters or steps contained in the tables of PLATE E, in the exact order they are treated of in this work, showing the different ways in which the said steps are performed whether forwards, backwards, sideways, or round, etc. in which you will see the steps treated of in words written down in characters and figures, which will not only convey a stronger idea of the steps, but also be very entertaining to the curious reader.

TABLE I. The HALF COUPEE.
FIG. 1. *Forwards with either foot.*
FIG. 2. *Backwards with either foot.*
FIG. 3. *Sideways to the right, and sideways to the left.*

TABLE II. The COUPEE.
FIG. 1. *The coupee forwards with either foot.*
FIG. 2. *The same backwards with either foot in two movements, or plain as Fig 1.*
FIG. 3. *Sideways before in two movements with either foot, or plain as Fig 4.*
FIG. 4. *Sideways behind with either foot.*

TABLE III. The BOUREE.
FIG. 1. *Forwards with either foot.*
FIG. 2. *Backwards with either foot.*
FIG. 3. *Sideways before with either foot.*
FIG. 4. *Sideways behind with either foot.*
FIG. 5. *Sideways before and behind with either foot.*
FIG. 6. *Sideways behind and before with either foot.*
FIG. 7. *Twice behind and the third step forwards with either foot.*
FIG. 8. *Bouree and bound with either foot forward.*

TABLE IV. The MARCH and POINT and MARCH.
FIG. 1. *Forwards with either foot.*
FIG. 2. *Point sideways with either foot.*
FIG. 3. *Forwards with either foot.*

TABLE V. The BOUND.
FIG. 1. *Forwards with either foot.*
FIG. 2. *Backwards with either foot.*
FIG. 3. *Sideways before with either foot.*
FIG. 4. *Sideways behind with either foot.*
FIG. 5. *Twice to a measure.*
FIG. 6. *Thrice to a measure.*

TABLE VI. The CLOSE.
FIG. 1. *With either foot into the first position forwards.*
FIG. 2. *With either foot backwards into the first position.*
FIG. 3. *Forwards with either foot into the third position enclosed before.*
FIG. 4. *The same backwards with either foot enclosed behind, and a walk forwards to a measure.*

TABLE VII. The LEAP OR JUMP.
FIG. 1. *Forwards.*
FIG. 2. *Backwards.*
FIG. 3. *Sideways to the right hand.*
FIG. 4. *Sideways to the left hand.*
FIG. 5. *The upright spring.*
FIG. 6. *Round in an upright spring.*
FIG. 7. *Two springs and a plain straight step forwards to a measure.*
FIG. 8. *Three springs to a measure forwards.*
FIG. 9. *The upright spring and plain step forwards to a measure.*
FIG. 10. *Two springs to a measure forwards.*

Table VIII. The RIGADOON STEP of one spring open in the same place.
Fig. 1. *Upon the same place with either foot in the first position.*
Fig. 2. *Upon the same place with either foot enclosing into the third position forwards.*
Fig. 3. *The same enclosing into the third position backwards.*
Fig. 4. *Upon the same place enclosing into the third position, first before and then behind, upright spring, and change of the hind feet first with either foot.*
Fig. 5. *The same with either foot, first behind and then before, upright spring into the first position, and plain step forwards to a measure.*
Fig. 6. *The same in the first position.*

Table IX. The RIGADOON STEP of two springs.
Fig. 1. *Forwards with either foot.*
Fig. 2. *Backwards with either foot.*
Fig. 3. *Sideways crossing before with either foot.*
Fig. 4. *Sideways crossing behind with either foot.*

Table X. The GALLIARD and FALLING STEP.
Fig. 1. *Forwards with either foot.*
Fig. 2. *Backwards with either foot.*
Fig. 3. *Sideways to the presence with either foot.*
Fig. 4. *Sideways with either foot in a quarter turn facing the sides of the room.*
Fig. 5. *Sideways with either foot in a half turn to the bottom of the room.*

An explanation of the characters or steps contained in the tables of PLATE I, as first *slipping before*, and then *slipping behind*, etc.

Table XI. The SLIP BEFORE, SLIP BEHIND, and HALF COUPEE.
Fig. 1. *Sideways with either foot before and behind to the presence.*
Fig. 2. *The same with a bound behind and before with either foot.*
Fig. 3. *Sideways with either foot before and behind in a quarter turn to each other.*
Fig. 4. *The same behind and before in a half turn to the bottom.*
Fig. 5. *Sideways with either foot twice slipping behind.*
Fig. 6. *The same slipping twice before.*

Table XII. The HOP or CONTRETEMP.
Fig. 1. *Forwards with either foot from the third position.*
Fig. 2. *The same backwards with either foot.*
Fig. 3. *With either foot advancing to the sides of the room in a quarter turn.*

Fig. 4. *The same with either foot to the bottom in a half turn.*
Fig. 5. *Sideways crossing before with either foot to the presence.*
Fig. 6. *The same with either foot in a quarter turn facing the sides.*
Fig. 7. *The same in a half turn with either foot to the bottom.*
Fig. 8. *With either foot stepping sideways and a draw behind.*
Fig. 9. *The same in a quarter turn to the sides.*
Fig. 10. *Sideways crossing before with either foot from the fourth position.*
Fig. 11. *The same with a bound.*
Fig. 12. *From the fourth position advancing up the room with either foot.*
Fig. 13. *The same with a bound.*
Fig. 14. *Backwards from the fourth position with either foot.*
Fig. 15. *The same with a bound.*

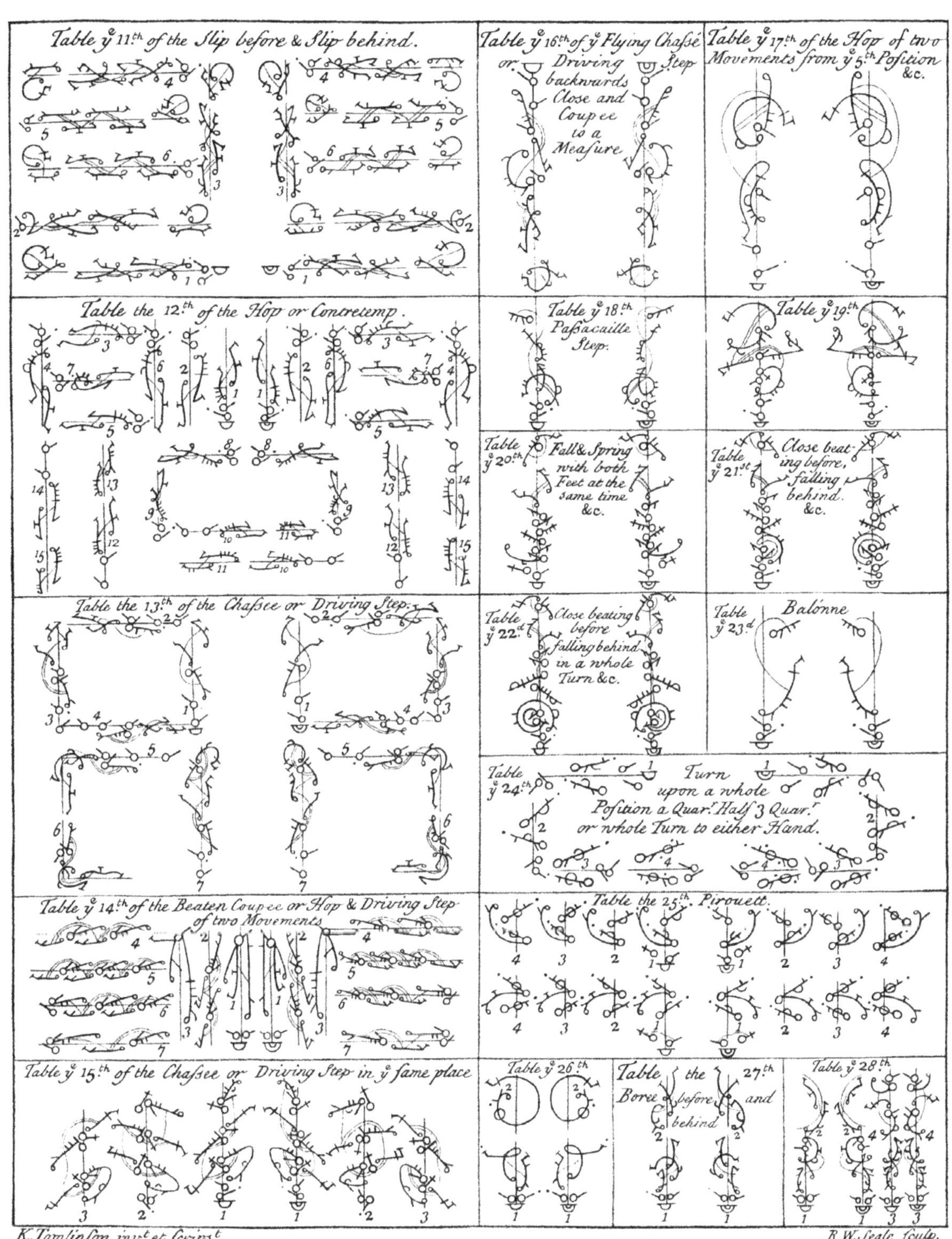

K. Tomlinson inv.t et scrips.t   R. W. Seale sculp.

THE

ART of DANCING

EXPLAIN'D.

BOOK the SECOND.

CHAP. I.

Of the MINUET STEP.

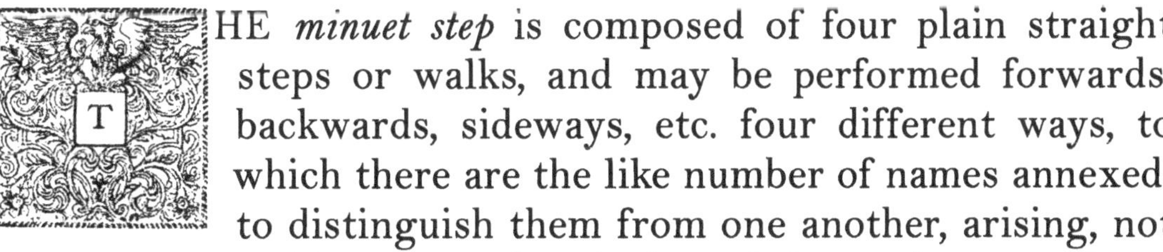

HE *minuet step* is composed of four plain straight steps or walks, and may be performed forwards, backwards, sideways, etc. four different ways, to which there are the like number of names annexed, to distinguish them from one another, arising, not improperly speaking, from the placing of the marks upon them: For example, a movement or sink and rise, being added to the first step of the three belonging to the minuet step, produces a *bouree*; and the like to the fourth and last a *half coupee*, which together compose what is commonly called the *English minuet step.* The second method of its performance is with a *bound*; that is to say, instead of the half coupee or movement to the last step made upon the floor, as in the aforesaid, you bound instead thereof, which is the only variation from the foregoing.

The third method is quite the reverse, because, instead of the bouree, the *half coupee* is made first and afterwards the *bouree*, or as the French term it, *one and a fleuret,* which is usually called the *French step.*

The fourth way of performing this step is by adding another movement to the third step of the aforesaid fleuret, or the fourth of the minuet step; and it will then be notwithstanding the same step, only of three movements. As to the two first foregoing steps, I shall say little concerning them, for the following reasons: In the first place, because they are now rarely, if ever, practised amongst persons of the first rank, and seem to be, for the present, entirely laid aside; not as being ungraceful, or that the dancer could not give pleasure to the beholders, or raise to himself a reputation in their performance, but merely through alteration of fashion, which varies in this respect, as in dressing, etc.

Secondly, because they have been, in some measure, already explained in the beginning of this book by the bouree and a bound, which, from what I then observed, appears to be the same as the minuet step here treated on, except that it there answers to a measure or bar, but here to two, as the time is much brisker than in the aforesaid slow movements; and, as to their agreement with the notes, it is very different from what I have to say, upon that head, to the two last steps following; the first of which is the third of the aforesaid, namely *one and a fleuret,* or a *half coupee* and *bouree*, usually called the *new minuet step*, and the same that is now danced in all polite assemblies†. As it has become the favourite step, my being somewhat more particular in its description, than of the foregoing, may not be lost time; for the minuet is one of the most graceful as well as difficult dances to arrive at a mastery of, through the plainness of the step and the air and address of the body that are requisite to its embellishment, as will further appear from the sequel.

But to return to the subject in hand; having, I say, already observed, that the *minuet step* is composed of four plain steps, without showing the method of their performance, or their agreement with the notes of the tune, I shall now proceed to describe both of these, which are to be accomplished in the following manner: The weight of the body being upon the left foot in the first position the right, which is at liberty‡, begins the minuet step, by making the half coupee or first of the four steps belonging to the minuet, in a movement or sink and stepping of the right foot forwards*, the gentle or easy rising of which, either upon the toe or heel, marks what is called *time* to the first note of the three in the first of the two measures, which is of triple time or of three notes to a bar; the second note is in the coming down of the heel to the floor◊, if the rise was made upon the toe, but if upon the heel or flat foot, in the tight holding of the knees before the sink is made that prepares for the fleuret or bouree following, in which is counted the third and last note of the measure aforesaid; and the said bouree or second part of the minuet step, if I may so say, is made upon the second measure of the tune, as the half coupee was to the first, so that it is visible, from what has been said before, that one *minuet step* is of equal value to two measures or bars of the tune.

The sink or beginning of the movement, that prepares for the

---

† See the characters of this step in Character Plate O, Table II, number I.   ‡ See the first figure in Plate I of Book I.   * See the second figure in Plate IX of Book I.   ◊ See the second figure in Plate I of Book I.

fleuret or second part of the minuet step, for so I shall for the future call it, being made, there only remains to rise from the sink aforesaid in the stepping forwards of the left foot$^\Delta$ to the first note of the second measure, and first of the fleuret or three last steps of the four that compose the minuet step; the second step of the said *bouree* or *fleuret* is made, swift forwards with the right foot$^\phi$, to the same note; and the third and last step of the *bouree*, or second part of the minuet step with the left foot$^\Delta$, is to the third and last note of the same measure of the tune, concluding the *minuet step* with the weight upon the said foot, as at first$^\nabla$. It is to be noted, that it always begins with the right and ends with the left foot; and it is performed faster or slower according to the tune that is played, which the dancer is obliged to follow.

Having described the foregoing step *forwards*, I shall now proceed in it *sideways* to either hand; and, in the first place, to the right side of the room, or rather obliquely, that is to say, from the upper left corner of the room to the right lower facing to the upper right corner of it, or rather in the middle between directly sideways facing the upper end of the room and, as said above, from corner to corner: For example, instead of the left side of the upper corner and the right to the lower, the left side or shoulder points about the middle of the upper left corner and sideways directly cross the room; which will be easily understood by a supposed line across the room, for the right shoulder consequently pointing the same way below the line, instead of facing the right upper corner, as before, is now to the middle or space between the said corner and directly up the room; which will likewise be comprehended, by supposing a right line up the floor, and the face a little turned looking towards the left shoulder, or, more

---

Δ See the first figure in Plate IX of Book I. ϕ See the second figure in Plate IX of Book I. ∇ See the first figure in Plate I of Book I.

properly speaking, upon the gentleman or lady with whom we dance; and the said turn, or rather complaisance, gives a most agreeable twist or contrast to the fashion of the body in this step, and not a little beauty to that part of the *minuet dance* upon which it falls[∂] but of that more hereafter.

Having described the action or posture of the body in which this step must be performed, if to advantage, I shall proceed in explaining the motion or stepping of the feet upon the aforesaid tract or line; which is *sideways* to the right hand, instead of *forwards*, as in the foregoing, which is the principal difference[♦]. However, as it may not in all probability be so fully comprehended by what has been said in the foregoing step, it may not be improper to take some further notice of it in this place, *viz.* that it is to be taken from the first position, that is to say, the weight being upon the left foot the right, which is at liberty[◇], commences by making a sink and step, open off from the left foot, on which the body rests, *sideways* to the right[℘].The rise of the sink marks time to the first of the three notes; and the rest are the same, as when done forwards, the half coupee or first part of the minuet step being made to the first measure of the tune, as aforesaid, ending in the same position upon the right foot, with the left disengaged[ƒ] to perform the bouree or second part of the said step *sideways*, in like manner as in the foregoing *forwards*; which it does in making a sink and step to the right hand sideways crossing behind the right on which the body rests[⅗], the rise of which is to the first note of the second measure. The right foot then makes a plain open step, *sideways* to the same hand[⊕], upon the second note, leaving the left upon the point, in the very place the body rested before, in readiness to make the

---

[∂] See the gentleman and lady in Plate VI.　　[♦] See the characters of this step in Table II of Character Plate O, number II.　　[◇] See the first figure in Plate I of Book I. For the action or posture of the body, see the gentleman and lady in Plate VI.　　[℘] See in some measure the second figure in Plate VI of Book I. [ƒ] See the second figure in Plate I of Book I. Action as at beginning.　　[⅗] See the first figure in Plate XI of Book I. Action the same.　　[⊕] See the second figure in Plate VI of Book I.

second step, and is about the distance of a point in the march$^\Delta$; upon which the third and last step of the bouree and minuet step is made to the third note of the second measure of the tune, by drawing the left foot, pointed as it is firm to the floor into the fifth position behind the right■, receiving the body, and concludes in the first position, as at first[†]; and it may be continued as long as the dancer pleases.

The third and last method of performing this step is as follows: Instead of obliquely, as in the last explained to the right hand, it is here diametrically or sideways crossing the room directly to the left hand, facing, not as in the aforesaid, but instead thereof full either up or down the room, as it shall happen[‡].

This step, in performance, differs from the last described in this, that the right or beginning foot, which before made the half coupee off to the right, now instead thereof makes a sink and step sideways to the left hand, crossing behind the left foot[*], which supports the body, marking time to the first note of the same measure, and filling up the remaining second and third notes, entirely the like as in the foregoing, except that, instead of the first position as in them, it here ends in the third with the left foot foremost or enclosed at liberty to perform the bouree, in the same manner to the left side of the room, as before to the right$^\Diamond$. The said bouree or second part of the minuet step begins, by making a sink and open step, off sideways from the right on which the weight rests to the left hand[§], the rise or receiving of the body upon which marks time to the first note of the second measure, and the right foot makes the second step of the bouree to the second note, in drawing it pointed$^\oint$ crossing behind the left[*], from the place where it supported the weight,

---

Δ See the first figure in Plate VI of Book I. ■ See the first figure in Plate XI of Book I. † See the first figure in Plate I of Book I. ‡ See the characters of this step in Table II of Character Plate O, number III. * See the second figure in Plate XI of Book I $\Diamond$ See the first figure in Plate IV of Book I. § See in some degree the first figure in Plate VI of Book I. $\oint$ See the second figure in Plate VI of Book I.

before the first step of the fleuret was made; and the third and last step of the bouree and fourth of the minuet step is made, by stepping the left foot open off from the right$^\nabla$, in like manner as the commencing of the fleuret, only without a sink, ending in the first position, as at the beginning of the step, upon the left foot[†], which step may be continued either diametrically or circularly, as occasion offers.

We are now arrived at the fourth and last of the before mentioned steps, namely, that of *three movements* or bendings and risings; which is also commonly called the *new step*, from its being used now as much, or very little less than the last explained of *two movements* only, and more especially when performed to the left hand sideways before and behind, in that it composes a part of the *minuet dance*, as now practised, of which I shall have occasion to speak more particularly hereafter.

In the interim I shall proceed in describing the present *minuet step of three movements*, which, as I have already said, is only the addition of a movement or a sink and rise more to the last step of the bouree or second part of the minuet step; yet it will require a further explanation, by reason that it differs very much from the last explained, in its agreement with the notes of the tune; for, though that may properly be divided into two parts or divisions through the half coupee, in that it, together with the sink which prepares for the succeeding bouree, answers to the first measure of the tune, and the fleuret or second part of the minuet step to the second, and consequently is of equal value, though no more than a single step, with the other three remaining, it is not the like here, because the four steps that compose the minuet step are partly of an equal space or distance one from the other, as in counting of *one, two, three, four,* and cannot so justly be divided

---

into two parts as the foregoing, which notwithstanding is but one minuet step, as I have said before, separated for the more familiar and easy comprehending thereof; which said advantage we must lose in this step, it being so entirely of a piece that a division here would be as unnatural, as the aforesaid is natural, as will appear by the description I am about to give of it, which in the first place shall be *forwards*[∂]; and it is to be performed in this manner. For example, the weight of the body being upon the left foot in the first position, the right disengaged and free[♦] begins, as aforesaid, in making a sink and step forwards directly up the room[◇]. The rising or receiving the weight upon the toe or instep marks the time to the first note of the three belonging to the first measure; the second is in the fall of the heel[℘] and sink which prepares for the second step of the four belonging to the minuet step, which is made by stepping of the left foot forwards, in the same manner as the first[ƒ]; and the rising or receiving of the body upon the instep is to the third and last note of the first measure. The third step of the said four is made with the right foot stepping a plain straight step forwards[ȣ] upon the toe to the first note of the three in the second measure; the second is in the coming down of the heel of the said right foot[℘] and sink that prepares for the fourth and last step which is with the left foot, in stepping forwards from the sink aforesaid[ƒ]; and the rising or receiving of the weight upon the toe is to the third note of the second measure of the tune, concluding in the same position from whence it began[♦], in order for a continuance, which may be either more or less, according to the largeness or smallness of the room in which the dance is performed.

The two other ways in which this step is performed are

[∂] See the characters of this step in Table II of Character Plate O, number I. A sink and rise must be supposed.   [♦] See the first figure in Plate I.   [◇] See the second figure in Plate IX, in some measure. [℘] See the second figure in Plate I.   [ƒ] See the first figure in Plate IX.   [ȣ] See the second figure in Plate IX.

diametrically or *sideways*; the first of which$^\oplus$ is in the like manner as the minuet step of two movements, or one and a fleuret, to the left side of the room, that is to say, the right foot always crossing behind the left; but as I have already in that step described the method in which the feet are to be stepped, it will be needless at present to say any more than to show its difference in counting to the notes, from the former, which from what I have said above appears to be very different from the step now treated on, as I shall endeavour to demonstrate by the following particulars.

In the first place, we are to suppose a movement added to the last step of the bouree, or second part of the minuet step, and the first step with the right foot† to be made upon the toe to the first note; the second is in the coming down of the heel‡ and sink upon the right foot, which prepares for the second step made with the left*, as was explained in the aforesaid, the rising or receiving of the weight upon which marks the third note of the first measure, leaving the right foot, as in the aforesaid, upon the point$^\lozenge$. The drawing or bringing of the right foot pointed, as it crosses behind the left§, is the third step, and marks time to the first note of the second measure; and the second note is in the sink upon the said right foot, preparing for the fourth and last step that is made, in rising and stepping sideways from the said sink upon the left foot*, to the third note, concluding in the first position$^\phi$ as at commencing.

The next way of performing this step only differs from the foregoing, in that, instead of the right or beginning foot's making the first step *behind,* as in the last, it is here made *before*$^\Delta$, from whence it is called *before and behind;* and this crossing or stepping of the foot *before* renders the step much more agreeable and

---

fuller of variety than the aforesaid, arising by reason of the twists and turns the body naturally gives and receives in the performance thereof.

But since this step is much more used in the dancing of a minuet than the aforesaid, I shall endeavour to give as plain a description of it as possible; in order to which I shall not only repeat the stepping or motion of the feet, but also suppose, instead of two bars or measures to a step in the minuet, as in the aforesaid, only one bar or measure, which in effect is the same thing; for what matters it, whether we count three twice over, or six but once; or whether the half time is beat to one, two, three, or to four, five, six, which last method, in my humble opinion, I take to be much more familiar and easy to be comprehended than the other, in that there is not any repetition of the first or second measure; but, however that be, I am sure it will afford a greater variety, and possibly may inform some of what, perhaps, they were ignorant of before.

But to proceed in the description of the step now treated on: For instance, the weight and position, as aforesaid[▽], facing either to the upper or lower end of the room, it begins in making a sink and step sideways, with the right foot crossing directly before the left[∂] to the same side of the room, and producing a twist or turn of the body towards the said step[♦] which receives the weight upon the toe, marking time to the first of the above-mentioned notes. The second is in the coming down of the right heel, in the third position before the left[◇] and sink for the succeeding step, which is made by stepping the left foot, open off sideways from the right on which the body is, to the left side of the room[℘]; the rising or receiving of the body either upon the toe or heel

---

▽ See the first figure in Plate I, Book I.　　∂ See the first figure in Plate XI, Book I.　　♦ See in some measure the twist or turn of the body in the said figure.　　◇ See the second figure in Plate V, Book I. ℘ See the first figure in Plate VI, book the same. [*Editor's note:* It's understood that here, *book the same* refers to Book I, the aforementioned book, rather than to the same book at present, that is, Book II.]

marks the third note, leaving the toe of the right foot upon the point*ƒ*, in the same place the body was before the second step was made. In the stepping of the left foot last mentioned it is to be observed, that the body is conveyed or rather, more properly speaking, makes a becoming feint in the air not much unlike that made in the minuet step of one, and a fleuret to the right, only there the bend or sway the body makes in the air was to the right℞ upon the half coupee, or first of the four steps which compose the minuet step; but here it is upon the second to the left, and the look or turn of the head, which in the former was to the left, is in this to the right†: The toe, I say, being left pointed, as aforesaid, makes the third step in the minuet, by being drawn pointed crossing behind the left foot, and receives the body in a twist upon the fourth note or half time, as above‡. The fifth note is in the sink that prepares for the last step of the four which compose the step we now treat of, and is made in like manner as the second step with the left foot to the third note, in rising and stepping open off sideways* from the sink aforesaid upon the left toe to the sixth and last note, except that the right toe is not left pointed as in the former, but ends in the first position as at beginning◊; and the last method of counting the notes or time to the step will bear, as well throughout all the minuet steps before described as the present.

Having explained the minuet steps which form the circle of this dance, I shall next take notice of some of the most remarkable steps used, by way of embroidery or further grace thereto, as the *hop*, *double bouree*, or *fleuret* advancing or in the same place, *balance*, etc.

ƒ See the second figure in Plate VI, Book I.   ℞ See in some measure the sway or twist of the body in the first figure in Plate XI, Book I.   † See in some degree the twist or sway of the body in the second figure of Plate XI, Book I.   ‡ See the second figure in Plate XI of Book I.
* See in some measure the first figure in Plate VI, Book I.   ◊ See the first figure in Plate I, Book I.

CHAP. II.

Of the HOP *in the* MINUET.

THE *hop* in the *minuet* needs little further explanation, since it has been already described in the rigadoon hop of two springs; I shall therefore refer to that, because it is the very same as the hop under consideration, only, when performed in a minuet, there must be a *bound* added and a different method in counting of the notes; for, instead of performing the first and second springs to one bar or measure, as in the aforesaid, they are divided, that is to say, the first spring or hop is to the first bar of the minuet tune, and the next spring and the bound which is added are to the second. They are all here to be reckoned but as one step[§], which is in its performance thus: For example, the weight and position being as aforesaid[ϕ], the spring is made in like manner upon the first note; but, instead of the right or advanced foot's being set down upon the second note, it is now put down to the third[Δ], the second being counted in the progress the right foot made in the air, concluding one half of the hop in the sink upon the aforesaid third note, that prepares for the second spring which is made, as in the aforesaid, to the fourth or beginning note of the second measure by taking of the left foot up from the floor into the third position behind the right and advanced foot upon which the weight of the body now is[▽]. The left being upon the point and at liberty makes the bound, as was shown in treating of that step, the sink or preparative for which marks the fifth

---

§ See the characters of this step in Table 3 of Character Plate O, number I.   ϕ See the first figure in Plate V, Book I.   Δ See the second figure in Plate IX, Book I.   ▽ See the second figure in Plate V, Book I.

note; and the sixth is in the spring or bound upon the left foot, by rising or springing off from the right on which the weight rested before the said spring was made, concluding as at first[∂].

This hop in the minuet may be performed *backwards*, in the same manner as described *forwards*, except that, instead of commencing with the right foot from the third position behind, it must be from the same position before[♦]; but the rest being entirely the same there needs nothing more to be said of it here, since it has been fully explained in the rigadoon step of two springs forwards, by which it may be easily understood how it is performed backwards[◇].

[∂] See the first figure in Plate V, Book I.   [♦] See the second figure in Plate IV, Book I.   [◇] See the characters of this step in Table 3 of Character Plate O, number II.

CHAP. III.
Of the DOUBLE BOUREE
upon the same place.

THIS step is taken from the third position before and ends in the same behind, answering to two measures of the tune, the same as the minuet step, and is here esteemed but as one step; though it is otherwise when it is performed in a saraband, or suchlike slow movement, for then one of them alone is to a measure without any dependence on the other, beginning with either the right or left foot, as occasion offers. But it is not so in the minuet, for the first bouree or fleuret must commence with the right foot as an equivalent to the half coupee; and the second bouree to the remaining fleuret or second part of the minuet step, as usual, with the left foot, completing six steps in the same space of time as the foregoing minuet step of four, and consequently much swifter in its performance†, which is thus: The weight of the body being upon the left foot in the third position, the right enclosed before it and disengaged‡ begins in making a *sink* or *bend* of both knees, from whence the right in rising steps directly open off sideways, either more or less according to the tune: For example, if to the above-said slow time, it may then be the length of a step in walking, or of a point in the march*; but not so now, by reason of the quickness of the tune. Therefore, about half the length of the said step, receiving the weight of the body upon the instep

---

† See the characters of this step in Table 3 of Character Plate O, number III.   ‡ See the second figure in Plate IV, Book I .   * See the second figure in Plate VI, Book I.

or toe of the right foot to the first note, the left on which the weight was remains in the same place, only the toe is pointed◊; the second note is in the raising of the said left toe and setting down or receiving of the weight upon the left heel, and also leaving the right foot upon the point where it marked the first note§; from whence it is drawn swift into the third position behind the left∮, at the same time pressing to the toe strong to the floor, the receiving of the weight upon which is to the third note, concluding the first bouree and measure in a smooth easy sink upon the right foot, and bending the left the same instant the right receives the body in order to begin the second bouree.

The second bouree is like the aforesaid, in rising from the sink by stepping of the left foot off sideways to the same handΔ, receiving the weight upon the toe or instep to the fourth note and beginning of the second measure of the tune, and leaving the right toe upon the point as aforesaid▽; the fifth is in the raising the said toe and setting down or receiving the weight upon the right heel, leaving the left toe pointed, as in the first bouree, or where it marked the fourth noteΔ; from whence it is drawn swift into the third position behind the right foot∂, pressing the toe strong to the floor at the same instant; the receiving of the weight upon which is to the sixth note, and concludes the second measure of the tune in the same step of the dance, in the position as at commencing.

It must be observed, that if this step is performed twice over, as in that under consideration, the sink falls upon the sixth note of the second bouree, the same as upon the third in the first.

Having described the foregoing step *upon the same place*, it may perhaps be acceptable to the reader, if I add thereto the said *bouree running* or *flying* along the room◆, it being often used

---

◊ See the first figure in Plate VI, Book I.   § See the second figure in aforesaid plate.   ∮ See the first figure in Plate IV, Book I.   Δ See in some respects the first figure in Plate VI, Book I.   ▽ See the second figure in the same plate.   ∂ See the second figure in Plate IV, Book I.   ◆ See the characters of this step in Table 3 of Character Plate O, number IV.

in dancing of a minuet by those who have attained to such a perfection in this art, as to render them capable of judging the most proper places of making use of it; and it only differs from the former by *advancing*, instead of being upon the same spot of ground.

The *running bouree* may be performed either from the position treated on in the foregoing step, or from the first as occasion offers; but I shall at present only explain it from the latter, that is to say, the first position: The weight being upon the left foot, as in the aforesaid[†], it begins by making a sink and step with the right foot forwards[‡]. The rise or receiving of the body upon the toe marks the time or first note; the second step, made with the left foot[*] plain upon the toe, marks the same note; and the third step, with the right foot[‡] plain in the like manner upon the toe, marks the third and last note, concluding the first bouree in the same position upon the right foot[◊], in a readiness to begin the second bouree. The latter bouree commences by sinking upon the third note and step of the former, from whence it steps forwards, as the aforesaid[§], the rise of which upon the left toe is to the fourth note; the second step plain with the right foot[‡] marks the fifth in the like manner, and the third step plain with the left foot[*] the sixth; and it concludes in the first position as at first[†], from whence it may be continued.

---

† See the first figure in Plate I, Book I.   ‡ See in some measure the second figure in Plate IX, Book I.
* See the first figure in Plate IX, Book I.   ◊ See the second figure in Plate I, Book I.   § See in some measure the first figure in Plate IX, Book I.

CHAP. IV.
Of the BALANCE.

THE *balance* is composed of two plain steps, to which are added two movements or sinkings and risings commencing from two different positions, namely, the first and second position or point, as in the beginning of a march; and the said steps and movements are equal in value to one minuet step, and fill up two measures of the tune the same as in that[§].

The *balance* is performed thus: For instance, the weight of the body being in the first position, as above, upon the left foot[Δ], the right disengaged makes the first movement and step by sinking or bending of the knees, and stepping with the right foot directly opening off sideways[∇], facing either to the upper or lower part of the room, as it shall happen. The rising or receiving of the weight upon the toe or heel marks time to the first note; and, if upon the toe, the second is in the coming down of the heel[∂]; or, if made upon the heel, it is in the tight holding of the knee after the rise to the first note is made, leaving the left toe upon the point[∂], on the very same place the body was at the beginning of the step[∇]. The third note, which concludes the first measure and part of the step, is in the sink that prepares for the second step of the balance, namely, with the left foot from the point aforesaid, in which it touches the heel of the right foot[♦] and then steps open off sideways[∇], receiving the weight of the body, either upon the toe or heel to the fourth note, in the same

---

[§] See the characters of this step in Table 3 of Character Plate O, number V.   [Δ] See the first figure in Plate I, Book I.   [∇] See in some degree the second figure in Plate VI, Book I.   [∂] See the first figure in Plate VI, Book I.   [♦] See the second figure in Plate I, Book I.

place from whence it was brought from the point. The coming down or fall of the left heel is to the fifth note, if the rise be made upon the toe; if not, in the tight holding of the knee, as aforesaid, ending in the first position, as at beginning[†]. The sixth note is in the sink or preparation for the succeeding step, whether it be the same or any other; and, when this step is performed with a quarter or half turn, as it frequently is, it must always be turning to the left hand, if commencing with the right foot, as it does in the present.

---

† See the first figure in Plate I, Book I.

CHAP. V.

Of the two COULEES *or* MARCHES.

TO perform two *marches*, instead of a minuet step, in a suitable and proper place in dancing of a minuet, I take to be an agreeable variation or change; but, as the manner of performing a *march* has been already shown, I shall refer to what has been before observed upon that step, and only take notice, that it must begin with the right foot to the first measure, and with the left to the second. The first of these is to be made upon *one, two,* and *three*; and the second upon *four, five,* and *six,* in the like method as already explained in the step of this name‡.

---

‡ See the characters of this step in Table 3 of Character Plate O, number VI.

CHAP. VI.

Of the SLIP behind and HALF COUPEE forwards to the right and left hands, each to a MINUET STEP.

THIS step is composed of three plain steps, as the bouree, which are generally done to a measure, as that, in other dances; but otherwise here, in that it is equal in value to a step in the minuet, and consequently, like that, takes up two measures or bars of the tune[*]. It is performed facing either up or down the room, as in dancing of the minuet it shall fall out, but usually to our *partner*, and may be taken from the third or first position: For instance, the weight being upon the left foot, with the right at liberty resting upon the heel of the said left foot, as in the march[◊]; or, if from the first, instead of behind, as we have observed, it is equal to the foot on which the body is, facing to the upper end of the room, which shall here suffice as an example[§], and begins the *slip*, or first and second steps of the three that compose this step, by making a sink and step sideways open off to the right side of the room[ϕ], rising upon the toe or heel to the first note, and leaving the left foot on which the weight was[§] upon the *point* in the same place[Δ]. It rests there, during the counting the second note; and the third is in the swift drawing of the said left foot pointed cross behind the right[▽], concluding the second step of the three to the first measure, in receiving

---

* See the characters of this step in Table 3 of Character Plate O, number VII.   ◊ See the first figure in Plate V, Book I.   § See the first figure in Plate I, Book I.   ϕ See the second figure in Plate VI, Book I.   Δ See the first figure in Plate VI, Book I.   ▽ See the first figure in Plate XI, Book I.

the body in an agreeable twist or turn$^\partial$ with both knees bent; that is to say, in the crossing, as aforesaid, the left shoulder, in bringing forward before the right, is more raised by the lowering or falling of the other.

The first movement being thus ended, with the knees bent upon the third note, in order to the performance of the coupee, or second part of this step, which is made to the second measure by rising from the sink aforesaid and stepping of the right foot forwards$^\blacklozenge$, the rising or receiving of the body on the toe or heel marks the fourth or beginning note of the second measure; and the fifth is in the coming down of the said heel to the floor, if the rise was upon the instep in the first$^\diamondsuit$ or third position$^\wp$, with the left foot at liberty the same as the right at commencing. The sixth note is in the sink which prepares for the same step with the other foot; and you are likewise to observe that, in the performance of the half coupee or second part of the foregoing step, the body returns from the said twist in bringing the right shoulder, which was behind and somewhat inclined downwards, to be equally forwards to the left and the same in height: For example, when we stand in a natural and erect posture.

But to return to the *slip* to the left hand, which is the very same as to the right already explained, it begins in rising from the sink aforesaid, stepping open off sideways to the left hand^f; and the rising upon the toe or heel of the left foot marks the first note, leaving the right toe upon the point$^\aleph$, as the foregoing did the left, making a pause or rest whilst the second note is counted. The third note is in the drawing or crossing of the right foot behind the left$^\oplus$, receiving the body in the aforesaid twist$^+$ and bending of both the knees, in which the right shoulder

---

∂ See the contrast or sway in the first figure of Plate XI, Book I. $\blacklozenge$ See in some measure the second figure in Plate IX, Book I. $\diamondsuit$ See the second figure in Plate I, Book I. $\wp$ See the second figure in Plate V, Book I. f See in some measure the first figure in Plate VI, Book I. $\aleph$ See the second figure in Plate VI, Book I. $\oplus$ See the second figure in Plate XI, Book I. $+$ See the sway or twist of the second figure of Plate XI, aforesaid.

is raised in advancing, as in the foregoing, to the right hand the left shoulder† was on concluding one half of the step to the first measure of the two; and the second is in the half coupee that is made as in the aforesaid, by rising from the sink which fell upon the third note and stepping of the left foot forwards‡. The rise receiving of the weight upon the toe is to the fourth note of the next measure; the fifth is in the falling of the heel*, and the sixth in the sink for the succeeding step, concluding upon the left foot, as at beginning, in one of the said positions◊.

Having now shown the method of performing this step in dancing of a minuet, both to the right and left hands (as indeed it cannot be done without the other by reason they both change the feet but as one minuet step, two bourees, or two marches) since this step is much used in tunes of common and triple time, as rigadoons, bourees, sarabands, and passacailles, etc. and also, instead of being performed to two measures, as in this dance, is often found to one bar only§ and of consequence varies in the method of counting from the aforesaid, it will not be improper to say something of it here, especially as it has hitherto been omitted: For example, in bourees and rigadoons the rise of the first movement marks time to the first note, as in the foregoing; but the second differs in this that, instead of the toe's being pointed during the counting of the second note, it is drawn swift behind the foot on which the weight is full upon the said note, receiving the body in the twist⨔ and bending of the knees, as aforesaid. The rise of the half coupee, which in the foregoing was to the second measure, is now to the third note, and the fourth note falls in the sink for the succeeding step; or if done to two measures here, as in the minuet, then, instead of counting only upon the point, the second note before its drawing behind the third must

---

† See the first figure in Plate XI, Book I.   ‡ See the first figure in Plate IX, Book I.   * See the first figure in Plate I, Book I.   ◊ See the first figure in Plate I or Plate V, Book I.   § See the characters of this step in Table 3 of Character Plate O, number VIII.   ⨔ See the first and second figures in Plate XI, Book I.

also be reckoned, immediately upon which the *slip* is made, as in the foregoing, to the fourth and last note. The rise to the half coupee marks time to the first note of the second measure; the second is in the fall of the heel, the third in the rest the body makes upon it, and the fourth in the sink for the succeeding step.

But if to the above tunes of triple time it be performed to two bars, it is much the same, as in the minuet, only more solemn and grave, and the foot that is upon the point follows the rise in a slow progress, pressing the floor upon the second note and beginning of the third; but before the expiration thereof it is brought swift behind the foot on which the weight is, concluding the first measure as in the minuet; and the half coupee is to the second measure the same, only, as I have said, more grave and slow.

When this step is performed to one measure, as in the aforesaid tunes of triple time, the easy rise from the first step made open off sideways is upon the first note; and the point or second step attends the said rise in a slow progress, during the counting of the second note, and then is drawn swift behind, before the expiring of the said note in a full sink or bending of the knees; and the third is in the rise of the half coupee made from thence by stepping forwards, as aforesaid, half of which is borrowed in the sink for the next step in the movements last mentioned. This step is sometimes done to both hands, as in the minuet; but it is often found single.

CHAP. VI.

Of DANCING the MINUET in general.

HAVING explained the different ways in which the steps of a *minuet* are to be performed, I shall now say something of that dance in general and proceed to show how the said steps form the circle or figure thereof by linking them one to another in order as they fall; and in the first place observe, that the minuet now in use is composed of three different steps that form the figure of it, which is mostly circular or in the shape of an S reversed or a Z[†], upon which said S or Z the above-named steps present themselves, as follows: That is to say, after making our honour or curtsy to the presence[‡] or upper part of the room in which we dance, and afterwards to our partner[*], the dance begins directly. Instead of stepping back again into your place, as the custom was formerly, and also instead of standing to wait the close or ending of a strain of the tune, begin upon the first time that offers, in that it is much more genteel and shows the dancer's capacity and ear in distinguishing of the time, and from thence begets himself a good opinion from the beholders, who are apt to judge favourably of the following part of his performance; whereas the attending the concluding or finishing of a strain has the contrary effect.

However the latter is by much the safer way for those whose ear is not very good, the concluding of a strain of the tune being much more remarkable than the middle part; for, if they

---

[†] See the second and fifth divisions of Character Plate U.   [‡] See the gentleman and lady in Plate II.
[*] See the gentleman and lady in Plate IV.

should happen to begin out of time, it is a thousand to one if they recover it throughout the dance. But on the other hand, had they waited a remarkable place of the tune, and taken the time at beginning, they might have come off with reputation and applause; for many dance the minuet step in true and regular time, though out of time to the *music,* which is occasioned by not hitting with it right at first; and not being able to recover it afterwards, they dance the whole minuet out of time. Their dancing on this account loses its effect upon the beholders; for, if the steps and the notes do not perfectly agree, in their performing, one with another, they can produce no harmony, and if no harmony, no pleasure to those they design to entertain.

But to the step and figure, as aforesaid, the honour or curtsy being made as above, the lady faces the gentleman, who, just before the dance commences, presents his right hand, or makes a motion as though he would if he was not at too far a distance, and begins the dance in making the half coupee and fleuret (and rest of the steps leading to what I call the *introduction*) open off sideways to the right hand in the manner already described, facing the lady or right side of the room, who performs the same to the left◊; and in the following step they return again in two minuet steps of three movements to the left, all behind, the last of which ends to the upper part of the room§ to which both advance in one and a fleuret◈. About this time the gentleman presents his right hand to the lady∧ and performs four more of the said steps▽; the first whereof is either advancing, as the foregoing, or sideways open off to the right hand facing the presence or upper end, as aforesaid, the rest turning gradually

---

◊ See the characters or steps marked 1 in Plate IV of Book II, or first division of this dance in Character Plate U.　　§ See the characters or steps marked 2 and 3 in Plate IV of Book II, or first division in Character Plate U.　　◈ See the characters or steps marked 4 in Plate IV of Book II, or first division in Character Plate U.　　∆ See the gentleman and lady in Plate V.　　▽ See the characters or steps marked 5, 6, 7, 8 in Plate V, or first division in Character Plate U on the man's side.

the same way, till he arrives at the left upper corner of the room facing the bottom thereof[∂]. During this he hands or introduces the lady into the dance in the most agreeable manner he possibly can, by leading or conducting her in the circle round him in her performance of the like number of steps[♦], that is to say, of one and a fleuret forwards; and, about the end of the second or third step after giving hands, he breaks off or lets go[◇] the lady who continues on a step more to the lower right corner of the room, and then makes a half coupee and bouree to the same hand sideways to the upper end of it[℘], provided the break or letting go of the hands was upon the second step[ƒ], as I have observed; but, if on the third[⅞], the half coupee and bouree or fourth of the steps aforesaid is made directly facing the upper part of the room[⊕], as I have said[+], concluding the first division or part of the minuet dance in the hat's being put on in a graceful manner.

There is no general rule in the performance of this dance, as to its length or shortness; however I shall reduce and divide it into six parts or divisions[■], by way of distinction one from another, each consisting of eight minuet steps, which to a minuet tune of the like numbers of bars will answer the first strain played twice over[≼].

[∂] See the gentleman or first figure in Plate VI.　[♦] See the steps upon the lady's tract marked 5, 6, 7, 8 in Plate V, or first division of the characters or steps in Character Plate U.　[◇] See the characters or steps marked 6 or 7 in Plate V, or first division in Character Plate U.　[℘] See the character or step marked 8 in Plate V, or first division in Character Plate U.　[ƒ] See the character or step marked 6 upon the lady's tract or figure in Plate V.　[⅞] See the character or step marked 7 in Plate V.　[⊕] See the step marked 8.　[+] See the lady in Plate VI.　[■] See the whole dance included in Character Plate U.　[≼] See the music contained in Plates IV and V, or first division in Character Plate U.

C H A P. VII.

Of the figure of S reversed or second division.

HAVING explained the introduction or first part of this dance, I shall now proceed to the second; which in figure is circular or, as I have said, in the form of an S reversed, or Z, upon which fall the steps that adorn this part of the dance, and are performed as follows: For instance, the gentleman at the upper left corner of the room faces the lady who is at the lower right in the third position, where the foregoing ended with the right foot disengaged and enclosed before the left[†], and they commence in performing about four of the minuet steps of three movements before and behind sideways crossing the room to the left hand; that is to say, the *gentleman* performs to the right side of the room and the *lady* to the left[‡], who by turning a small matter gradually upon the third and fourth of the said steps meet in the middle of the room facing one another[*], and pass obliquely upon the right hand of each other; that is, the lady to the uppermost right corner, and the gentleman to the lower left[◊], continuing on the remaining half circle or figure in four minuet steps of one and a fleuret forwards[§]. The lady, as I have said, passes on round by the right upper corner till she arrives at the left, looking full to the bottom of the room[∮].

The last of the foresaid steps[Δ] may also be made open off sideways to the right hand, turning a quarter of a turn the same

---

[†] See the gentleman and lady in Plate VI. [‡] See the characters or steps marked 1, 2, 3, 4 in Plate VI.
[*] See the gentleman and lady in Plate VII. [◊] See the tract or figure in Plate VII, or second division in Character Plate U. [§] See the characters or steps marked 5, 6, 7, 8 in Plate VII, or second division of Plate U. [∮] See the lady in Plate VIII. [Δ] See the character or step marked 8 in Plate XIII.

way; that is, the lady from facing the left side of the room[∇] turns down it, concluding in the third position as above. The gentleman does the same, passing by the lower left side in his way to the right, and concludes as aforesaid, only up the room[∂].

But, instead of either of the former ways, this part of the dance is frequently performed in making the first of the four steps forwards, after passing each other, and then not continuing the remaining circle on forwards, or to the last one and a fleuret open off to the right hand sideways, as before; but instead thereof three of the said minuet steps are made directly opening off sideways to the right hand, by making half a turn upon the half coupee, or beginning of the first of them, from the upper end of the room, the rest continuing on to the upper left side facing the lower end. The gentleman performs the same way except that, after the half turn from the bottom, he makes the said three steps to the lower right side of the room facing the lady, or up it, answering the playing of the second strain of the tune twice over[♦], which now has been played once through, and concludes the second division of the dance; and it is likewise to be observed that, in the performance of these eight minuet steps, the gentleman and lady only alternately change places[◇].

[∇] See the lady and gentleman in Plate XIII.   [∂] See the gentleman in Plates VII and XIII.   [♦] See the music in Plates VI and VII, or second division in Character Plate U.   [◇] See the gentleman and lady in Plate VIII.

C H A P. VIII.

Upon PRESENTING the RIGHT ARM
or third part.

THIS second foregoing step being explained we enter upon the third, which consists in the ceremony of *presenting* or giving the right hand; and in it there is no small beauty and air, as to the graceful and easy raising of it, in order to take hands, and also the gentle and natural fall on letting them go. As for the tract or figure it varies from the former, in its being circular but particularly towards the latter end, upon which tract the steps we now treat of are to be performed, as follows: For example, the gentleman at the lower part of the room on the right side, and the lady at the upper left side, facing each other◊, begin the first step either obliquely open off sideways to the right hand, or else instead thereof make four minuet steps of three movements before and behind crossing the room to the left hand; that is to say, the gentleman to the left side of the room and the lady to the right†, turning a little upon the third and fourth minuet steps, so as to face each other near the middle of the room‡. Instead of passing forwards to the cross corners, as in the second division, they turn a quarter off to the upper and lower ends of the room upon the last movement of the fourth minuet step: For instance, the gentleman to the presence or upper part, and the lady to the lower*, to which each advance pursuing their respective tracts

---

† See the characters or steps marked 1, 2, 3, 4 in Plate VIII, or third division of Plate U.　　‡ See the gentleman and lady in Plate XI.　　* See the gentleman and lady in Plate IX.

in taking as large a circumference, as the joining of hands will admit.

In performing the four remaining minuet steps forwards[◊], which are of one and a fleuret, the right arm is to be raised in the manner before observed, about the turning off or ending of the fourth minuet step of three movements[§], as a sign or warning to the lady of the gentleman's *presenting* his hand, which is given by an easy bending of the elbow before it is presented near the end of the fifth minuet step, continuing on round the sixth and seventh minuet steps until the gentleman faces the upper right corner of the room and the lady the lower left. About this time the hands are let go and the arm falls gently to the side, whilst the eighth step is performed obliquely off sideways to the right hand[ƒ] and lower right corner of the room, the gentleman's head being a little turned looking upon the lady who does the like to the upper left corner, concluding in the third position as at commencing this division, only much nigher to each other, and the shoulders pointing to the upper and lower right and left corners of the room, as was already shown in the explanation of this step; which part or division of the dance, as here treated on, falls upon the first strain of the tune, the second time of playing, and answers to the strain twice over[Δ].

As for the taking off or keeping on the hat I shall not take upon me to determine, leaving it to everyone's choice to act as they shall think most agreeable, since it entirely depends upon fashion and fancy; but, as I have a right as well as others humbly to offer my thoughts on this point, I shall declare in favour of the former, in that it has the appearance of much more complaisance and air than keeping the hat upon the head, which in my humble opinion seems more flat and disrespectful; and the

---

◊ See the characters or steps marked 5, 6, 7, 8 in Plate IX, or third division of Plate U.   § See the last step in Plate VIII, marked 4, and first of Plate IX.   ƒ See the gentleman and lady in Plate VIII.
Δ See the music to the steps in Plates VIII and IX.

taking off and putting on of the hat with a good air likewise gives a singular grace to the dance, which is all lost by its remaining upon the head.

But if it should be objected, that it is inconvenient and troublesome to take off the hat with the right hand, by reason it must be changed to the left before the right can be at liberty to present to the lady: *I answer*, it is easy to be done; or it may be taken off with the left hand as well as the right, and then once changing will serve, which may be upon the letting go or breaking off hands, that is to say, in making one and a fleuret open off to the right hand. The said step finishes the part of the dance now treated of; and the hat is to be taken off with the left hand on giving the right falling naturally and slow down to the side, and holding the hat at arm's length during the time of changing, as was above observed.

CHAP. IX.

Of the fourth division or PRESENTING *of the* LEFT ARM.

AS the last explained treated of the presenting or giving the *right hand,* the present or fourth division is upon *presenting* of the *left,* which in its performance is thus: For instance, being upon the left of each other, the hat in the right hand, the position and presence of the body the same as at the beginning of the third part, only, as I have said on the conclusion thereof, something nigher together, and the body a little more turned to the right, the gentleman who faces the upper part will be to the same side of the room, but the lady, as she faces the lower part, is to the left†; to both of which each advance in eight minuet steps, returning upon the same circle or tract that conducted them hither, which is enlarged by the aforesaid turning‡ and making the first minuet step which is of one and a fleuret forwards; and on the commencing thereof the left arm is raised* in a slow and easy motion, in order to be *presented* or given, which is much upon the second minuet step by a gentle bending of the elbow, as in the aforesaid.

But, instead of the second's being a minuet step of one and a fleuret, you may make the *minuet hop,* which, if well executed, is an agreeable variation proceeding round in the continuation of three minuet steps more of one and a fleuret, at the full extent

---

† See the gentleman and lady in Plates VIII and X.   ‡ See the steps marked 1, 2, 3, 4, 5, 6, 7, 8 in Plate X, or fourth division of Plate U.   * See the gentleman and lady in Plate X.

or length of the arms, till arrived very near the place of setting out, that is to say, whilst the gentleman faces to the upper right corner of the room and the lady the lower left◊; upon which hands are broke off or let go, and, extended as they are, gently fall to their proper places. The hat is put on again with the right hand, upon the ceremony of the arms being ended; and the three remaining minuet steps are performed obliquely open off to the right hand sideways§, as upon the last step of the preceding division⨎, or directly across the room to the right and left sides, concluding in the position and place from whence the third division of three movements to the left begun; or, instead of the eighth and last's being made, as I just observed the double bouree was performed, it would fall very naturally here and be no small embellishment to this part of the dance, or any other steps to fill up the timeΔ. I mean when performed by such as have arrived at a capacity of doing it perfectly, otherwise it is better ommited; but nothing can be more graceful than the former, as appears from what has been said in the explanation of that step; and it affords a further variety, in that the tune has now been twice played through on the conclusion of the division or part now treated of▽, which was to the second strain both times over∂.

◊ See the steps marked 3, 4, 5 on the different tracts in Plate X, or in the fourth division of Plate U.
§ See the steps marked 6, 7, 8 in Plate X, or fourth division of Plate U.   ⨎ See the action of the gentleman and lady in Plate VIII.   Δ See the characters of this step in Table 3 of Character Plate O, Number 3.   ▽ See the music to the first, second, third, and fourth divisions in Plate U.   ∂ See the music to the part of the dance contained in Plate X.

C H A P. X.

Of the fifth division or second S.

AS this part of the dance has been already explained by the second division, which in figure and step is altogether the same, except that, instead of the gentleman's being at the upper end of the room as in the foregoing part, the lady is now there and the gentleman at the lower[†], from whence both commence as in the aforesaid, I might here refer to what I formerly said, in that a further explanation seems entirely needless, since it will easily be comprehended from the former as some may imagine, it being no more than to perform the said steps in the method above described; yet, for the better understanding thereof, if I accompany the dancer or reader through this part of the dance a second time, it will not I hope be thought a tedious or unnecessary repetition. The gentleman and lady, situated as was already observed, both commence in performing the said four minuet steps of three movements before and behind sideways crossing the room to the left hand; but the gentleman now, instead of moving to the right side of the room, as in the second division, moves to the left, the lady doing the same to the right[‡]; and as I have said, by turning a small matter gradually upon the third and fourth of the said minuet steps, they meet in the middle of the room, as in the aforesaid, facing one another[*] and pass obliquely upon the right hand of each other, *viz.* the gentleman to the upper right corner and the lady to the lower

---

† See Plate VIII.　　‡ See the characters or steps marked 1, 2, 3, 4 in Plate VIII, or fifth division in Plate U.　　* See the gentleman and lady in Plate XI.

left, continuing on the remaining half circle or figure in four minuet steps of one and a fleuret as aforesaid forwards[◊], the gentleman, as I have said, passing on round by the right upper corner until arrived at the left facing down the room[§].

The last of the said four steps may also be made open off sideways to the right hand, turning a quarter of a turn the same way as the gentleman from facing the left side of the room[ϕ] down it, and finishing in the third position[Δ]; and the lady the like, passing by the lower left in her way to the right side and concluding, as aforesaid, only up the room[▽].

But, instead of either of the foregoing ways, this part of the dance is usually performed in making the first of the four steps forwards after passing each other[∂], and then not continuing the remaining on a circle forwards, or to the last one and a fleuret open off to the right hand sideways, as before[♦], but instead thereof three of the said minuet steps are performed directly opening off sideways to the right hand in making half a turn upon the half coupee, or beginning of the first of them, from the upper end of the room, the remaining continuing on to the upper left side facing the lower end. The lady does the same, except that after the half turn from the bottom she performs the said three steps to the lower right side of the room, looking up it or to the gentleman; and, having again alternately changed places as before, the gentleman is left at the upper left corner or side of the room and the lady at the lower right[◇], concluding to the first strain of the tune twice over which is now begun a third time[℘].

◊ See the characters or steps marked 5, 6, 7, and 8 in Plate XI, or in the fourth division of Plate U. § See Plate VI. ϕ See the action in Plate XIV, and also the character or step marked 8. Δ See in some measure Plate VI. ▽ See the aforesaid Plates IV and XIV. [*Editor's notes:* Plate IV is not aforesaid; it's ambiguous whether that is written in error or is an indication that in fact the author meant here Plate VI or meant earlier IV.] ∂ See the character or step marked 5 in Plate XIV. ♦ See the steps or characters marked 6, 7, and 8. ◇ See the gentleman and lady in Plate VI ℘ See the fifth division of Plate U, or the under written music to Plates VIII and XI.

CHAP. XI.

Of the sixth division or *PRESENTING* of *BOTH ARMS* and conclusion.

THE sixth and concluding part of the minuet dance principally consists in the ceremony of *presenting* or giving *both hands*, as the third and fourth parts did in giving the *single arm*, and they are much alike in figure and form: For instance, the gentleman and lady facing each other in the third position, where we left them in the three last explained[f] minuet steps, begin in the performance of the like number of movements sideways each to the left hand, the gentleman to the right side of the room and the lady to the left; and, near the end or finishing of the said three minuet steps, both turn off to the same hand to which they were performed[ɤ], as in the fourth minuet step of three movements belonging to the third division, opening gracefully in order to enlarge the figure and *present both hands*[⊕] as the other was for *one*, only making the fourth minuet step which is of one and a fleuret forwards to that part of the room to which the presence of the body is directed; that is to say, the *gentleman* to the *lower* and the *lady* to the *upper*[+], upon the beginning of which said step both arms are raised in the easy gracefulness observed in the single arm, as the sign or warning of giving both hands[■], which is done upon the commencing of the fifth or succeeding step.

---

[f] See the gentleman and lady in Plate VI pursuing their different tracts or figures to the steps marked 1, 2, 3, and 4.　　[ɤ] See the character or step marked 6 in the sixth division of Plate U.　　[⊕] See more particularly the steps marked 1, 2, 3, and 4 in the sixth division of Plate U.　　[+] See the gentleman and lady in Plate XII.　　[■] See the action in the figures of Plate XII.

In this part of the dance there may be a *minuet hop,* instead of one and a fleuret, continuing on round upon the right side of each other, until the gentleman faces the upper part of the room and the lady the lower[†], which will be about the conclusion of the sixth minuet step; during which the arms are raised near the height of the shoulder, and the elbows a little elevated or raised forming a circle or whole round.

In this posture the seventh and eighth minuet steps are also performed, the gentleman making one and a fleuret backwards, or rather a small matter to the right, whilst the lady performs the same steps forwards[‡], upon which the hands are let go; and the gentleman, in making the slip or beginning of the eighth minuet step, takes off his hat with the right hand which falls gently down to the side, as aforesaid, in order to make the reverence or bow to the presence or upper end of the room, which is upon the third and fourth minuet step. At the same instant the lady coupees to the gentleman in a half turn to the right from the lower part of the room facing up it, and leaves the right foot upon the point[*] finishing the remaining half of the *step* and *dance* in the reverence or curtsy made in drawing the said right foot behind the left, on which the body rests, into the third or fifth position[◊]; after which the honour or respect is made to each other and the ceremony ended[§], as also the tune which has now been played three times over[ϕ].

As to the hat, I should rather approve of its not being taken off here till the breaking off or letting go of both hands; however this is likewise submitted to the dancer's choice, as well as the presenting of the single arm, whether he takes it off, or keeps it on, throughout the whole dance.

[†] See in some measure the gentleman and lady in Plate IX.　　[‡] See the steps marked 5, 6, 7, and 8 in Plate XII, or steps with the same figures in the sixth division of Plate U.　　[*] See the second figure in Plate VI, Book I.　　[◊] See the first figure in Plate IV, or second of Plate XI, Book I.　　[§] See Plates II, III and IV.　　[ϕ] See the music to the steps of Plates VI and XII, or last division of Plate U.

C H A P. XII.

Of the *MISTAKES* in *DANCING* of a *MINUET*, *with their occasions and rules to prevent them.*

IN the foregoing chapters I have shown the method or manner in which the minuet dance is to be performed, when reduced to a just and regular dance; yet in effect it is no more than a voluntary or extemporary piece of performance, as has already been hinted, in regard there is no limited rule, as to its length or shortness, or in relation to the time of the tune, since it may begin upon any that offers, as well within a strain as upon the first note or commencing thereof. It is the very same with respect to its ending, for it matters not whether it breaks off upon the end of the first strain of the tune, the second, or in the middle of either of them, provided it be in time to the music; but nevertheless there are frequently *mistakes* in the performance of this dance, arising from want of a just notion of the figure and some certain rule in performing the steps upon the said figure, and more particularly those steps which are designed by way of ornament or further grace, which instead of that often prove its disgrace. Nothing is more common than to see the gentleman or lady detained in the performance of some step, in order to illustrate the dance; and so consequently not reaching that part of the room, on which the crossing is made, time enough[Δ], instead of per-

---

Δ See the gentleman and lady in Plates VII and XI.

forming one and a fleuret open off sideways to the right hand$^{\triangledown}$, or some suchlike step, or making a feint off to the right hand in the same minuet step quite round forwards falling into the minuet step of three movements all behind facing the right or left side, as it shall fall out, by which time the former will be arrived at the place of crossing which will then be in its due time; whereas the running in either before or behind our partner, as before, would have caused a confusion.

This disorder also frequently happens in performing the common minuet step, as when one of the dancers does not fill out the room and figure in the performance of an equal number of steps to the other; for, if this be not observed, it will produce the like effect as the former; or if, as I have observed, in presenting the right hand or giving of both, a sufficient warning is not had by raising of the hand or hands, as aforesaid, one minuet step before the hands are given[†], the dancers are often nonplussed and put out of the figure, while on the contrary a presence of mind with the observation of these *rules* will prevent all such blunders and confusions.

There is yet one observation more, with which I shall conclude what I have to say upon this head, which may be of some service in preventing the said accidents, *viz.* the marking whether the minuet step of three movements before and behind sideways to the left hand, which introduces or leads to the giving the right hand, was facing up or down the room, because in going the circle or figure round to the right you certainly come to the same place[‡], whether it be facing to the upper or lower part of the room, ending the division in the minuet step of one and a fleuret obliquely off sideways to the right hand and looking the same way as described in that step; and also the like in the

---

$^{\triangledown}$ See the gentleman and lady in Plates VI and VIII.   † See the divisions or chapters which treat of giving the hands.   ‡ See for example the gentleman and lady in Plate VIII.

performance of the minuet steps round to the left, in which the said hand is given[*].

As the foregoing are the principal places, in which young dancers usually mistake, I thought the making some observations on the *occasion*, and the *rules* or *methods* to be observed in preventing them, might not be unacceptable; for, admitting that masters may have frequently taught their scholars the same lesson, yet according to the old saying, *Words soon pass into oblivion, but what is put down in print remains more strongly fixed upon the mind.*

There is much more that might be said upon this subject; but, as the aforesaid is sufficient, to avoid being tedious I shall only proceed to the making a few further observations, in regard to the foregoing described steps, which as yet have not been introduced into the dance above explained nor any place assigned them therein: For instance, the march, balance, slip behind and step forwards being to the right hand, and the same to the left and a double bouree forwards, every one of which steps, as was already observed, depend upon fancy, as there are some parts of the dance much more proper than others, it may not be foreign to my present purpose to take notice of them; and in the first place introduce the march, which seems to claim three places in the said dance, the choice of which rests in the performer, for it is to be observed that no step of this sort is ever performed more than once or twice in dancing of a minuet. For example, should the said dance be performed in one assembly or company twice or thrice over, its steps ought to be varied as much as possible, that is, provided the dancer is capable thereof; otherwise, as I have already observed, it is much better performed plain; but to what I was saying the two marches will

---

[*] See the beginning in the gentleman and lady in Plate X, concluding in Plate VIII.

be agreeably made advancing upon the seventh minuet step of the second division, the first of the three ways there described, that is, of one and a fleuret continuing all round forwards.

The eighth minuet step may be of one and a fleuret open off sideways to the right hand, as aforesaid, facing either to the upper or lower end of the room, as it happens; the next place it challenges is the second measure of the fourth division, instead of the *hop* which is then left out; and the third is upon the last step but one of the fifth division or second S, entirely in the same method described in the second division.

The *balance* is also frequently made much about the same place or eighth minuet step, either sideways facing each other, or advancing and retiring; and the next is the *slip behind* and step forwards to the right and left hands, each to a minuet step and fall in their performance upon the aforesaid second and fifth divisions, only in the second of the three methods explained in the second part of the dance, by breaking off the minuet step of one and a fleuret upon the ending of the sixth minuet step, instead of a seventh it makes the said slip to the right hand turning to each other from the contrary sides of the room, and the slip to the left hand is instead of the eighth minuet step.

This step may also be performed with no small advantage to the dance, instead of the seventh and eighth minuet steps of the fourth division which are there obliquely; and the double bouree forwards may be made upon the seventh minuet step of the second or fifth division, concluding the eighth minuet step in one and a fleuret to the right hand, as aforesaid, or instead of the fifth minuet step, after which the remaining are as described in the second division or S.

The third way of this step's performance is by a half turn

upon the half coupee or beginning of the sixth minuet step of one and a fleuret, opening off sideways to the right, or in the sixth division after the hop instead of the minuet step.

The foregoing graces or steps being now united and brought into the aforesaid dance, and having their proper places assigned therein, I shall conclude with one observation more, *viz.* that it is in its performance longer or shorter, according to the dancer's pleasure. In order to this instead of performing the second division but once, as in the dance before described presenting the right hand, it may be performed twice or thrice, only it must be noted that the fifth division upon breaking off the left hand is performed the like number of times; that is to say if the second twice, the fifth the like, and if thrice the same after giving the single hand; but the shortest way is once, as described in the foregoing dance.

The said dance and its steps, as I have already observed, altogether depend on fancy, and are in their performance various and uncertain; for it is left to the pleasure of every one to perform them in the order here set down, in any better method of their own, or without any steps. Indeed, it must be confessed that the steps well performed in a minuet are great *ornaments* to that dance, in filling it with variety; yet at the same time it must be owned the performing the plain minuet steps alone is extremely graceful, if well accomplished, and in effect the most *gentleman-like,* or at least the safer of the two.

C H A P. XIII.

Of TIME, or
some account of what TIME is,
with rules to be observed in keeping it.

TIME is a large space or distance without variation or change; and, as it has been from the beginning of all things, it will remain till a period be put thereto and it ceases to be. This mighty space the great author thereof, in his exceeding wisdom, has divided or measured into equal parts and proportions, as days into hours, months into weeks, quarters into months, years into quarters, etc. which divisions or parts move or travel round in a continual but just and regular motion or pace, succeeding each other without ceasing until they arrive at the utmost limits or confines of time, which will then be no more.

But leaving these sublime thoughts to draw more closely to the point or subject in hand, I shall endeavour to illustrate it by one day or measure of the foregoing *space* or *time*, in supposing every hour therein to be bars or measures of a dance or tune; and that they are as short in length or time, as measure in common or triple time. I shall likewise show that by one hour may be comprehended the scale both of common and triple time.

For instance, the former thus:

COMMON TIME.

$$\left\{\begin{array}{l} 1 \text{ \textit{Semibreve.}} \\ 2 \text{ \textit{Minims.}} \\ 4 \text{ \textit{Crotchets.}} \\ 8 \text{ \textit{Quavers.}} \\ 16 \text{ \textit{Semi-quavers.}} \end{array}\right. \qquad \left\{\begin{array}{l} 1 \text{ \textit{Hour.}} \\ 2 \text{ \textit{Half hours.}} \\ 4 \text{ \textit{Quarters of the hour.}} \\ 8 \text{ \textit{Half quarters of the hour.}} \\ 16 \text{ \textit{Half half quarters of the hour.}} \end{array}\right.$$

The above is the whole *proportion* of *common time* or of four to the measure, as usually found in books of music; yet we often find in pieces of music the sixteen *semi-quavers* doubled two and thirty *demi-semi-quavers*, and then the hour will be divided into the like number of parts.

In *triple time* the hour must be supposed to be divided into three thirds or parts, by reason it only consists of three in a bar or measure.

The example is as follows:

TRIPLE TIME.

$$\left\{\begin{array}{l} 1 \text{ \textit{Pricked Minim.}} \\ 3 \text{ \textit{Crotchets.}} \\ 6 \text{ \textit{Quavers.}} \\ 12 \text{ \textit{Semi-quavers.}} \end{array}\right. \qquad \left\{\begin{array}{l} 1 \text{ \textit{Hour in three thirds.}} \\ 3 \text{ \textit{Thirds or parts of the hour.}} \\ 6 \text{ \textit{Half thirds or parts of the hour}} \\ 12 \text{ \textit{Half half thirds or parts of an hour.}} \end{array}\right.$$

This is the *proportion* of *triple time* or three in a measure, as usually put down; yet sometimes it amounts to twenty-four *demi-semi-quavers.*

Having now shown that the hours of the day may be esteemed as so many measures of a tune or dance, it must consequently be understood that a day of twelve hours contains the like number of measures; and, admitting that the tune or dance consisted of seventy-two bars, six divisions or days would complete it. This comparison may possibly be thought by some foreign to the purpose, though it is indeed very just and suitable; and I question not but upon further consideration it will appear so to the judicious reader, for since the subject in hand is *time* and there is nothing more certain than the *day* and its *hours*, the latter will of course imprint in the mind stronger and juster ideas of the former.

However, it may perhaps be objected and at first view with great show of reason, that the *time* in dancing is various and liable to be changed to faster or slower, according to the performer's fancy; whereas the *day* and *hours* are immutable or without any change. I answer, for this very reason, as I have just observed it will give them a truer notion of the justness of time, and be a means to prevent their starting from or dragging behind it, which is often done by such whose ears are pretty good, as well as by those who have very bad ears, though it is the natural fruit of the want of an ear which of all other things is most difficult to cure, it being more a gift of nature than art. This caused the ancients to say, *The gods gave a genius to music and dancing*; and it is of that importance in the latter as to render it impossible to please without keeping *time*, nor is it to be called *dancing* without it.

From what has bccn said it appears, that to have a just and true idea of time is of no small consequence in order to dance well, and that too much cannot be said upon this head; which is, I think, a sufficient motive for me to proceed in a few further observations upon it, which if duly considered, I am confident, will be found of remarkable service.

In the first place then, you are to take notice, that of the foregoing *proportions* of time one is *common* and the other *triple*, from whence arise all the times and movements made use of in dancing. From the former of these flow very slow *entrees* containing two steps in each measure called *quadruple,* or of two times, on account of their slowness or admitting of a supposed bar in the middle of the said measure; but the rest as allemaignes, gavots, galliards, bourees, rigadoons, etc. are only of one time, as not allowing of more than one step to a measure by reason they are much lighter movements than the aforesaid quadruple, of which they are esteemed but as half a measure. The latter consists of loures, or slow jigs, courants, sarabands, passacailles, chaconnes, minuets, passepieds, etc. the first of which, namely loures or slow jigs, are of two times or steps to a measure and agreeable with quadruple, so that in effect there are three sorts of times in dancing, *viz. common, triple,* and *quadruple* proceeding from the two former; yet they are all reckoned but as *common* and *triple time* and only beat as such, except that some are slower and others quicker, which is the subject I am now about to explain.

Common time, for instance, is of four notes to the bar or measure, as has already been observed in the explanation of the steps upon that time; and the rise or beginning of the step, in dancing, from a sink always marks time to the tune, as well as the fourth or last note is in the sink or preparative for the rise or beating time to the succeeding step, which no sooner is performed than the dancer proceeds to the next, as in walking; and so on till the dance is completed, keeping a just and equal distance or space between every beginning and ending of a measure of the dance, as has been observed by the hours of a day, which is called *time,* the same way, as not making the rise or marking of the time, from a sink upon the first note which in all measures is out of time, and also performing the steps of a dance sometimes faster or slower than at others; but this is as morally impossible for one of a good ear, as it would be for a well-timed watch to go out of time. Dancing may justly be considered as a *watch*; for as, when the latter is set agoing by the springs, the wheels move round measuring out the hours or divisions of a day in certain and equal spaces, during the time it goes: So the springs and steps of a dance ought to be continued after it is put in motion by music, till the whole is ended, which may easily be accomplished. But the difficulty arises here; for example, supposing a person, would set his watch agoing at twelve at noon, having no rule nor any thing to direct him in it but beholding of the sun, is it not a thousand to one but he would be either before or after the time? The case is the very same in dancing, as to those who have not a *genius* or *ear* to music; and though I durst[9] engage to make such a one acquire the former, namely to dance in just and regular time, yet I would not answer for his commencing upon the right time by reason, as I have observed in the comparison of the *sun*, it is a point of a very nice nature and in reality not to be done with any certainty, if the ear is not first helped and improved by a knowledge of that science; no more than the former without a skill in *dialling*[10].

Having by the going of a watch shown the true and exact time in which the steps of a dance ought to be performed, and the difficulty of suiting the movement of the *dance* to that of the *tune*, I shall proceed to give the rules to be observed in beating or keeping time to the foregoing proportions of time, which I take to be the first step in the affair under consideration; and I shall begin with the *gavot*, upon which movement the time is sometimes beat directly upon the first of the four notes belonging to the measure, but most usually after letting pass or flip half a measure, that is to say, the third and fourth notes. For the better understanding of this I shall name two or three dances of the

---

Editor's notes: 9. *Durst*, archaic spelling of darest, that is, to dare.　10. *Dialling*, referring here to the practice of sun-dialling, that is, telling the time by the sun.

latter sort, *viz.* the *Princess Royal* composed by Mr. L'Abbé, the *Princess Ann* by Mr. Siris, and the gavot to the dance, named the *Prince Eugene*, of my own composition, and they all begin with odd notes to which in the dance a plain step or walk is made, whilst the person who beats time raises the heel or toe on playing the odd notes of the tune, in order to strike full upon the time or first note of the ensuing measure; which is done in the fall or coming down of the heel or toe, either of which remains upon the floor during the counting of the first and second notes or half measure. While the third and fourth notes, or concluding half are counting the heel or toe is raised to mark time to the succeeding bar, as at first, and so on till the whole tune or dance is ended, keeping an exact and equal motion up and down neither faster nor slower, and counting the said first, second, third, and fourth notes successively over and over during the same; so that the heel or toe rises upon the third note, remains in the air the fourth, comes down to the first, and rests the second, etc. as before.

The *galliard* movement is entirely the same, as to the beating part, but not as to the odd notes, for instead of two, as in the foregoing, there is only one here; an instance whereof we have in Mr. Isaac's galliard, upon which the heel or toe is raised to beat the time upon the first note, as aforesaid. These two movements are rather more solemn and grave than the following, namely, allemaignes, bourees, rigadoons, etc. but with regard to the method of beating time the very same, for they usually begin with an odd note; and if not, it's only borrowing the last note of the foregoing measure for raising the heel or toe, as aforesaid.

It is here to be noted, that it can never be reckoned out of time, whether the said four notes of the measure be counted faster or slower, provided they are continued through the dance, as begun at first; for though the fancy of masters often differs upon this point, yet every movement has its proper time.

From what has been said it fully appears, that the first note or beginning of a bar is the time or mark the dancer must hit; and in order thereto, as the performer in music, in playing of the tune, prepares for beating time by taking up of the toe or heel, so does the dancer in making a sink or bending of the knees to beat or mark time to the tune, as well as to perform the first or introducing step of the dance; but whether it be done by a rise upon the toe, a hop, or any other step, it matters not, in that it is to be observed, the rise from a sink beats time in dancing, as the fall of the heel does in music.

Before I proceed to *triple time*, it will be necessary to say something further of *quadruple*, which from its graveness is reckoned as two times, as was already observed; and I know no more proper or suitable method of explaining it, since in time and value it is equivalent to two measures of *common time*, than the counting every note double as *one one, two two, three three, four four*, and supposing them what in effect they really are, four minims, for in this sort of time the *crotchets* are of equal length to the *minims*, and would be as before observed, if the time was beat in the middle of the measure. For instance, on the commencing of the third minim it is no longer *quadruple* but *common time*; from whence it follows, that the *minims* must be beat in their timing, as one measure, the same as the *crotchets*, though in length and value double to them.

Tunes of quadruple time rarely, if ever, begin with odd notes, as the foregoing tunes of common; and, for an example, I shall name a tune or two of this kind, as the *Entree d'Apolon*. But as that dance may not probably be known to such as this book is principally designed for, I shall name a second of the same sort, namely the *Godolphin*, composed by the late Mr. Isaac, upon which may be practised the time of this movement; to which end the heel is raised to mark the time, as already explained, after which it remains on the floor the playing of the first and second minims or half measure. The third and fourth minims are in the two motions the heel or toe makes in rising, in order to mark the ensuing measure: For instance, the first rise is made strong and brisk upon the beginning of the latter half of the measure or third note; the second rise is made further up into the air, in the same manner as the first, to the fourth and last note; upon the expiration whereof the toe or heel comes down marking the time to the next bar, counting *one one, two two,* etc. as before, whilst the whole tune is completed.

Having shown how the dancer suits his steps to the notes of the music, it will be of no use to say anything further of that here; and therefore I shall only observe, that as there are in this sort of tunes two steps to each measure, the first is beat, as usual, down, but the second is marked up in the air, on the beginning of the third minim, as above explained.

Being now arrived at *triple time* or of three in a measure, I have little to say, having already in the foregoing proportions of time described the manner of beating or marking time; for it is altogether superfluous and unnecessary to enlarge, since it is entirely in the same method, except to make a few observations touching the most material difference in the movements thereof; and first observe, that the *courante* is a sort of *quadruple* movement which consists of three minims, instead of the like number of crotchets, as in the rest following; which minims are usually divided into double the quantity of *pricked crotchets* and *quavers,* mixed or blended promiscuously together, according to the composer's fancy, producing this movement and played as three minims, which renders it very solemn and grave; and, in its counting or beating in time it is the same as the foregoing *quadruple,* only it is a minim less and generally begins with an odd quaver or half note. Upon this the heel or toe is raised, as aforesaid, to mark the time or first note in the coming down of the toe or heel, counting *one one, two two*, during which, two-thirds of the measure the foot rests upon the ground. In the third and remaining minim or part, the heel or toe is raised in readiness to mark the measure following, which is performed successively on, in like manner, keeping just and regular time, etc. as was shown before; but, for an example, I shall name the *La Bourgogne* by Mr. Pécour and *Brawl of Audenarde* by Mr. Siris.

The next grave movements are sarabands, passacailles, and chaconnes, each of three crotchets to a measure, and every one a degree lighter than the other: Nevertheless the method of beating time is the same as described above in the courante movement, only instead of minims to crotchets and of the time's commencing after an odd note, it is marked directly as in *quadruple*; that is to say, excepting chaconnes, which always begin with odd notes. Examples of the two former sorts are the *Princess Ann*, the *Follie d'Espaigne*, and *Passacaille d'Armide*, all which dances were composed by Mr. L'Abbé; and also of the latter the *Princess Ann's Chaconne* by the same author is an instance, where a whole measure is let slip before the time commences.

The next minuets and passepieds are still brisker, the first being of three crotchets to a bar or measure, and the second of three quavers; and the first usually begins without odd notes, but the second never. The time of these movements, in dancing, ought never to be beat after every bar but every other measure, by reason, as has been said, one minuet step takes two measures of these movements; and it is to be noted that, as in quadruple, the time is to be marked the first measure down, and the second up, instead of twice down. It must be further observed that if the strains of the minuet or passepied consist of eight, as they most frequently do, four minuet steps are equivalent to a strain once over; from whence it follows, that the beginning of a strain, whether the first or second it matters not, is always the time the dancer is to mark or hit, and from thence to proceed on from one second bar to another upon the time, neither varying to faster nor slower, than at first setting out, during the performance of the whole dance; and if the minuet or passepied is of more measures, it is nevertheless performed in the same manner. There are plenty of examples of the former kind, as is of the latter the *Royal George,* that is, the conclusion and beginning of the *Bretagne;* the first by Mr. L'Abbé, the second by Mr. Pécour, to which I shall add one more of my own composition, namely, the *Passepied Round.*

As to tunes of *triple time* agreeing with *quadruple, viz.* loures or slow jigs, they are of two measures, or of six crotchets in the bar, the first three whereof are beat down and the remaining up, each answering to a measure of a saraband, and a movement usually beginning in odd notes. For instance, the *Entree Espagnol* and *Pastoral Dance,* the latter by the late Mr. Isaac; and the *Union* by the same author is of this nature, though it does not begin with odd notes as the dances aforesaid. As the foregoing discourse shows that loures or slow jigs are agreeable to quadruple time, I shall next proceed to observe, that jigs and airy light tunes of the like number of notes to the measures, as the aforesaid, agree with rigadoons in common time, and beat as such in marking the first three down, and the remaining up; as for example, in jigs or forlanes, the *Princess Amelia* composed by Mr. L'Abbé and the dance of that movement by Mr. Pécour; and the *Shepherdess* composed by myself is likewise an example of this sort.

There is yet another movement that occurs to my memory, namely, the *canary,* which is of a very brisk nature, consisting only of three or six quavers in a measure, but usually the latter, slipping before the time is beat three quavers or half a measure, and marking the three first down and the rest up; and the last movement of the *Royal Galliard* by the late Mr. Isaac is an example of this kind.

There is still a movement unobserved, of the like quantity of notes to a measure, *viz.* the *hornpipe*, which is of three minims or six crotchets in the bar, and, in marking or beating time, agrees with a tune of triple time or of three, as for instance a saraband, in which the foot remains down, during the counting of *one, two*, and upon the *third* rises to mark the ensuing measure, etc. The second parts of the *Union* and *Richmond* are both dances of a *hornpipe* movement, and of the late Mr. Isaac's composition.

Besides the foregoing rules of beating time it may be of service to such as have but *indifferent ears*, when they are about to dance in any assembly or private room, or in their dancing, to *hearken* to the *tune*, that they may know the time in which the dance is to be performed; which they may more easily do by reason the music rarely fail of beating time to the tune they are playing, or at least ought not, because hearing the beating or striking of the toe or heel against the floor are visible and certain marks of the dancers commencing.

Moreover, in dancing, if the partner with whom we dance be a good performer, we should take care to keep our steps and figure agreeable with theirs; and I am of opinion, if a person has the least notion of the steps he is performing, it will be very easy for him to observe, whether they begin and end together, which I believe may be useful in dancing.

However, as I have said before, the most sure method I take to be *listening* to the *music* and *time* beat thereto, though that itself is uncertain, nothing being more common than the *hearing* of a tune begun in one time, and, before it is ended, to be near as fast again; which renders it impossible for the best dancers whatsoever to dance as they ought, for instead of their finding the note upon which they should step, it is pushed or driven from under their feet during every step they take, and of consequence causes them to lose that natural and careless air so agreeable in dancing, notwithstanding they keep up with the tune, as being never certain of its time. Indeed, it must be owned to be the dancer's business to dance to the *tune;* yet it is nevertheless the music's part to beat and keep constant and true time, as well at the latter part of a tune as at first. By this means the dancers, sure of the time they dance to, perform not only with pleasure and ease to themselves, but also give a double satisfaction to the spectators in beholding the dancers; for although the latter are at a considerable distance from each other, yet the former will observe that every movement or sink and rise the dancers make is exactly the same in one as well as the other; the former in order to mark time, and the latter in marking of it. Moreover every turn, step, spring or bound seen in one will be at the same instant observed in the other, in such an exact symmetry and harmony of the parts agreeing with the notes of the music, as to cause the most agreeable surprise in the beholders of the two dancers; or admitting a dozen or more in number, by observing them all to move as only one person. This is the natural effect of good dancing adorned with all its beauties, in that the music seems to inspire the dancing, and the latter the former; and the concurrence of both is so requisite to charm those who behold them, that each of them in some measure suffers by a separation. For example, the *eye* can receive no pleasure in the *music* any more than the *ear* in *dancing;* but in conjunction there is at once an attack upon both these senses.

Though this is only an imperfect draught of *fine dancing,* yet it may serve to show how frequently this art suffers by the *unskilfulness* of its performers, whether it arise from the want of a true knowledge of the steps, a bad ear, or from any other cause; and this it was that gave birth to my treatise on dancing, in which the principal and most remarkable steps in that art are described and taken in pieces. I have also shown how the steps of each measure are made to *common* or *triple time*; and in the *minuet* I have given an explanation of all the steps of that dance; and shown, though in effect it is not so, how it may be reduced into a regular dance. In discoursing upon *time*, I have given examples in the most known tunes of every movement, upon which it may be practised or beaten; and in the rules for the same I have fully made appear, how the steps of the foregoing discourse, although in pieces, are there united and set together again, moving in just time to the sound of music, as the watch is put in motion by its springs. Upon taking some further notice of the elevation, movement, and graceful fall of the arms, together with some observations concerning *country dancing*, I shall conclude this work, in hopes that, as the chief, nay, *only* motive of undertaking it was the *public good*, it may answer the desired end; the accomplishing whereof will be a sufficient recompense for the great pains, trouble, and expense I have been at in completing the same; and, as there never hitherto appeared in the world, at least in our language, a piece of this nature, I flatter myself it will meet with the more acceptance.

CHAP. XIV.

Of the movement of the ARMS in DANCING.

HAVING shown the method in which the different steps are to be taken and performed, I shall now proceed to show how the movements of the *arms* ought to accompany the said steps in dancing; lest this work should be compared to the legs and body of a man without arms.

However, as on the one hand, I shall make it my study to omit nothing that can contribute to complete this work, I shall at the same time, on the other, only observe what I apprehend to be material without tiring the reader's patience on a subject which cannot be completed without the very best masters. The correspondence of the *legs* and *arms* in dancing is a point of so nice a nature that any awkwardness or improper movements therein would destroy the beauty of the whole, since that dancing cannot be good which is decrepid or lame in any of its parts, any more than a gentleman or lady can be justly esteemed completely genteel who are naturally and easily disposed in some parts and disagreeable in others; so that, in fine, it is the very polish and finishing stroke.

For the better comprehending of this we must first take notice that, in whatsoever position we stand before the elevation or raising of the arms, the palms or insides of the hands are to our side in a genteel, easy shape or fashion, the whole arms hanging from under the shoulders without force downwards, or too much relaxation upwards, but natural and easy in a readiness for the elevation†.

The next observation relates to the position of the hands after their elevation or being raised; and we should find them with the palms of the hands to the presence or right forwards with the arms both open or extended, in the like manner we have described them by the sides, neither too much raised nor too much sunk beneath the shoulders, but graceful and easy, and being so disposed ready to perform the first motion, which in the movement of the arms above corresponds with the sink or bending of the knees below‡. This is done by moving or raising the whole arms; and, in the fall of the said arms to their first situation after their elevation, the palms of the hands, instead of right forwards as before, are now to the floor; which is effected by a slow and easy turning of the said wrists during the motion of the said arms downwards completing the movement or motion of the arms, from whence all other movements take their rise or beginning; so that, if the graceful raising or elevation of the arms from the sides to the palms right forwards be by a slow and even raising of the wrists, turning outwards or backwards till they arrive at their proper height as before described‡, their becoming fall must in like manner* be in the turn of the wrists and palms of the hands downwards in a slow and even motion inwards, or forwards, whilst the palms are to the sides, as at first†, greatly resembling the fall of a feather or the coming down of a bird, their fall is so smooth and easy; and it is a wonderful grace to dancing when well performed.

To avoid being tedious or overloading this subject with too many observations I shall reduce the various movements of the arms to three or four, *viz.* first, the movement of the wrists from

---

† See the figures in Plate I, Book I.   ‡ See Plates II and XV in Book I.   * See Plates XV and II in Book I.

the elbows round upwards[§]. Secondly, the movement of the arms inwards in their motion upwards[ϕ]. Thirdly, the completing the said movement of the arms inwards by the movement of the wrists round upwards mentioned before[§]. And fourthly, the *irregular* or *contrary* movement[Δ].

Now, as to the method of performance and timing of the movement of the wrists round upwards, it is by a slow and even motion or movement of the *knuckles* or *forefingers* and *thumbs* upwards round from a small bend of the *wrists* and *elbows* corresponding therewith[ϕ]. The commencing is upon *one*, the movement round backwards[ϕ] finishing in a flirt or careless motion of the wrists and arms in their return to their former situation, as in the position of the arms after their elevation; upon *two*[§] and *three*, if to *triple time*, in the motion or preparative for the movement of the arms next ensuing, as it will conclude in like manner upon *four*, if to *common time*.

The next movement is made by the easy fall of the *elbows* at the same time or instant; and the *knuckles* or *forefingers* and *thumbs* lead the way in a smooth and easy motion from below upwards, forming a quarter or half circle or bow[▽]. The *hands* in a handsome fashion may be supposed the ends or points of the said half circle or bow; and it is to be noted that this movement is only about the one half of the aforesaid. But, as that began by forming the circle round upwards *above* the position of the arms, the elbows during the movement of the wrists remaining elevated until the flirt or finishing is made, on the other hand in *this movement* of the arms, the half circle, or motion the wrists make, is *below* the position of the arms; and, instead of the elbows remaining elevated, as before, together with the whole arms, they fall or sink down in a slow, smooth, and easy

---

§ See Plate XV in Book I.　　ϕ See Plate X in Book I.　　Δ See Plates IV, V, VI, IX, XII, XIII, and XIV in Book I.　　▽ See the figures in Plates X and XI in Book I.

motion, whilst the *forefingers* and *thumbs*, as aforesaid, at the same time move upwards in the like slow and deliberate manner, finishing together with the *hands above* and the *elbows below* in order to the throwing the arms open off again, as in hops, chassees, and the like, for which these are the proper arms. The bringing them in on the conclusion of the foregoing step, as just described▽, is in order to the said throwing them out on the time or beginning of the next step§ for which this is the preparative, though the movement of the arms to the palms of the hands downwards must always be first made by way of further preparation, concluding open and extended, till the measure is expired; and from hence it appears, that these two movements usually answer each seperately to a measure or step, forming together much about a whole circle. The former half, as I have said, moves under the position of the arms, and the latter half above in the movement of the arms round upwards in the form and manner above described; and these are the second and third movements I proposed to explain.

The *irregular*, or fourth and last movement, is produced from the two former, *viz.* by the fall of the elbow of one hand as the knuckle moves upwards, whilst the other at the same time performs the motion of the arm round upwards; which compose a fine *contrast*, concluding both at the same time△ with one hand bended and the other extended△. This beautiful contrasted movement changes, every step alternately, first one hand and then the other, and is the proper movement of the arms in half coupees, marches, bourees, and the like; only it must be observed that the bended arm is the *contrary arm* to the *beginning foot* in any of the steps† aforesaid, excepting backwards or sideways, because then the *opposition* or *contrast* is between the same *hand*

---

† See Plates IV, VI, IX, XII, and XIV in Book I.

and *foot*, as was already shown in treating of *walking*‡. The movement of the arms round upwards* is made use of in pirouttes, bourees with a bound, and all suchlike steps.

Although there are various other methods or manners of moving the arms in dancing, yet as these, like the five *positions* with regard to the *feet*, are as it were the principal, it is needless (nor indeed is it agreeable to my present design) to enlarge, especially on a subject which, as I have already said, cannot be sufficiently described by *words* but must be completed by the very best masters; and therefore to avoid trifling, as I have described and given some hints of the method or manner of moving the arms which will agree with all the steps made use of in genteel dancing, I shall refer the rest to the personal instructions of a master properly qualified, who must complete what is here wanting, not only in relation to the movements of the arms but also those of the feet between which there is, as I have already observed, a perfect connection and harmony. The fingers and toes, wrists and ankles, elbows and knees, shoulders and hips, in dancing must move all of a piece; and in fine, the completing of this is the end I had chiefly in view in composing this work.

---

‡ See Plate XIII in Book I. * See Plate XV in Book I.

CHAP. XV.
Of COUNTRY DANCING.

THOUGH my original design was only to have spoken of genteel dancing, yet as *country dances* are at all assemblies or balls introduced as it were a part of or belonging to the former, (and indeed I think it may very properly be esteemed as a luxuriant or careless branch growing out from the other) and has become as it were the darling or favourite diversion of all ranks of people from the court to the cottage in their different manners of dancing, and as the beauty of this agreeable exercise (I mean when performed in the *genteel character*) is very much eclipsed and destroyed by certain *faults*, or *omissions*, in the performers not hitherto, if I remember right, taken notice of in any books; I shall, at the request of some persons of figure in my subscribers, endeavour to point out those neglects which render this diversion, to fine dancers, either altogether disagreeable, or much less pleasant, because one or two couples, either through *carelessness* or *want of better instructions*, will put the whole set in disorder.

This will always be occasioned by the couples below those who lead up the dance, when they omit moving up into the first couple's places, on their casting off, and down again in their casting up to their places as at first; or the like, if the first or leading couples cross over and figure in. In a word, whenever the leading couples move downwards, the couples coming up to lead the dance should move upwards and, when they move up again, the couples who do not lead the dance ought to move down again, attending the motion of the dancers going down with the dance, who in return will attend them in like manner, when they arrive at the upper end to dance in their turns. The nice observation of this presents to the beholders an agreeable prospect of the whole company in motion at once, instead of the confusion that happens when this is neglected; as when in giving the right hand and left in going round downwards from above, or upwards from below, instead of continuing on and giving first the right and then the left hand to those you meet, you turn back, or if in conversation with your partner, or otherwise, you be not attentive and ready to begin at the conclusion of any part or division of the dance; which frequently falls out for, when the coming up couples have concluded the dance with those going down, they often forget that they are immediately to begin again with the next above them, and so for *want of attention* breed confusion and at the same time expose themselves to the spectators.

Indeed good breeding, in regard to those with whom we dance, requires our *not being careless*; and yet my fair readers and others I hope will excuse me, if I tell them I fear this is too often the case, since with due circumspection and care it is impossible not to follow almost any country dance, though I must own when I was a youth I thought it *conjuration*[11]. If we place ourselves at the bottom, and, instead of talking, take a survey of the dance, whatever it is in its performance, over and over again, first with one couple and then with another, it is impossible, I say, but we must be able to go down with it, when it comes to our turns, as well as avoid disorders in our gradual ascent to the upper end; it being only to observe and distinguish one from another the things of which the different parts of all dances whatsoever

---

Editor's notes: 11. *Conjuration* - it is likely the author uses this word in the late Middle English sense, which means a conspiracy or a plot, from the Latin *coniurationem*, rather than the more familiar meaning of a spell or incantation, from the French *conjuracion*.

are composed whether *casting off* or *up, figuring in, hands across* or *round, right hand and left, flying, pursuing, clapping of hands, heys, leading up* or *down, back to back, changing of places, falling back, meeting again,* or whatever it be, by dividing one part of the above catalogue from the other. And with a little practice you will soon be able not only to follow country dances but also lead them up, though you never danced them before: For instance, if a gentleman or lady at the upper end propose a dance to their partner unknown to one of them, you need only ask how it begins, and they will acquaint you, and whether it be *falling back, meeting again, crossing over,* or whatsoever else, you will readily perform it. For this reason I would advise all young people and others who are not perfect in *right hand* and *left, figuring in, heys,* and the like, before they attempt to dance in public, to make themselves well acquainted with and able to perform all the different parts or divisions of country dancing; which they may privately learn amongst one another, if they don't care to practise in public, and thereby not only render this diversion more agreeable to themselves, but also more pleasing to those who accompany them in this exercise.

Besides as I have before hinted, instead of giving a confused idea to the beholders it will afford an agreeable landscape or prospect of so many pairs of fine gentlemen and ladies gracefully in motion to the sound of music, and completing each part of the dance in time to the measure, or strains of the tune, as it were of one accord: As of even rows longwise when falling back and meeting again; half circles, when casting off or up again; figures of eight or binding of a hedge, as in figuring in, or the heys; irregular figures, when one flies and the other pursues; round circles, when hands are joined; cross figures, when the right or left hands are joined moving round; Beating time in contrast, as when hands are clapped first in time with their own, and next crosswise with their right hand against their partner's, or others again clap their own hands, and afterwards strike the left in contrast; leading crosswise in rows, in order of marching up the room and the like down, with various other beautiful circles and figures. If a fine picture, beautiful fields, crystal streams, green trees, and embroidered meadows in landscape or nature itself will afford such delightful prospects, how much more must so many well-shaped gentlemen and ladies, richly dressed, in the exact performance of this exercise, please the beholders, who entertain them with such a variety of living prospects.

Having in the above sketch or draught attempted to raise some noble ideas of country dancing, when performed in a proper manner, and in the foregoing instructions pointed out and removed all the most material *faults* and *omissions* in the performance of this branch of our art, which either obstruct the pleasure of the dancers or beholders, I think I have finished what I designed, *viz.* the improvement and pleasure of others. I shall therefore conclude this work, not in the least questioning but my good intentions will meet with a favourable reception from the public, especially from those who receive benefit or profit thereby.

FINIS.

T HESE are to certify, that the foregoing or second part of the work entitled, THE ART OF DANCING EXPLAIN'D, *was* designed and composed long before the treatise entitled, THE DANCING MASTER, *appeared as we believe and that, having carefully perused and examined the same, we found that, on the twenty-seventh day of* January, 1727–8, *it was written in its present form.*

Witness our hands,

ALEX. JACKSON,   } Dancing-Masters.
JOSEPH JACKSON, }

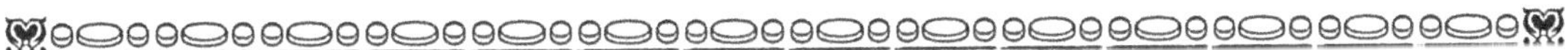

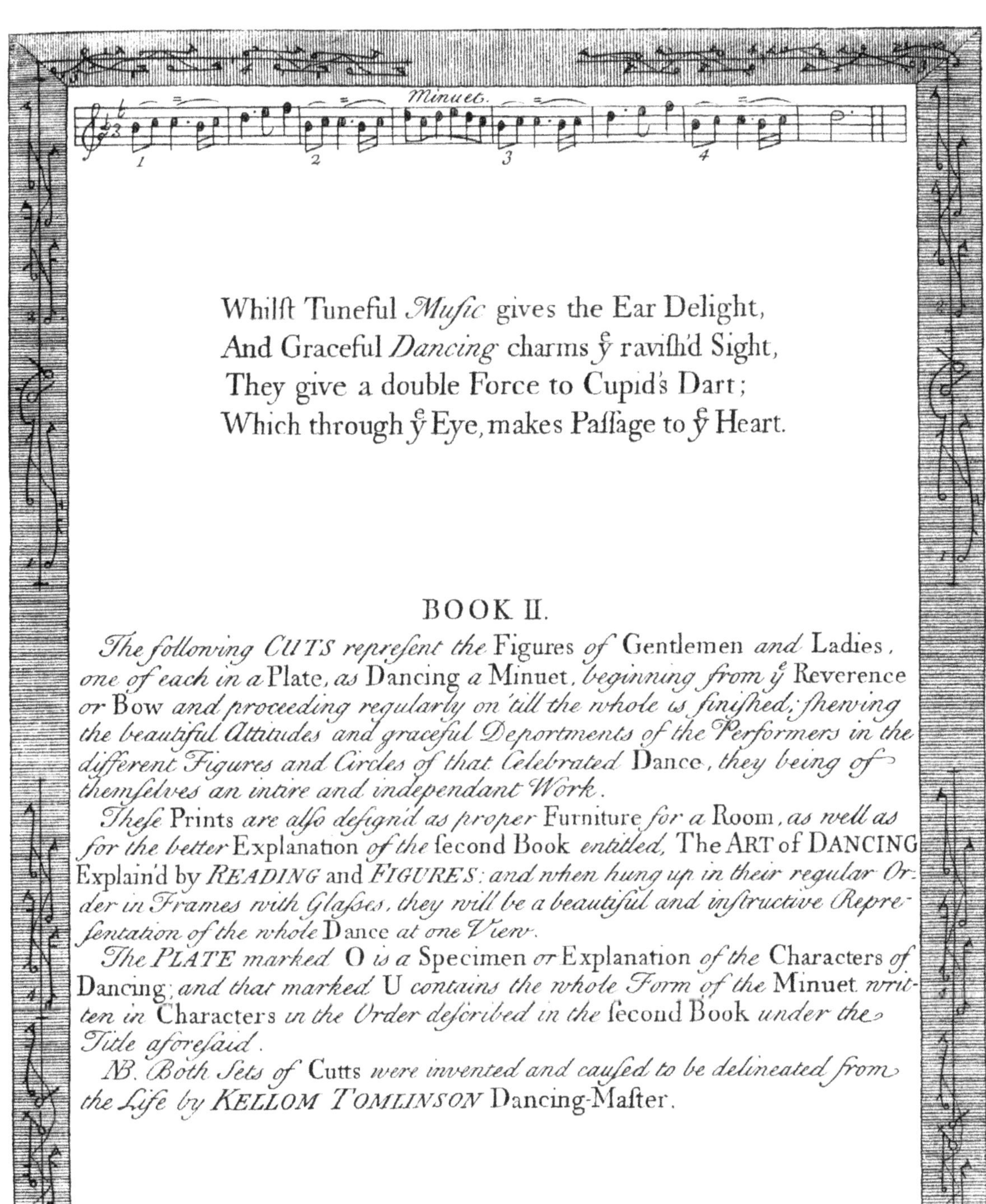

Whilst Tuneful *Music* gives the Ear Delight,
And Graceful *Dancing* charms ẙ ravish'd Sight,
They give a double Force to Cupid's Dart;
Which through ẙ Eye, makes Passage to ẙ Heart.

BOOK II.

The following CUTS represent the Figures *of* Gentlemen *and* Ladies, *one of each in a* Plate, *as* Dancing *a* Minuet, *beginning from ẙ* Reverence *or* Bow *and proceeding regularly on 'till the whole is finished; shewing the beautiful Attitudes and graceful Deportments of the Performers in the different Figures and Circles of that Celebrated* Dance, *they being of themselves an intire and independant Work.*

These Prints *are also design'd as proper* Furniture *for a* Room, *as well as for the better* Explanation *of the* second Book *entitled,* The ART *of* DANCING *Explain'd by* READING *and* FIGURES: *and when hung up in their regular Order in* Frames *with Glasses, they will be a beautiful and instructive Representation of the whole* Dance *at one View.*

The PLATE *marked* O *is a* Specimen *or* Explanation *of the* Characters *of* Dancing; *and that marked* U *contains the whole Form of the* Minuet *written in* Characters *in the Order described in the* second Book *under the Title aforesaid.*

NB. Both Sets of Cutts *were invented and caused to be delineated from the Life by* KELLOM TOMLINSON *Dancing-Master.*

To my once honoured Scholar the Right Honourable the Lady Elizabeth Heathcote,
Daughter to the late Earl of Macclesfield, and Thomas Heathcote Esqr. her Ladyships
Eldest Son, this Plate is most humbly inscribed by her Ladyships ever obliged Servant
Kellom Tomlinson.

To my ever respected Scholars Mr. Simon Every of Egington *in the County of* DERBY. *Son to the* Reverend Sir Simon Every Bart. *and* Miss Ann Every *his Sister.* This PLATE *is gratefully inscrib'd by their much oblig'd Servant.* Kellom Tomlinson

To my very much respected Scholar Legh Master Junior, of Newhall in Lancashire Esq.r and to Miss Elisabeth Master his Sister. ________ This PLATE is most gratefully inscribed, by their ever obliged Servant ________ Kellom Tomlinson.

To my Ever Honoured Scholars the Honble Edward Aston Son and Heir to the Lord Aston, and the Honble Miss Aston his Sister, This PLATE is most gratefully Inscribed by their Honour's most Obliged Servant.
Kellom Tomlinson.

To Mr. Cotton, Son to Rowland Cotton of Etwall in the County of DERBY Esq.r and to my much respected — Scholar Miss Catherine Cotton, his Sister, this PLATE is humbly inscribed by their most obliged Serv.t H. Tomlinson.

To the R.t Hon.ble Brownlow Lord Burleigh Son to the Earl of Exeter, and the R.t Hon.ble the Lady Margaret Sophia Cecil his Sister, this Plate is most humbly Inscribed by their Hon. most oblig'd Servant ———— Kellom Tomlinson.

To the Most Noble & Puissant Lord George Talbot, Earl of Shrewsbury & Baron Talbot in ENGLAND, & Earl of Waterford & Wexford in IRELAND; & to my much Honoured Scholar y.e Lady Mary Talbot, his Lordships Sister, This PLATE is most humbly inscribed by their obliged Serv.t Kellom Tomlinson.

To Corbet Owen of Ynysmaingynne *MERIONETHSHIRE* and Riwsaison *MONTGOMERYSHIRE Esq.r* and my ever respected *Scholar* Miss Elizabeth Owen *his Sister, this PLATE is gratefully inscribed* by their most obliged Servant *Kellom Tomlinson* ——

To my much honoured Scholar the most Noble and Puissant Lord William Stafford Howard, Earl, Viscount and Baron of Stafford, and to the Right Honourable the Lady Mary Stafford, his Lordship's Sister, this PLATE is most humbly inscribed by their very much obliged Serv.t Kellom Tomlinson

To my once Honoured Scholars the Marquiss de Seyssel & Mademoiselle de Seyssel, Son & Daughter
to his Excellency the Marquiss d'Aix late Envoy Extraordinary from ye KING of SARDINIA to ye Court of GREAT
BRITAIN, & now Governour of MILAN. This PLATE is most humbly Inscrib'd by their most oblig'd Servt. Kellom Tomlinson.

To the Honourable M.r Belasyse, and the Honourable Miss Belasyse, Daughter to Thomas Viscount Fauconberg, and my once honoured Scholar Catherine Viscountess Fauconberg, this PLATE is most humbly inscribed by their Honours very much obliged Serv.t Kellom Tomlinson

To the Hon.ble M.r de Courcy and the Hon.ble Miss Mary Elizabeth de Courcy Daughter to the Lord Kingsale
this Plate is, with great Respect, inscribed by their very much obliged Servant
Kellom Tomlinson.

To my ever respected Scholars, Henry Every of Egington in the County of Darby Esqr. Son
and Heir to the Reverend Sr. Simon Every Bar. and Miss Mary Every his Sister, this Plate
is most humbly inscrib'd, by their very much Obliged Servant,
Kellom Tomlinson.

To James Stanley *Esqr Son & Heir* to Sr Edward Stanley *Bart & to my much respected Scholar*
Mifs Elizabeth Stanley *his Sister.*
This PLATE is humbly inscribed by Their most obliged servt Kellom Tomlinson.

THE STEPS TREATED OF IN BOOK II.

An explanation of the characters or steps contained in the tables of PLATE O, in the regular order treated on in Book II.

TABLE II. FIG. 1. The MINUET STEP of two movements or ONE and a FLEURET.

FIG. 2. *The same open off sideways to the right hand.*

FIG. 3. *The same crossing behind to the left sideways.*

FIG. 4. *The same of three movements crossing behind to the left.*

FIG. 5. *The same of three movements before and behind to the left.*

TABLE III. Steps by way of GRACE.

FIG. 1. *The hop or contretemp in the minuet forwards.*

FIG. 2. *The same backwards.*

FIG. 3. *The double bouree upon the same place, the first, FIG. 1. the second, FIG. 2. forwards.*

FIG. 4. *The double bouree forwards the first FIG. 1. and the second FIG. 2.*

FIG. 5. *The balance, the first FIG. 1. and the second FIG. 2.*

FIG. 6. *The two marches, the first FIG. 1. and the second FIG. 2.*

FIG. 7. *The slip behind and step forwards to either hand.*

The slip behind to the right, FIG. 1.

The step forwards, FIG. 2. slip behind to the left, FIG. 3.

The step forwards, FIG. 4.

FIG. 8. *The same in two measures.*

PLATE U contains the whole form of the minuet in the exact order treated on in Book II.

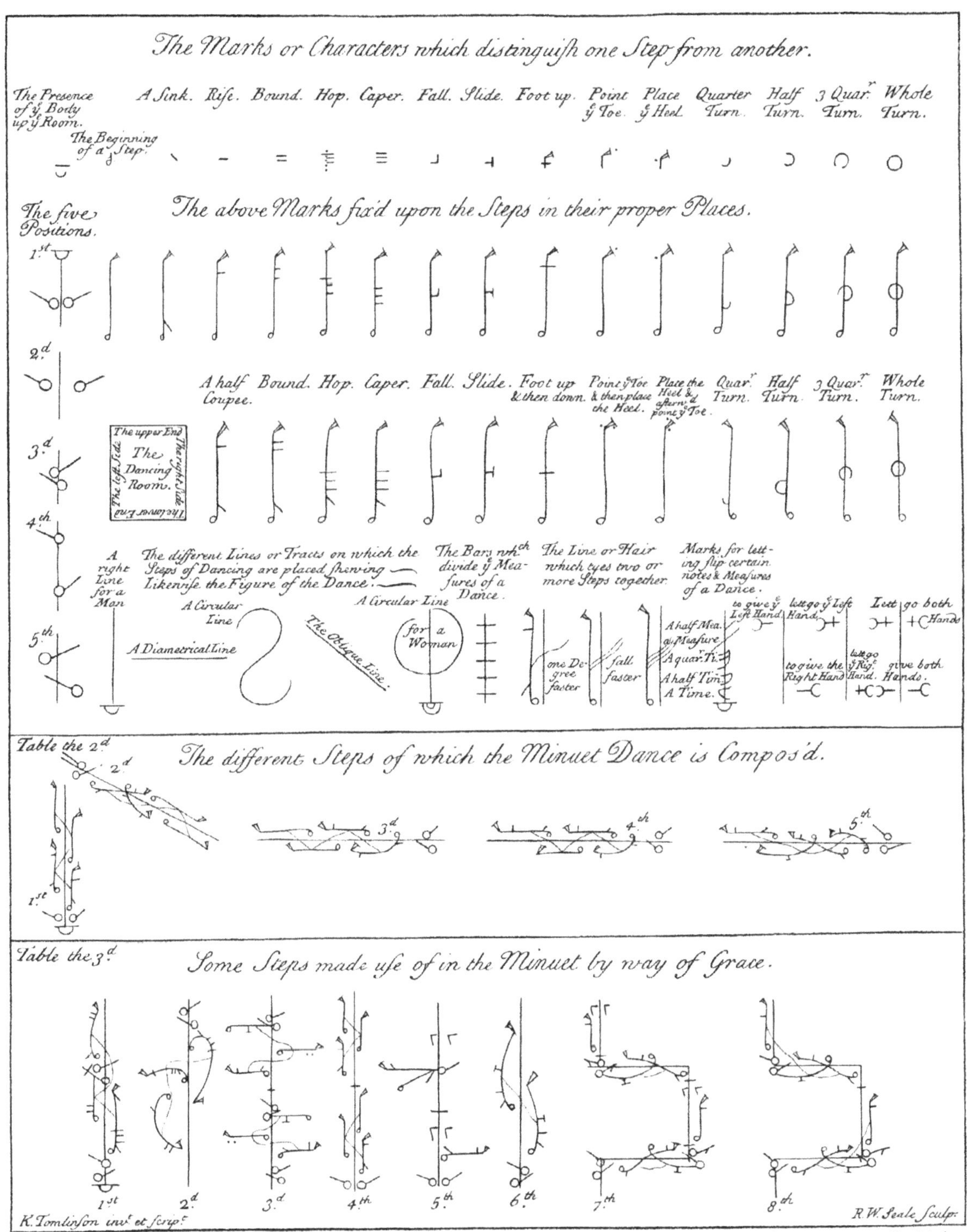

The NOBILITY and GENTRY, who are desirous their Children should learn the *Characters* of DANCING, of which the above is a Specimen, and willing to honour the *Author* in learning of him, shall pay no more than ye usual Prises for *Dancing* only, *viz.* at their own Houses one *Guinea* and an *half* 12 Lessons: and in Proportion if they are pleased to come to him, for in his humble Opinion teaching to *play by Ear* and to *Dance without Book* are equally wrong & ought to be discontinued. Young *Dancing Masters* also may be instructed in the *Art of Dancing & Writing* by *Characters*.

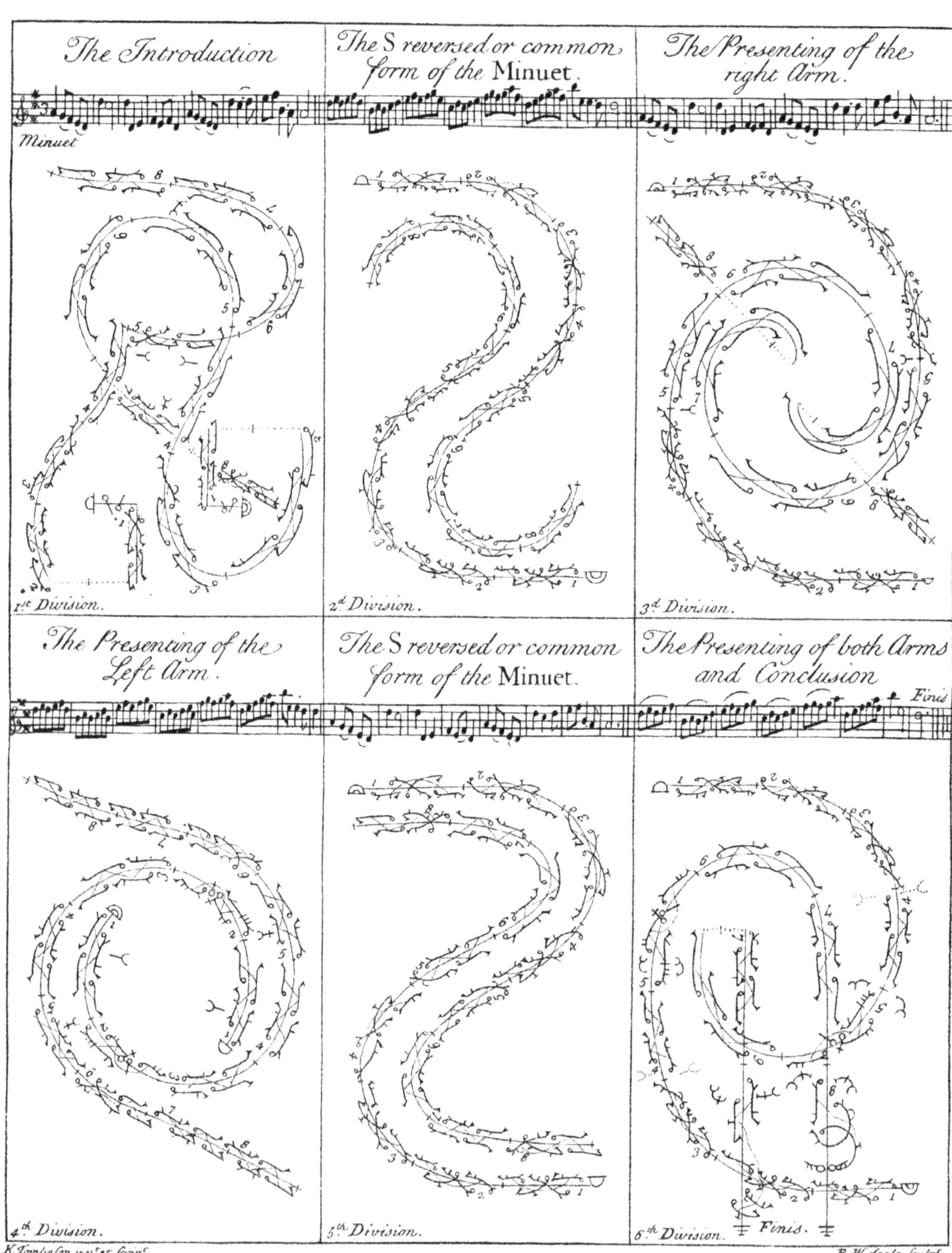

The above is the whole Form and regular Order of the Minuet
written in Characters & Figures, as describ'd in Book II.

This book has been typeset in a custom-amalgamated font, named Kellom after this project, comprised of characters from Bell MT, Big Caslon, and personalized figures, to approximate the font of the original text. Additional footnote characters use Cambria Math.